UNDERSTANDING INCOME STATEMENTS

UNDERSTANDING

JOHN WILEY & SONS, INC.

NEW YORK   CHICHESTER   BRISBANE

INCOME STATEMENTS

FRANKLIN J. PLEWA, JR. and
GEORGE T. FRIEDLOB

TORONTO   SINGAPORE

Copyright © 1995 by Franklin J. Plewa, Jr. and George T. Friedlob
Published by John Wiley & Sons, Inc.

Library of Congress Cataloging in Publication Data

Plewa, Franklin James, 1949–
    Understanding income statements/by Franklin Plewa, Jr. and George T. Friedlob.
        p. cm.
    Includes biographical references.
    Includes index.
    ISBN 0-471-10383-7 (cloth)—ISBN 0-471-010384-5 (pbk.)
    1. Income accounting.   2. Financial statements.   I. Friedlob, G. Thomas.   II. Title.
Hf5681.I48P55   1995
657'.3—dc20   94-29850

ACKNOWLEDGMENTS

We appreciate the patience of our families and the help of Trisa Starnes, graduate assistant at Idaho State University.

PREFACE

This book is for readers who have little or no accounting knowledge. For this reason, we assume nothing about the educational background of our readers. Those with exposure to business topics will see more quickly the relevance of the material, but the book will be useful to all financial statement users.

We emphasize the use of accounting information in making decisions, but focus on the income statement because we feel that it is the most important financial statement. Still, an analysis of the income statement must be done in the context of the total financial picture. The income statement should be studied only in the light of all the information presented in the annual report.

The reader will see that financial statements, and particularly the income statement, are not precise measurements or valuations. One of our objectives is to show the areas where accountants must make estimates and choose among competing accounting alternatives. We show how these estimates and alternatives might affect a user's analysis.

Judgement plays an important part in interpreting the economic consequences measured by the accounting process. Although financial statements appear to be the result of precise measurement and valuation, at times they are not, and the accountant's judgement can result in different interpretations of the same events.

Our main objectives in writing this book are:

1. To present the general principles that govern financial accounting and reporting.

2. To show how accounting data are created, accumulated, and used in the creation of the financial statements.

3. To show how information contained in the income statement is often the result of choices made by a company's management and how these choices affect the reader's analysis.

4. To show how data from a company's income statement are used by managers and third parties such as stockholders, bondholders, suppliers, and other creditors.

5. To show how information in the income statement is used for financial analysis.

6. To illustrate how accounting operates in our economy and influences economic decisions.

The first six chapters are devoted to general purpose financial statements and the principles underlying their preparation. Chapters 7 through 14 discuss the components of the income statement. Chapters 15 and 16 relate to earnings per share and the relationship of the income statement and the statement of retained earnings. The statement of cash flows is discussed in Chapter 17 while Chapter 18 presents a discussion of consolidated financial statements. Chapter 19 introduces the contents of the annual report. Supplemental information found in the footnotes is discussed in Chapter 20. Financial statement analysis is discussed in Chapters 21 and 22 and the quality of earnings in Chapter 23. Finally, we conclude with a discussion of international financial statements in Chapter 24.

Excerpts from actual annual reports are used extensively to illustrate points made in the text. Our intention is to create a working reference that enables you to understand the income statements and annual reports of public companies. We hope you make good decisions and a lot of money!

CONTENTS

1

THE ACCOUNTING PROCESS

The accounting process provides information that management, creditors, investors, and other interested parties use to evaluate the success and efficiency of a company. This chapter introduces the reader to the accounting process used to produce a company's financial statements. Later chapters focus on the income statement and parts of the annual report that assist in understanding and evaluating the income statement.

To be able to understand and evaluate a company's income statement, you must understand basic accounting. Our purpose is not to provide a lengthy, in-depth discussion of accounting, but merely to give you the basic structure so you can understand the rest of this book.

Structure of Accounting

Accounting is based on a simple relationship that explains the different types of accounts used to prepare financial statements. Accountants record economic events (called *transactions*) as they occur. These recordings are then summarized and presented as the company's financial statements. Such summarization enables interested parties to understand the economic activities of a company.

All economic resources that a company owns come from somewhere. The basic accounting relationship between resources and their sources (called the accounting equation) can be stated as:

$$\text{Resources Owned} = \text{Sources of the Resources Owned}$$

The dollar amount of the resources owned must equal the dollar amount of the sources of those resources. In accounting, the term for the resources owned by the company is *assets.* Companies obtain assets from two sources: borrowing (incurring debt) and owner investment. The dollar amount of assets must equal the dollar amount of debt plus owners' investment, resulting in the following equation:

$$\text{Assets} = \text{Debts} + \text{Owners' Investment}$$

The accounting term for debts is *liabilities. Owners' equity* is the accounting term for owners' investment. Owners' equity includes both the owners' direct investment and the reinvestment of company earnings not distributed to owners. In accounting terms the equation (sometimes called the balance sheet equation) is as follows:

$$\text{Assets} = \text{Liabilities} + \text{Owners' Equity}$$

Your understanding of the *balance sheet equation* is of paramount importance to your understanding of accounting and the financial statements. The use of this equation allows us to create a balance sheet (one of the basic financial statements) and provides us with a system of checks on the accuracy of the accounting system. This system of checks is called the *double-entry system,* because each economic event must affect the balance sheet equation in two ways in order to keep the equation in balance. To demonstrate this, assume that you start a company by investing $150,000.

The $150,000 investment affects two components of the equation: it increases assets (cash is an asset of the company) and owners' equity (the source of the investment). If we fail to increase either assets or owners' equity, the equation will not balance.

$$\text{Assets} = \text{Liabilities} + \text{Owners' Equity}$$
$$\$150,000 = \$-0- \qquad \$150,000$$

Assume next that the company purchases a warehouse for $45,000 cash. In this situation, the asset warehouse must be increased and the asset cash decreased. One asset is exchanged for another asset with the same value. You can see that the equation is still in balance.

	Assets	=	Liabilities	+	Owners' Equity
Beginning Balance	$150,000	=	$-0-		$150,000
Warehouse	+45,000				
Cash	−45,000				
Total	$150,000	=	$-0-	+	$150,000

Now assume that your company needs a six-month loan from the bank to assist in starting operations. The amount of the loan is $20,000. Assets and liabilities are both increased; that is, the asset account, Cash, is increased and the liability account, Bank Loan Payable, is increased. The increase in the Bank Loan Payable account shows that the company received cash (the resource or asset) from the bank (the source) and incurred a liability that will be repaid in six months.

	Assets	=	Liabilities	+	Owners' Equity
Beginning Balance	$150,000	=	$-0-		$150,000
Cash	20,000				
Bank Loan Payable			20,000		
Total	$170,000	=	$20,000	+	$150,000

You can see that the balance sheet equation is still in balance. When the bank loan is repaid, the Cash account is decreased, as is the Bank Loan Payable account, and once again the equation is in balance. It should be clear that this double entry system affects at least two accounts for every economic event.

Revenues are increases in owners' equity that result from increases in assets from doing business. For example, a company sells a product or performs a service and in return receives cash or a promise to be paid cash at a later date. The promise to pay by the buyer is called an *account receivable* and is an asset. In this situation you can readily see that the accounting equation is still in balance, because the account Cash or Accounts Receivable is increased and the sales or service revenue increases owners' equity.

Expenses are decreases in owners' equity that result in decreases in assets (or increases in liabilities) from doing business. For example, a company incurs many types of expenses in attempting to generate revenue from selling a product or providing a service to its customers. These expenses might include salaries and wages expense, commissions expense, selling expenses, and income tax expense. As an example, assume your company earns $75,000 providing consulting services to a client and incurs salaries expense of $32,000, paid in cash. In addition, commissions totaling $10,000 are also incurred, but will not be paid until next month. The effect on the balance sheet equation is:

	Assets	=	Liabilities	+	Owners' Equity
Beginning Balance	$170,000	=	$ 20,000	+	$150,000
Cash	+75,000				
Consulting Revenue					+75,000
Salaries Expense					−32,000
Cash	−32,000				
Commissions Expense					−10,000
Commissions Payable			+10,000		
Total	$213,000	=	$ 30,000	+	$183,000

The balance sheet equation is still in balance. Revenues and expenses are similar to assets, liabilities, and owners' equity in that they are types of accounts. Thus, the accounting equation can be expanded to include revenues and expenses, as follows:

$$\text{Assets} = \text{Liabilities} + \text{Owners' Equity} + \text{Revenues} - \text{Expenses}$$

This equation contains all the account types that you will encounter in published financial statements.

We will use the basic accounting equation in Chapter 2 when we discuss the financial statements in greater detail. The material in this chapter should also be reviewed in preparation for the discussion in Chapter 3.

Assets

Liabilities

A company has many types of assets and each type is reported in a separate account. Every account has its own name. A dollar amount tells the balance in each account. Assets of a typical company include cash, inventory, property, plant, and equipment, such as computers. As you have seen, a company increases its assets by borrowing and by earning revenues. Company assets are decreased by paying off debt, by paying expenses, and by owner withdrawals. Moreover, one asset can be exchanged for another, as in our example, when a company purchases a warehouse for cash.

Companies report their liabilities in separate accounts, just as they do for assets. Liabilities are also called "payables," and it is not unusual to find the word "payable" in the title of a liability account. Typical liability accounts include Accounts Payable (amounts owed to vendors and others), Bank Loan Payable, Salaries Payable, Notes Payable, and Bonds Payable. Liabilities are increased in several ways, including borrowing or incurring an expense with a promise by the company to pay for the goods or services at a later date. Liabilities are decreased by paying off a liability. In addition, one liability can be exchanged for another. For example, a company may refinance an obligation. In effect, it exchanges one type of loan obligation for another, normally with a change in the terms of the agreement.

Owners' Equity

Because the owners of a corporation are stockholders, the owners' equity of a corporation is normally referred to as *stockholders' equity*. There are two basic stockholders' equity accounts. One is the Common Stock account. The Common Stock account is increased when the owners (stockholders) invest cash in the company. Recall that revenues increase owners' equity and expenses decrease owners' equity. The Retained Earnings account consists of the excess of revenues over expenses (called net income, net earnings, or profit) that has not been distributed to the owners. We say that these earnings have been "retained" in the business, and this amount is recorded in the Retained Earnings account. Retained earnings is explained in greater detail later in this book.

2

BEGINNING WITH BUSINESS CASH FLOWS—
AN ILLUSTRATION

A company needs sufficient cash flow to transact daily business with its customers, meet operating expenses, and pay debts. In addition, if the business is a manufacturing or merchandising concern, cash flow is needed to purchase raw materials for manufacturing or for resale. Business managers understand the need to carefully manage cash flows to meet these demands; however, other parties are interested in the cash flows of a business too. These interested parties include lenders, suppliers, employees, and current and potential owners. Lenders want loans repaid, suppliers wish bills to be paid, employees desire to receive their salaries and wages, and owners want an adequate return on their investment. Therefore, these groups keep a close eye on cash.

To demonstrate how a business generates and expends cash, we provide an example, which can also be a valuable preview of the chapters ahead.

Assume the following regarding All-American Sporting Goods, Inc.:

Background—Mike Brady started a sporting goods business that has been in existence for three years at the end of the current year. Mike employs three salespersons who earn salaries for selling the store's various types of sporting goods. Mike invested $250,000 and incorporated the business as "All-American Sporting Goods, Inc."

On January 1 of the first year of operations, the business purchased a building for $95,000 cash. At that time, the building was supposed to last for approximately 25 years. On the same date, store equipment was also purchased for $10,000 cash. The store equipment was estimated to last 10 years.

The company has had an excess of revenues over expenses totaling $101,900 over the last two years. Mike Brady has made no withdrawals nor received other compensation during those two years.

Third Year—The current year is the third year of operations. The company's fiscal year end is December 31. Our reference point for the purpose of financial reporting is December 31 of the third year of operations.

The following information relates to the transactions occurring over the current year:

1. Cash on hand at the beginning of the year totaled $250,000.
2. On January 1 of the current year Mike Brady, acting for the corporation, signed a note payable for $40,000, agreeing to repay $20,000 plus interest on the note on the next January 1, and the remaining balance on the following January 1. Interest expense for the current year is $2,500. The proceeds of the note are to be used for expansion purposes.
3. The company purchased for cash additional store equipment costing $2,800 on January 1 of this year. The new store equipment was estimated to last for seven years.
4. During the year Mr. Brady invested an additional $5,000 in the business.
5. *Sales:* During the year sales of sporting goods totaled $120,000. Cash of $100,000 was collected during the year, of which $5,000 represented amounts owed to All-American by customers at the beginning of the

year. This left a balance of $25,000 owed to the company at the end of the year. The cost of the goods sold totaled $40,000 for the year.

6. *Salaries:* Salaries paid to employees totaled $35,000. Of this amount, $3,000 was earned by the employees in December of the previous year but not paid until January of the current year. At the end of this year, employees' December-earned salaries totaled $2,000. These salaries had not been paid at December 31 and will be paid in January of next year.

7. *Maintenance, insurance, and other operating expenses:* Also during the year costs for maintenance, insurance, and other operating expenses totaled $19,000, all paid in cash.

8. *Purchases:* All-American purchased on account various types of sporting goods from suppliers at a cost of $50,000. The company paid $51,000 to suppliers during the year, which included a payment of $8,500, representing the amount due at the end of the preceding year. The balance of $7,500 will be paid in January of next year. The company had goods on hand at the beginning of the current year costing $20,000.

9. *Federal and state income taxes:* Taxes for the year amounted to $10,290. These taxes will be paid in April of the following year. Income taxes owed at the beginning of the year (for the previous year) totaled $7,000 and were paid in April of the current year.

10. *Owner's withdrawals:* Mike Brady withdrew $40,000 cash as compensation for his efforts and investment.

At the end of the third year of operations, Brady's accountant prepared a report showing the cash receipts and disbursements for the company for the year.

ALL-AMERICAN SPORTING GOODS, INC.
STATEMENT OF CASH RECEIPTS AND DISBURSEMENTS FOR THE YEAR

Cash was received from:	
An additional investment by the owner	$ 5,000
Sales and payments on account for the prior year	100,000
Loan proceeds	40,000
Total cash received	145,000
Cash was used for:	
Payments of federal and state income taxes	7,000
Payments to suppliers for the current and prior years	51,000
Purchase of additional office equipment	2,800
Payment of salaries for the current and prior years	35,000
Withdrawal by owner	40,000
Payment of maintenance, insurance, and other operating expenses for the current year	19,000
Total cash used	$154,800
Decrease in cash for the year	$ (9,800)

How Did All-American Sporting Goods, Inc. Do This Year?

We see from the accountant's report that cash decreased during the year by $9,800. At first glance, you might conclude that All-American had a bad year. But in order to determine whether that conclusion is valid you must dig a little deeper, because the Statement of Cash Receipts and Disbursements does not answer two very important questions:

1. Did the business earn a profit for the year?

2. What was the financial condition of the resources and sources of the resources of the business at the end of the year?

Cash Flows Versus Profit

Actually, cash flow and profit of a company for a period are measures of the same business activity. It is very unusual for the cash flow of a company to equal its profit (or loss) for a period. This is because the vast majority of companies do business on *credit*. They sell products or services on credit, with amounts uncollected at the end of the accounting period called "accounts receivable." In addition, many companies buy goods that they resell and incur some operating expenses on account, and therefore have a liability to pay for the goods they purchase and the services they use. These amounts owed to others are liabilities. Specifically, they are called "accounts payable."

So you can see that the cash received during a current period does not measure revenues earned during that period. The amount of cash received includes amounts from the prior period's sales and does not include amounts owed to the company by customers that will be received in cash in the next period.

Likewise, cash paid is not a measure of expenses, because it includes payments of amounts owed from the prior period and does not include amounts owed at the end of the current period. These liabilities will be paid in the next period.

In determining whether a company has earned a profit, dis-tinctions are made between the sources of cash receipts and between the purposes of disbursements. Remember that the sources of cash are company operations, investments by own-ers, and borrowings. A company does not count as revenue the cash received from creditors and owners. You can see by look-ing at All-American's statement of cash receipts and disburse-ments that two of the sources of cash receipts are borrowing and owner's investment. Disbursements include payments to suppliers and to employees for salaries. Payments were also made for income taxes, maintenance, insurance, and other op-erating costs, and these payments are certainly related to ex-penses. However, a withdrawal by the owner and the purchase of office equipment do not constitute payments for expenses. The payment to the owner is in return for his investment, and the payment for office equipment is for an asset that will be used over an extended period of time. It does not make sense to treat the cost of the office equipment as an expense in just one year, but instead to "spread out" and consume the cost of the office equipment over its estimated useful life.

You can see then that the statement of cash receipts and dis-bursements is inadequate to learn whether All-American has earned a profit (revenues in excess of expenses). This type of accounting is called "cash basis" or "cash accounting." Adjustments must be made to the amounts in the statement, and other items not appearing in the statement must be included to determine profit. Making these adjustments involves the use of *accrual accounting*. Accrual accounting records the accounts receivable from making sales on credit, and requires the recording of liabilities for unpaid expenses and purchases in determining the correct amounts of revenues, expenses, and profit. Accrual accounting recognizes revenue in the period it is *earned*, regardless of when the cash is received, and recognizes expenses when they are *incurred*, regardless of when the cash is paid.

All-American's statement of cash receipts and disbursements does not adequately portray the resources and sources of those resources at the end of the current year. We do know the amount of cash on hand at the end of the year, but we do not know what the balances are for other asset, liability, or equity accounts.

Chapter 3 introduces the general-purpose financial statements and discusses the income statement and the balance sheet. These statements and a statement of cash flows (statement of cash receipts and disbursements) are generally presented in the annual report.

3

GENERAL PURPOSE FINANCIAL STATEMENTS—AN ILLUSTRATION

Stockholders, creditors, economists, financial analysts, suppliers, and customers all look to the financial information in a company's annual report to satisfy their information needs. Because the financial statements and accompanying footnotes must satisfy such a diverse group of users, annual reports are rigidly structured by both accounting rules and legal requirements.

The annual report includes discussions on a variety of topics, some based on accounting figures, and some not. These generally include management's evaluation of the results of operations for the current year, as well as the company's plans for the future. In addition, the company's independent external auditors (Certified Public Accountants, or CPAs) evaluate all the financial information provided in the annual report. A CPA's report is an expert opinion on the presentation and completeness of the financial statements and footnotes. This opinion is an important part of the annual report.

The core of an annual report is the financial statements, which must conform to accounting and reporting standards established primarily by the Financial Accounting Standards Board (FASB) and the Securities and Exchange Commission (SEC). Some feel that because of the high degree of structure found in the financial statements, reporting requirements are a mixed blessing. The rigid structure of financial reporting means that the specific needs of each user group cannot be addressed, so that each group of users may find something lacking in information content. But because of the high degree of structure and the involvement of the CPA, users of financial statements can be sure that the information they receive adheres to the fair presentation prescribed by the accounting profession.

Understanding General Purpose Financial Statements

Understanding financial accounting depends on your ability to read and interpret three basic financial statements. The basic accounting equation is discussed in Chapter 1. In this chapter we reintroduce the example from All-American Sporting Goods, Inc. and continue our discussion.

Background—Mike Brady started a sporting goods business that has been in existence for three years at the end of the current year. Mike employs three salespersons who earn salaries for selling the store's various types of sporting goods. Mike invested $250,000 and incorporated the business as "All-American Sporting Goods, Inc."

On January 1 of the first year of operations, the business purchased a building for $95,000 cash. At that time, the building was supposed to last for approximately 25 years. On the same date, store equipment was also purchased for $10,000 cash. The store equipment was estimated to last 10 years.

The company has had an excess of revenues over expenses totaling $101,900 over the last two years. Mike Brady has made no withdrawals or other compensation during those two years.

Third Year—The current year is the third year of operations. The company's fiscal year end is December 31. Our reference point for the purpose of financial reporting is December 31 of the third year of operations.

The following information relates to the transactions occurring over the year:

1. Cash on hand at the beginning of the year totaled $250,000.
2. On January 1 of the current year Mike Brady, acting for the corporation, signed a note payable for $40,000, agreeing to repay $20,000 plus interest on the note on the next January 1, and the remaining balance on the following January 1. Interest expense for the current year is $2,500. The proceeds of the note are to be used for expansion purposes.
3. The company purchased additional store equipment costing $2,800 for cash on January 1 of this year. The new store equipment was estimated to last for seven years.
4. During the year Mr. Brady invested an additional $5,000 in the business.

5. *Sales:* During the year sales of sporting goods totaled $120,000. Cash of $100,000 was collected during the year, of which $5,000 represented amounts owed to All-American by customers at the beginning of the year. This left a balance of $25,000 owed to the company at the end of the year. The cost of the goods sold totaled $40,000 for the year.

6. *Salaries:* Salaries paid to employees totaled $35,000. Of this amount, $3,000 was earned by the employees in December of the previous year but not paid until January of the current year. At the end of this year, employees' December-earned salaries totaled $2,000. These salaries had not been paid at December 31 and will be paid in January of next year.

7. *Maintenance, insurance, and other operating expenses:* Also during the year costs for maintenance, insurance, and other operating expenses totaled $19,000, all paid in cash.

8. *Purchases:* All-American purchased on account various types of sporting goods from suppliers at a cost of $50,000. Suppliers were paid $51,000 during the year, which included a payment for $8,500, representing the amount due at the end of the preceding year. The balance of $7,500 will be paid in January of next year. The company had goods on hand at the beginning of the current year costing $20,000.

9. *Federal and state income taxes:* Taxes for the year amounted to $10,290. These taxes will be paid in April of the following year. Income taxes owed at the beginning of the year (for the previous year) totaled $7,000 and were paid in April of the current year.

10. *Owner's withdrawals:* Mike Brady withdrew $40,000 cash as compensation for his efforts and investment.

At the end of the third year of operations, Brady's accountant prepared a report showing the cash receipts and disbursements for the company for the year.

ALL-AMERICAN SPORTING GOODS, INC.
STATEMENT OF CASH RECEIPTS AND DISBURSEMENTS FOR THE YEAR

Cash was received from:	
An additional investment by the owner	$ 5,000
Sales and payments on account for the prior year	100,000
Loan proceeds	40,000
Total cash received	145,000
Cash was used for:	
Payment of federal and state income taxes	7,000
Payments to suppliers for the current and prior years	51,000
Purchase of additional office equipment	2,800
Payment of salaries for the current and prior years	35,000
Withdrawal by owner	40,000
Payment of maintenance, insurance, and other operating expenses for the current year	19,000
Total cash used	$154,800
Decrease in cash for the year	$ (9,800)

In Chapter 2 we introduced accrual accounting and explained how it gives a company's financial condition or position at the end of the year, and helps us assess whether a company has earned a profit during the year. Accrual accounting (as opposed to cash accounting) culminates in an income statement and balance sheet presented as part of general-purpose financial statements. These statements and a statement of cash flows (statement of cash receipts and disbursements) are generally presented in the annual report. In its simplest form, the statement of financial position may be viewed as reporting the possessions the company owns at the end of the year, what the company owes, and what remains as the equity of the owner. The statement of financial position is the condition of the company at a point in time, in this example December 31 (or year end). The statement of financial position is also called a *balance sheet* because the resources are equal to (balance) the sources of the resources.

ALL-AMERICAN SPORTING GOODS, INC. STATEMENT OF FINANCIAL POSITION AT DECEMBER 31

Resources or Possessions

The company's possessions that will be used or exchanged for cash in the following year:

Cash on hand	$240,200
Amounts owed to All-American, receivable next year	25,000
Inventory of sporting goods purchased and unsold at year end	30,000
Total	295,200

The company's possessions that will be used over the next years:

Cost of building	95,000
Less: adjustment for building wearing out	(11,400)
	83,600
Cost of office equipment	12,800
Less: adjustment for office equipment wearing out	(3,400)
	9,400
Total possessions	$388,200

Sources

The company owes others within one year:

Payments to suppliers for purchases of sporting goods	$ 7,500
Salaries to employees for services rendered this year	2,000
Income taxes for the current year	10,290
Interest payable on the loan	2,500
First payment on loan	20,000
Total	42,290

The company owes other more than one year from now:

Second payment on loan*	20,000
Total owed to others	62,290

The owner's share of the company's possessions:

Mike Brady's equity in the company	325,910
Total owed to others plus owner's share	$388,200

*Interest on the building loan of $2,500 for the current year has been incurred by All-American and earned by the lender and therefore is shown as an obligation. That is, the $2,500 is an expense to the company because it has had the use of the money for one year. The company will not owe any interest on the balance ($20,000) until the end of the next year, which is why the obligation beyond one year includes only the principal portion of the final loan payment.

The balance sheet numbers are derived in the following manner:

Resources or Possessions

Cash:
(Beginning balance + receipts − disbursements)
$250,000 + $145,000 − $154,800 = ... $240,200
Amounts owed the company:
(Beginning balance + sales − cash received)
$5,000 + $120,000 − $100,000 = ... 25,000
Inventory of sporting goods:
(Beginning balance + purchases − cost of sporting goods sold)
$20,000 + $50,000 − $40,000 = ... 30,000
Total 295,200

Building: 95,000
Less: adjustment for building wearing out
The building has an estimated life of 25 years. Therefore, accountants "spread" the cost of the building over its life. This means that the cost of the building is expensed at a rate of $3,800 ($95,000/25 years) per year. Since the building has been owned for three years, the accumulated amount for wear and tear is 3 × $3,800 or ..... (11,400)
83,600

Office Equipment:
Beginning balance + purchases of equipment
$10,000 + $2,800 = ... 12,800
Less: adjustment for office equipment wearing out
The company initially purchased office equipment costing $10,000. The estimated life of the equipment on the date of purchase was 10 years; therefore $1,000 of the cost of the equipment would be charged to expense each year. Since the equipment has been owned for three years the accumulated amount is $3,000. In the current year, the company purchased additional office equipment at a cost of $2,800 with an estimated life of seven years. The amount of the adjustment for each year in the life of the equipment would be $400 ($2,800/7 years). The accumulated amount would be $3,000 + $400 or ..... (3,400)
9,400

Total possessions $388,200

Sources

Owed to others within one year:

Payments to suppliers:
(Beginning balance + purchases − payment of prior years' balance)
$8,500 + $50,000 − $51,000 = ... $ 7,500
Salaries:
(Beginning balance + salary expense from the income statement below − salaries paid)
$3,000 + $34,000 − $35,000 = ... 2,000
Income taxes:
(Beginning balance + income tax expense from the income statement below − income taxes paid)
$7,000 + $10,290 − $7,000 = ... 10,290
First payment on loan (given) 20,000
Interest payment on loan (given) 2,500
Total 42,290

Owed to others more than one year:

Second payment on loan (given) 20,000
Total owed to others 62,290

The owner's share of the company's possessions:

Mike Brady's equity in the company:
(Beginning balance + additional owner investments + revenues from the income statement below − expenses from the income statement below − owner withdrawals)

Mike Brady initially invested $250,000 as his equity in the company. The company has been profitable in the preceding years, with revenues exceeding expenses by $101,900. Therefore, the beginning owner's equity in the company is $351,900.
$351,900 + $5,000 + $120,000 − 110,990 − $40,000 = ... 325,910
Total owed to others plus owner's share $388,200

The income, or profit or loss, statement presents the revenues and expenses for a period of time (rather than at a point in time). The income statement for All-American is for the current (or third) year.

ALL-AMERICAN SPORTING GOODS, INC.
INCOME STATEMENT FOR THE YEAR
ENDED DECEMBER 31

Revenues:
Sales of sporting goods	$120,000
Expenses:	
Cost of sporting goods sold	40,000
Salaries	34,000
Maintenance, insurance, and other operating expenses	19,000
Interest	2,500
Adjustments for building and office equipment wearing out	5,200
Federal and state income taxes	10,290
Total operating expenses	110,990
Net income (or profit)	$ 9,010

Revenues
Sales: (given)	$120,000
Expenses:	
Cost of sporting goods sold (given)	40,000
Salaries (amount paid − amount owed at the beginning of the year + amount owed at end of year)	
$35,000 − $3,000 + $2,000 =	34,000
Maintenance, insurance, and other operating expenses (given)	19,000
Interest (given)	2,500
Adjustments for wear and tear on building and office equipment	
[$3,800 + ($1,000 + $400)] =	5,200
Federal and state income taxes	
(Amount paid − amount owed at the beginning of the year + amount owed at end of year)	
$7,000 − $7,000 + $10,290 =	10,290
Total operating expenses	110,990
Net income (or profit)	$ 9,010

The amounts appearing in the income statement were derived as follows:

Conventional General Purpose Financial Statements

As previously mentioned, the first statement is called a Balance Sheet, the second statement an Income Statement (or Profit and Loss Statement), and the third a Statement of Cash Flows.

These types of reports are prepared for all businesses. Reports prepared for large corporations such as Ford Motor Company and Nike, Inc. are produced following the same methodology as demonstrated in the preceding example. General purpose financial statements normally take the following form as illustrated in Exhibits 3-1, 3-2, and 3-3.

EXHIBIT 3-1 BALANCE SHEET—ALL-AMERICAN SPORTING GOODS, INC.

At December 31

ASSETS

Current Assets:		
Cash		$240,200
Accounts Receivable		25,000
Inventory		30,000
Total Current Assets		295,200
Noncurrent Assets:		
Building	$ 95,000	
Less: Accumulated Depreciation	(11,400)	83,600
Office Equipment	12,800	
Less: Accumulated Depreciation	(3,400)	9,400
Total Noncurrent Assets		93,000
Total Assets		$388,200

LIABILITIES

Current Liabilities:	
Accounts Payable	$ 7,500
Salaries Payable	2,000
Income Taxes Payable	10,290
Interest Payable	2,500
Loan Payable	20,000
Total Current Liabilities	42,290
Noncurrent Liabilities:	
Loan Payable	20,000
Total Liabilities	62,290

OWNERS' EQUITY

Brady, Equity	$325,910
Total Liabilities and Owners' Equity	$388,200

EXHIBIT 3-2 INCOME STATEMENT—ALL-AMERICAN SPORTING GOODS, INC.

For Year Ended December 31

Sales		$120,000
Less: Cost of Goods Sold		40,000
Gross Margin		80,000
Less: Operating Expenses		
Salaries		34,000
Maintenance, Insurance, and Other Operating Expenses		19,000
Depreciation		5,200
Total Operating Expenses		58,200
Operating Income		21,800
Interest Expense		2,500
Income Before Taxes		19,300
Income Tax Expense		10,290
Net Income		$ 9,010

EXHIBIT 3-3 STATEMENT OF CASH FLOWS—ALL-AMERICAN SPORTING GOODS, INC.

For Year Ended December 31

Cash Flows from Operating Activities:		
Cash Collected from Customers		$100,000
Less: Cash Paid for Expenses		
For Income Taxes	$ 7,000	
For Payments to Suppliers	51,000	
For Payment of Salaries	35,000	
For Payment of Maintenance, Insurance, and Other Operating Expenses	19,000	112,000
Cash Used by Operating Activities		(12,000)
Cash Flows from Investing Activities:		
Purchase of Office Equipment		(2,800)
Cash Flows from Financing Activities:		
Proceeds of Loan	$ 40,000	
Additional Investment by Owner	5,000	
Withdrawal by Owner	(40,000)	
Total Cash Flows from Financing Activities		5,000
Decrease in cash		(9,800)
Cash, Beginning of the Year		250,000
Cash, End of the Year		$240,200

You can see that the form of general purpose financial statements differs only slightly from the statements shown earlier in this chapter. The next two chapters discuss in greater detail the Balance Sheet, Income Statement, and Statement of Cash Flows of All-American Sporting Goods, Inc.

4

THE BALANCE SHEET—AN ILLUSTRATION

As explained in Chapter 1, accountants use double-entry bookkeeping based on the relationship between the company's resources and the sources of those resources. Business resources (assets) are obtained by borrowing (creating a liability), by the investment of owners, and by the reinvestment of profits resulting from profitable operations (creating an equity by the owner). The relationship between assets, liabilities, and owners' equity is:

$$Assets = Liabilities + Owners' Equity$$

A balance sheet, or statement of financial position, is a report that shows a company's assets, liabilities, and owners' equity at a specific date or point in time. Exhibit 4-1 is the Balance Sheet for All-American Sporting Goods, Inc. that we introduced as Exhibit 3-1 in Chapter 3.

EXHIBIT 4-1   BALANCE SHEET—ALL-AMERICAN SPORTING GOODS, INC.

At December 31

ASSETS		
Current Assets:		
Cash		$240,200
Accounts Receivable		25,000
Inventory		30,000
Total Current Assets		295,200
Noncurrent Assets:		
Building	$ 95,000	
Less: Accumulated Depreciation	(11,400)	83,600
Office Equipment	12,800	
Less: Accumulated Depreciation	(3,400)	9,400
Total Noncurrent Assets		93,000
Total Assets		$388,200
LIABILITIES		
Current Liabilities:		
Accounts Payable		$ 7,500
Salaries Payable		2,000
Income Taxes Payable		10,290
Interest Payable		2,500
Loan Payable		20,000
Total Current Liabilities		42,290
Noncurrent Liabilities:		
Loan Payable		20,000
Total Liabilities		62,290
OWNERS' EQUITY		
Brady, Equity		325,910
Total Liabilities and Owners' Equity		$388,200

Classified Balance Sheet

A balance sheet is normally prepared with the accounts grouped according to their liquidity (ease of conversion into cash), length of economic life, or some other characteristic. When accountants prepare a balance sheet with the accounts grouped in this manner, we call the statement a *classified balance sheet*. Generally, most classified balance sheets contain the following asset, liability, and owners' equity categories, as shown in Exhibit 4-2.

EXHIBIT 4-2 ASSET, LIABILITY, AND STOCKHOLDERS' EQUITY CATEGORIES

ASSETS	LIABILITIES
Current Assets	Current Liabilities
Noncurrent Assets:	Noncurrent Liabilities
Investments	
Property, Plant, and Equipment	
Natural Resources	
Intangibles	
Other Assets	STOCKHOLDERS' EQUITY
	Owners' Equity

Each category contains individual accounts. For example, current assets include accounts such as Cash, Accounts Receivable, and Inventory. Property, Plant, and Equipment include a company's long-lived productive assets (such as land, buildings, and machinery). Owners' equity includes the Common Stock and Retained Earnings accounts.

Current Assets

Assets are listed in the balance sheet in order of decreasing liquidity. Current assets is the first category. A current asset will be either converted into cash or used (consumed) in the course of the business within one operating cycle or one year, whichever is longer. Most current assets will be converted into cash. Inventory is sold for cash or on account. Accounts receivable will be collected in cash. One exception is prepayments. For example, businesses, like individuals, normally pay for insurance coverage in advance, creating an asset—the right to have insurance protection for a future period. The value of the right (the amount of the prepayment) declines as time passes. The asset is used up, or consumed, in the course of the business.

Current assets are listed on the balance sheet in order of decreasing liquidity, or the ease with which the asset can be converted to cash. Cash is always listed first because it is already cash. Accounts receivable are listed second (one step away from cash—collection), and then inventories (two steps away from cash—sale and collection). Last is prepayments, which include payments for insurance, rent, and salary advances to employees.

You can see that the current assets of All-American consist of cash, accounts receivable, and inventory, totaling $295,200.

Noncurrent Assets

All assets not classified as current are noncurrent. Noncurrent assets have lives longer than one year or one operating cycle and, for the most part, are consumed by the business and not converted into cash. Noncurrent assets are of several types. The most common long-lived assets are property, plant, and equipment used to manufacture products. Other noncurrent assets include investments, intangibles, and other assets.

Investments—Companies may invest idle funds in various ways. A company can choose to leave its cash invested in a savings account or in certificates of deposit, or to invest the cash in stocks and/or bonds of other companies. If a particular investment is to be held for less than one year and then sold and converted to cash, it is classified as a current asset. On the other hand, long-term investments are included between current assets and plant, property, and equipment on the balance sheet. All-American has no investments.

Property, Plant, and Equipment—Most companies, especially manufacturers, own property, plant, and equipment. Land, buildings, machinery, office equipment, and all other long-lived physical assets used in the business appear in this category. When long-lived assets are purchased, they are recorded at cost. This cost is sometimes referred to as the asset's "historical cost." As explained in Chapter 2, this cost is "spread out" and consumed over the assets' estimated useful life.

Another way of looking at this process is that we are allocating a portion of an asset's usefulness to each period of its economic life. This is called depreciation. In ordinary usage depreciation means a decline in value, but to an accountant, *depreciation* is the assignment of the historical cost of a long-lived asset to periods of use. Depreciation results in matching the costs of business (expenses) with the benefits (revenues). The company records the using up of the historical cost of the asset, rather than recording the decline in value. Depreciation appears as an expense in the income statement. *Accumulated depreciation* is the amount of depreciation that the company has taken on its assets since they were purchased. It is the cumulative amount of the asset cost charged off as an expense when the asset was used and its benefit consumed. Contrary to popular belief, accumulated depreciation does not represent an amount of cash that the company sets aside to replace its assets.

All-American presents the cost of its building at $95,000 and the cost of the office equipment at $12,800. The related accumulated depreciation amounts are $11,400 and $3,400, respectively. Exhibit 4–3 shows the property, plant, and equipment information from the annual report of Digital Equipment Corporation.

EXHIBIT 4-3   CONSOLIDATED BALANCE SHEETS— DIGITAL EQUIPMENT CORPORATION

(in thousands)

	July 3, 1993	June 27, 1992
Property, Plant and Equipment *(Note A)*		
Land	$ 363,264	$ 372,989
Buildings	1,887,211	1,871,710
Leasehold improvements	532,369	592,971
Machinery and equipment	4,410,586	4,835,454
Total property, plant and equipment	7,193,430	7,673,124
Less accumulated depreciation	4,015,139	4,103,422
Net property, plant and equipment	$3,178,291	$3,569,702

NOTE A: **Property, Plant and Equipment**—Property, plant and equipment are stated at cost. Depreciation expense is computed principally on the following bases:

Classification	*Depreciation Lives and Methods*
Buildings	33 years (straight-line)
Leasehold Improvements	Life of assets or term of lease, whichever is shorter (straight-line)
Machinery and Equipment	3 to 10 years (accelerated methods)

Natural Resources—Many companies own stands of timber, oil fields, and coal, mineral, or other ore deposits. These assets are called natural resources or wasting assets. You can see from Exhibit 4-4 that Georgia Pacific Corporation and Subsidiaries has approximately 13% of its total assets consisting of timber and timberlands in both 1992 and 1993. The basis for recording these assets is the cost of acquiring the asset and placing it in service—including any costs of exploration or development. Wasting assets are consumed through extraction or production. Expensing the costs of natural resources is called *depletion*. For example, if a stand of timber costs $2 million and is expected to produce 4 million cords of wood, the depletion rate per cord is $.50 ($2,000,000/4,000,000 cords). If 500,000 cords are removed and sold in one year, the depletion expense for that year is (500,000 × $.50) $250,000.

EXHIBIT 4-4   BALANCE SHEETS—GEORGIA PACIFIC CORPORATION AND SUBSIDIARIES

	December 31	
(Millions, except shares and per share amounts)	1993	1992
Assets		
Current assets		
Cash	$ 41	$ 55
Receivables, less allowances of $32 and $35	377	331
Inventories		
Raw materials	367	321
Finished goods	786	792
Supplies	262	282
LIFO reserve	(213)	(203)
Total inventories	1,202	1,192
Other current assets	26	29
Total current assets	1,646	1,607
Timber and timberlands, net	1,381	1,402
Property, plant and equipment		
Land and improvements	237	247
Buildings	1,074	1,101
Machinery and equipment	9,550	9,420
Construction in progress	125	64
Total property, plant and equipment, at cost	10,986	10,832
Accumulated depreciation	(5,538)	(5,001)
Property, plant and equipment, net	5,448	5,831
Goodwill	1,832	1,891
Other assets	238	181
Total assets	$10,545	$10,912

The accompanying notes are an integral part of these financial statements.

NOTE: **Timber and Timberlands**—The Corporation depletes its investment in timber based on the total fiber that will be available during the estimated growth cycle. Timber carrying costs are expensed as incurred.

Intangible Assets—Intangible assets are long-lived productive resources that have no physical existence. Their value comes from rights and privileges granted to the company owning them. Examples include patents, copyrights, trademarks and tradenames, franchises, leaseholds, and goodwill.

Intangible assets are recorded at historical cost. Like plant, property, and equipment, the cost of an intangible asset is allocated over its estimated useful life. This allocation process is called *amortization*. Amortization is an expense similar to depreciation or depletion. Generally accepted accounting principles require that intangibles be amortized over the shorter of their (1) legal lives, (2) their economic (useful) lives, or (3) 40 years.

Other Assets—The items in this section of the balance sheet vary widely. This category includes all other assets not classified as current assets, long-term investments, property, plant, and equipment, natural resources, or intangibles. This category might include such costs as debt issue costs, software development costs, or land held for resale. All-American does not have items classified as other assets. Exhibit 4-5 is an excerpt from the balance sheet and the notes to financial statements of Lafarge Corporation, showing the company's Other Assets balance sheet category.

EXHIBIT 4-5 BALANCE SHEET—
LA FARGE CORPORATION

(in thousands)

	December 31	
	1993	1992
Assets		
Cash and cash equivalents	$ 109,294	$ 84,658
Receivables, net	253,207	244,694
Inventories	186,082	222,205
Other current assets	36,661	28,585
Total current assets	585,244	580,142
Property, plant and equipment, net	880,724	982,277
Excess of cost over net assets of businesses acquired, net	39,636	43,049
Other assets	168,114	161,973
Total Assets	$1,673,718	$1,767,441

See notes to Consolidated Financial Statements

NOTE: **Other Assets**

Other assets consist of the following (in thousands):

	December 31	
	1993	1992
Long-term receivables	$ 23,896	$ 26,788
Investments in unconsolidated companies	37,688	36,817
Prepaid pension asset	56,493	48,820
Property held for sale	26,235	26,053
Other	23,802	23,495
Total other assets	$168,114	$161,973

Property held for sale represents certain permanently closed cement plants and land which are carried at the lower of cost or estimated net realizable value.

Current Liabilities

Current liabilities are obligations of the company that are expected to be paid from current assets within one year of the balance sheet date. Current liabilities include accounts payable, short-term bank loans payable, interest payable, salaries payable, taxes payable, and the current portion of long-term debt (discussed in the following paragraph). All-American has current liabilities consisting of accounts payable, salaries payable, income taxes payable, interest payable, and loan payable. All-American's current liabilities total $42,290.

Noncurrent Liabilities

Noncurrent, or long-term, liabilities are obligations that the company does not expect to be paid for at least one year from the date of the balance sheet and that are not expected to be paid from current assets. Examples include loans, mortgages, and bonds payable. Most noncurrent liabilities require periodic payments of principal and interest. The portion of principal that is due within one year is a current liability. All-American has one long-term liability, a payment of $20,000 due more than one year from December 31.

The liability section of Thiokol Corporation's Balance Sheet is presented in Exhibit 4-6. Note which accounts are shown as current and noncurrent.

EXHIBIT 4-6   BALANCE SHEET—
THIOKOL CORPORATION,
CONSOLIDATED BALANCE SHEETS

(in millions)	June 30 1993	1992
Liabilities		
Current Liabilities		
Short-term debt	$ 27.0	$ 20.1
Accounts payable	33.2	42.6
Accrued compensation	48.0	50.4
Other accrued expenses	28.7	41.9
Income taxes	12.8	2.0
Current portion of deferred income taxes		100.6
Current portion of long-term debt	34.7	102.7
Total Current Liabilities	184.4	360.3
Noncurrent Liabilities		
Long-term debt	87.9	123.0
Deferred income taxes	62.7	36.9
Accrued interest and other	62.8	54.7
Total Noncurrent Liabilities	213.4	214.6

See notes to consolidated financial statements.

Stockholders' Equity

From the basic balance sheet equation

$$Assets \ = \ Liabilities \ + \ Owner's \ Equity$$

we can rearrange the categories to highlight owners' equity:

$$Assets \ - \ Liabilities \ = \ Owner's \ Equity$$

In this form, owners' equity is also referred to as the *net assets* of the company. In proprietorships only one owner's equity account is used to record the owner's interest in the company. In large, widely held public companies the owners' interests are represented by shares of stock, and the Common Stock account appears in the stockholders' equity section of the balance sheet. Retained earnings contains the excess of revenues over expenses and owner withdrawals from the inception of the company to the current balance sheet date. For corporations, owner withdrawals are called *dividends*, which are really distributions of earnings. Retained earnings is net earnings, minus dividends paid, to date.

In the All-American example, we assume Mike Brady received shares of stock for his initial investment of $250,000 and his additional investment of $5,000. We know that the excess of revenues over expenses for the first two years is $101,900 and that Brady made no withdrawals (received no dividends) during those years. In the third or current year, Brady withdrew $40,000 and the company earned a profit of $9,010. We can now recast the liability and equity section for All-American in Exhibit 4-7 using the Common Stock and Retained Earnings accounts.

EXHIBIT 4-7 LIABILITY AND STOCKHOLDERS' EQUITY— ALL-AMERICAN SPORTING GOODS, INC.

At December 31

LIABILITIES

Current Liabilities:
Accounts Payable	$ 7,500
Salaries Payable	2,000
Income Taxes Payable	10,290
Interest Payable	2,500
Loan Payable	20,000
Total Current Liabilities	42,290

Noncurrent Liabilities:
Loan Payable	20,000
Total Liabilities	62,290

STOCKHOLDERS' EQUITY

Common Stock[*]	$255,000
Retained Earnings[**]	70,910
Total Stockholders' Equity	325,910
Total Liabilities and Stockholders' Equity	$188,200

[*] $250,000 + $5,000
[**] $101,900 + $9,010 − $40,000

5

ILLUSTRATIVE INCOME STATEMENT AND STATEMENT OF CASH FLOWS

Accountants and users of financial statements generally feel that the income statement is more important than the balance sheet. A strong earnings record can overcome a high level of debt on the balance sheet and convince an investor to invest in the company. However, even a moderate level of debt may cause an investor to doubt that a company will survive if the company's earnings record is poor.

We saw in Chapter 2 that a company's cash flow and profit are measures of the same business activity, even though it is unusual for cash flows to equal profit (or loss) for any particular period. The implication is that the statement of cash flows contains important information that augments the information in the income statement.

In this chapter we conclude our consideration of the financial statements of All-American Sporting Goods, Inc. with a discussion of the income statement and statement of cash flows.

The Income Statement

The income statement for All-American, which appears in Exhibit 5–1, reports the results of business activities of All-American for a year of operations.

EXHIBIT 5-1 INCOME STATEMENT—ALL-AMERICAN SPORTING GOODS, INC.

For Year Ended December 31

Sales	$120,000
Less: Cost of Goods Sold	40,000
Gross Margin	80,000
Less: Operating Expenses	
Salaries	34,000
Maintenance, Insurance, and Other Operating Expenses	19,000
Depreciation	5,200
Total Operating Expenses	58,200
Operating Income	21,800
Interest Expense	2,500
Income Before Taxes	19,300
Income Tax Expense	10,290
Net Income	$ 9,010

The benefits and costs of operations are revenues and expenses; the excess of revenues over expenses is net income. If expenses exceed revenues, a net loss is incurred. Revenues measure the inflow of assets resulting from the earnings process; expenses measure the outflow. Net income causes an increase in net assets and owners' equity; a loss has the opposite effect.

You can see that All-American has earned a profit of $9,010. Revenues total $120,000, and the amount the company paid for the inventory it sold was $40,000. This expense is called "Cost of Goods Sold." The difference between Sales and Cost of Goods Sold ($80,000) is "Gross Margin" or "Gross Profit." This profit margin must exceed all other costs if the company is to earn a profit. Users of financial statements are interested in a company's gross margin and may track this amount from year to year. Another useful measure of company performance is the gross margin percentage, computed by dividing the gross margin by sales. All-American's gross margin percentage is 67%. Company performance in the same industry can be compared using this ratio.

All-American's operating expenses total $58,200 and are deducted from its gross margin to arrive at operating income of $21,800. Operating income is another item that users follow from period to period to assess company performance. Interest expense is a financing expense, not an operating expense, and is subtracted from operating income to get income before taxes of $19,300. Deducting the income taxes of $10,290 results in net income of $9,010.

Compare this form of income statement presentation to the initial presentation found in Chapter 3 prior to the discussion relating to conventional general purpose financial statements. A greater amount of detail is provided with the current format, and readers find it much more useful in making company comparisons.

Statement of Cash Flows

Chapter 2 discussed the statement of cash receipts and disbursements. At that time we mentioned that this statement was important in determining cash inflows and outflows for the year. The statement of cash flows identifies the sources and uses of cash and assists financial statement users by providing information about a company's liquidity and solvency.

Liquidity is the ability of a company to pay its short-term debts. A company that cannot pay its creditors is not liquid. *Solvency* is the company's ability to pay all its debts, both short- and long-term. Information on liquidity is shown by a company's current operating cash receipts and payments. Information on solvency is shown in the company's investing and financing activities.

Operating activities are associated with the earning of net income. As a general rule, all cash flows that are not caused by investing or financing activities result from operating activities. During the year, All-American had net income of $9,010, but a net cash outflow of $12,000 from operations.

Investing activities consume cash when noncurrent investments are acquired, and provide cash when noncurrent investments are liquidated. We use the term *investments* here in the general sense. That is, investments include the purchase or sale of noncurrent assets, such as plant, property, or equipment, as well as investments in other companies' securities. During the third year, All-American had one investing activity, the purchase of office equipment for $2,800.

Financing activities include most interactions between a company and its stockholders or long-term creditors. Financing activities provide the company with long-term capital (debt and equity). As you can see from Exhibit 5–2, All-American had three financing activities during the year. The company borrowed $40,000, had an additional investment by the owner of $5,000, and a dividend to the owner (withdrawal) of $40,000. The net effect of these activities was to provide a cash inflow of $5,000 from financing activities. Summing the operating, investing, and financing activities results in a net decrease in cash of $9,800.

EXHIBIT 5-2 STATEMENT OF CASH FLOWS—
ALL-AMERICAN SPORTING GOODS, INC.

For Year Ended December 31

Cash Flows from Operating Activities:		
Cash Collected from Customers		$100,000
Less: Cash Paid for Expenses		
For Income Taxes	$ 7,000	
For Payments to Suppliers	51,000	
For Payment of Salaries	35,000	
For Payment of Maintenance, Insurance,		
and Other Operating Expenses	19,000	112,000
Cash Used by Operating Activities		(12,000)
Cash Flows from Investing Activities:		
Purchase of Office Equipment		(2,800)
Cash Flows from Financing Activities:		
Proceeds of Loan	$ 40,000	
Additional Investment by Owner	5,000	
Dividend	(40,000)	
Total Cash Flows from Financing Activities		5,000
Decrease in cash		(9,800)
Cash, Beginning of the Year		250,000
Cash, End of the Year		$240,200

This ends our illustration of All-American's general purpose financial statements. The discussion should give you a foundation for chapters that follow. The rest of the book deals with the most important financial statement—the income statement.

6

ACCOUNTING CONVENTIONS
AND ASSUMPTIONS

Generally accepted accounting principles (GAAP) are the rules that govern how accountants measure, process, and communicate financial information. GAAP are probably much more extensive than you might think. They are the conventions, rules, and procedures necessary to define accepted accounting practice at a particular time. GAAP include both broad guidelines and relatively detailed practices and procedures. In a way, GAAP are much like our system of law, in that they are a set of rules used to govern behavior, according to what is acceptable to a majority of people.

In Chapters 3 through 5 we defined and identified what constitutes general purpose financial statements and their elements. Now it is important to understand the underlying bases for measuring and valuing each financial statement element. The amounts that appear in the financial statements are dependent on the accounting methods used, which in turn are dependent on the conventions and assumptions adopted by the accounting profession. To understand financial statements, it is necessary to understand the fundamental basis on which they are prepared.

The Accounting Entity Concept

Probably the most basic concept in accounting is the entity concept. This is because financial statements represent the results of operations and the financial condition of a specific company based on past economic transactions. The concept assumes that the company stands apart from other organizations, individuals, and its owners as a separate economic entity.

To understand the importance of the entity concept, consider the following situation. You are employed as a manager of a department store. After work you also operate a business repairing small appliances. You make deposits into your personal checking account for revenues you earn from your small business, and you pay expenses out of that same account. If you do not maintain separate records for your repair business, how will you know whether it is profitable?

Therefore, you maintain separate records for your business, as a separate entity.

Consider also General Motors Corporation (GMC) with its Buick, Cadillac, Chevrolet, Oldsmobile, Pontiac, and Saturn divisions. If each division was not treated as a separate accounting entity, GMC would not know which divisions were profitable and which were not.

An accounting entity is not determined by legal form. For example, only corporations and trusts are granted legal existence separate and apart from their owners. Legally, a sole proprietorship or a partnership is considered to be an extension of its owner or owners' personal affairs. Accountants do, though, account for the personal affairs of the owners as separate from the business affairs of each of these entities.

The Cost Principle

The cost principle states that assets and services acquired by an entity should be recorded at their *historical costs*. If a building is purchased by a business for $450,000, the accounting records reflect that amount as its cost for as long as that business holds that asset. The $450,000 is the asset's recorded value regardless of current or future changes in its market value, and as such, the valuation for accounting purposes may not be the same as the building's market value. This is an inherent limitation of historical-cost-based financial statements; however, accountants justify the use of historical cost on the grounds that it is objective.

The Objectivity Principle

When accountants state that financial statements are based on objective information, they mean that the activities that underlie the accounting records have been documented by objective evidence. This assures that the information found in the financial statements will be reliable and as useful as possible. The cost principle is consistent with the concept of objectivity, in that cost is normally the most objective measurement available. For example, assume that you purchase a building for your business for $75,000 cash. What makes the recording of the building at $75,000 objective? The exchange price was negotiated by a willing buyer and a willing seller, and the documentation supporting the exchange is verifiable by any outside party.

Unit of Measure Assumption

Going Concern Assumption (Concept)

Closely tied to the cost principle is the unit of measure assumption. Accountants assume that the U.S. dollar is the appropriate unit of measure employed in the financial statements of U.S. companies. Assets are recorded at their historical cost in U.S. dollars. Sometimes the assumption is referred to as the "stable monetary unit concept," because accountants assume that the dollar's purchasing power is relatively stable, and so exchange transactions as measured in dollars are not adjusted for inflation or deflation. That is, even if the U.S. economy is experiencing inflation, causing the purchasing power of the dollar to decrease, no adjustments are made in the accounting records for this fact.

The classification of assets and liabilities as current and noncurrent implies that the business will continue in existence in the foreseeable future. Many of the business' assets, such as land, buildings, and equipment, were purchased to use, rather than to sell. The going concern assumption presumes the company will remain in existence long enough to use its existing assets for their intended purpose. This assumption allows a company to record its assets at their historical cost and carry over to a certain period values assigned to those assets in previous periods.

If available evidence indicated that the company would not continue as a going concern, there would be no purpose in classifying assets or liabilities as current or noncurrent. In this instance, the assets would be converted into cash to satisfy the claims of creditors. The appropriate valuation for assets, then, would be their liquidation value, rather than their historical cost.

Time Period Concept

Without the time period concept, the only way one would know whether a company had earned a profit would be for the company to sell all of its assets, pay off its creditors, and return any excess to the owner or owners. Obviously, it is not feasible for a company to measure income in this manner; therefore, the economic life of a company is "sliced" into artificial time periods. The most common period of time for financial reporting purposes is a year. The year that starts on January 1 and ends on December 31 is called a calendar year. If a company's year-end is other than December 31, the accounting period is called a fiscal year. A company's year-end normally coincides with the low point in business activity. Many retailers have a fiscal year-end of January 31 because this is the low point in their year following after-Christmas sales in January.

Revenue Recognition Principle

The revenue recognition principle requires revenue to be recognized (recorded) when the activities necessary to sell a good or provide a service have been substantially completed. Revenue is recorded when earned, regardless of when cash is received. If your business receives $10,000 in cash in exchange for a promise by your company to provide excavation services next month, should your company record revenue? The answer is no, because revenue should be recognized only when your company has done virtually everything needed to complete its part of the transaction and the customer has accepted the work.

Matching Principle

The matching principle forms the basis for the recording of business expenses. Expenses are the using up of assets. The matching principle requires accountants to identify and measure expenses during a certain period and to match those expenses against the revenues earned during that period. These matched expenses are deducted from revenues of the period to determine net income or loss.

Sometimes there is a natural link between a revenue and an expense. For example, when a retailer sells a product, that product has a cost. The cost is the amount that the retailer paid to acquire the item. The cost of the product is matched against the sales price of the product. Accountants say that there is a "cause and effect" relationship; that is, if there is no sale there cannot be a cost of goods sold.

Other types of expenses do not have this natural linkage. Items such as factory rent and the cost of long-lived productive assets are examples of the type of costs that do not have a cause and effect relationship to the generation of revenue. These expenses are associated with a certain period of time. The factory rent is allocated over the period of benefit—the lease term. The cost of long-lived productive assets are expensed over their useful life—a process we call depreciation. The point is that these types of costs are systematically and rationally allocated to expense over the period of benefit.

Other costs that are not long-lived and do not have a causal relationship to revenue are immediately recognized as expenses. Supervisory salaries are an example of such costs. This type of expense is associated with a particular time period and charged to expense in that period. Supervisory salaries might be associated with a month; they cannot be directly linked with sales for that period, so they are treated as an expense of that month.

Substance over Form

Accountants report the economic substance of transactions without regard to their form. The most common example of this concept involves a leasing transaction whereby the company leases equipment for 10 years. Assume the lessor maintains title to the equipment. If the economic life of the equipment is 10 years and the lessee (the company) must pay for basic maintenance and insurance on the equipment, then in substance the company has purchased the machine. The lessor has transferred the basic rights and obligations of ownership to the lessee company. The transaction is simply an alternative way to purchase the equipment. The company records an asset and a related obligation in the same manner it would had it purchased the asset by borrowing from a bank. Legally, the form of the transaction constitutes a lease, while in substance the transaction is a purchase.

Conservatism

Conservatism in accounting refers to a downward measurement bias in recording economic transactions. The concept is used to prevent overvaluation of assets, undervaluation of liabilities, and overstatement of income. Generally, conservatism comes into play when a company is faced with alternative ways to account for a particular transaction. Many accountants feel that conservatism is used to counterbalance management's general tendency to be overly optimistic when accounting for transactions resulting from operations. They feel that sometimes management tends to look at the brighter side of economic events and that this attitude may lead to overstated asset values and net income.

The concept of conservatism is pervasive in accounting. The concept favors valuing assets at historical cost rather than higher market values. Losses are recognized for accounting purposes if they are likely to occur, and asset values are reduced if it appears that their future benefit has been diminished. An example is the write-down of obsolete inventory. Conservatism leads us to reduce the carrying value of the inventory and recognize a loss, even though a transaction has not occurred. An old accounting adage sums up the concept of conservatism: "Provide for all losses, and anticipate no gains."

Materiality Concept

The materiality concept requires accountants to record transactions of the company when these transactions are significant to the company's operations. Materiality is determined by the ultimate effect on the financial statements. Thus, an item is material to the financial statements when its inclusion (or exclusion) and presentation in the financial statements would cause a user to change a decision because of the inclusion (or exclusion) of that item of information. If an item is insignificant—accountants call such an item immaterial—the item would not affect a user's decision regarding the financial statements. The materiality concept allows accountants to avoid the necessity of scrupulously recording every single economic event in accordance with GAAP and thereby reduces record-keeping costs. A word of caution, though, in applying the concept of materiality. Some transactions taken separately are not material. For example, one $10 sale of merchandise might not be material to a company; however, 5,000 sales of the same merchandise over the year are certainly material in the aggregate. All sales should be recorded. On the other hand, the purchase of a metal wastebasket for $20 is a purchase of a long-lived asset. The economic life of a wastebasket is longer than one year. Does it make sense for the company to spend clerical time computing depreciation of the wastebasket? No, and because the $20 is immaterial, the company treats the $20 expenditure as an expense and not as an asset.

Consistency Principle

The consistency principle requires that a company use the same accounting procedures from period to period. The purpose of this principle is to foster comparability of a company's financial statements from period to period. The consistency principle does not imply that a company cannot ever change from one generally accepted accounting principle to another. But it does require that when a company changes an accounting principle, it must disclose the reason for the change and the related effect on net income.

Exhibit 6-1 is a footnote from the annual report of First Brands Corporation, describing the changes the company made in accounting for its inventory and income taxes.

NOTE

As of July 1, 1992, the Company changed its accounting for domestic inventories from the last-in, first-out (LIFO) method to the first-in, first-out (FIFO) method. The Company's non-chemical costs have steadily declined since its inception and chemical costs have declined for the past several years. The Company expects that the non-chemical cost trends will continue and industry forecasters predict that the chemicals which the Company purchases will be priced within a narrow range over the next few years. Based on these factors, the Company believes that the FIFO method of accounting for these inventories provides a better matching of inventory costs with product sales. The change has been applied retroactively by restating the financial statements for prior years. The effect of this restatement was to reduce retained earnings as of June 30, 1992 by $15,787,000.

In February, 1992, the Financial Accounting Standards Board (the "FASB") issued Statement No. 109 (SFAS No. 109) Accounting for Income Taxes. SFAS No. 109 requires a change from the deferred method to the asset and liability method of accounting for income taxes. Under the asset and liability method of SFAS No. 109, deferred tax assets and liabilities are recognized for the future tax consequences attributable to differences between the financial statement carrying amounts of existing assets and liabilities and their respective tax bases. Deferred tax assets and liabilities are measured using enacted tax rates expected to apply to taxable income in the years in which those temporary differences are expected to be recovered or settled. Under SFAS No. 109, the effect on deferred tax assets and liabilities of a change in tax rates is recognized in income in the period that includes the enactment date. The Company adopted SFAS No. 109 during fiscal 1993, by retroactively restating the financial statements for all prior years. The effect of this restatement was to increase retained earnings as of June 30, 1992 by $14,918,000. As a result of the foregoing accounting changes, the financial statements for the years ended June 30, 1992 and 1991 have been restated. The following summarizes the impact of adopting SFAS No. 109 and the effect of changing the accounting method for domestic inventories:

(in thousands)	1992		1991	
	Income Before Extraordinary Loss	Net Income	Income Before Extraordinary Loss	Net Income
As previously reported	$41,660	$23,358	$47,993	$46,229
Effect of change in accounting method for inventories, net of tax	(5,126)	(5,126)	(6,451)	(6,451)
Effect of adopting SFAS No. 109	2,681	5,246	1,126	1,001
As restated	$39,215	$23,478	$42,668	$40,779
Per share amounts as previously reported	$ 1.91	$ 1.07	$ 2.21	$ 2.13
Effect of change in accounting method for inventories, net of tax	(0.24)	(0.24)	(0.30)	(0.30)
Effect of adopting SFAS No. 109	0.12	0.24	0.06	0.05
As restated	1.79	1.07	1.97	1.88

Disclosure Principle

The disclosure principle maintains that a company's financial statements should provide enough information for users to make informed decisions about the company. The concept is important, because the numbers reflected in the financial statements often do not provide sufficient information to allow users to make knowledgeable decisions. Companies include narratives and additional disclosures, such as footnotes, for this reason. These disclosures provide additional insight into the meaning of the numbers reflected in the statements. Without these additional disclosures, the financial statements could be misleading to their users.

7

THE INCOME STATEMENT

There are two commonly encountered types of income statements, (1) the *single step* and (2) the *multiple step* or *classified* statement. The single step income statement is the simplest to read and is found in most annual reports. The multiple step income statement is found much less frequently but is the most commonly requested form of income statement when information users are able to specify the form of the information they are to receive. For example, lenders will commonly request a multiple step format from small companies applying for credit. We discuss both formats.

The Single Step Income Statement

A single step income statement is constructed by subtracting expenses from revenues. The expenses are grouped into either *natural* or *functional* categories.

Revenues

Less Expenses

Net Income

Natural Expense Classifications

A natural grouping places all like expenses together, regardless of the function from which the expenses emanate. For example, all selling, administrative, and manufacturing salaries and wages might be shown as a single total, "Salaries and Wages." The same could be true for all energy costs or all depreciation. Typical natural expense categories might be as in the following example.

CLASSIFICATION COMPANY INCOME STATEMENT

For Year Ended December 31, 19XX

Revenues		$100,000
Less Expenses:		
Salaries and wages	$40,000	
Depreciation	10,000	
Energy	20,000	
Supplies	10,000	
Taxes	5,000	85,000
Net Income		$ 15,000

The single step income statement for Bear Stearns Companies, Inc. in Exhibit 7-1 has expenses classified by natural categories.

EXHIBIT 7-1 SINGLE STEP INCOME STATEMENT WITH NATURAL EXPENSE CLASSIFICATION— BEAR STEARNS COMPANIES, INC.

In thousands, except share data	Fiscal Year Ended June 30, 1993	Fiscal Year Ended June 30, 1992	Fiscal Year Ended June 30, 1991
Revenues			
Commissions	$ 421,090	$ 374,752	$ 338,823
Principal transactions	1,164,143	972,160	540,944
Investment banking	349,736	306,454	186,021
Interest and dividends	902,482	1,001,673	1,284,375
Other income	19,451	26,920	29,790
Total revenues	2,856,902	2,681,959	2,379,953
Interest expense	710,086	834,859	1,141,029
Revenues, net of interest expense	2,146,816	1,847,100	1,238,924
Non-Interest Expenses			
Employee compensation and benefits	1,037,099	909,916	652,186
Floor brokerage, exchange and clearance fees	83,879	65,770	58,365
Communications	59,705	52,799	52,723
Occupancy	69,818	71,268	66,650
Depreciation and amortization	41,234	39,684	33,169
Advertising and market development	43,718	32,484	27,531
Data processing and equipment	27,051	35,313	32,428
Write down of real estate investment	25,221	7,000	
Other expenses	144,693	125,241	86,371
Total non-interest expenses	1,532,418	1,339,475	1,009,423
Income before provision for income taxes	614,398	507,625	229,501
Provision for income taxes	251,951	213,047	86,636
Net income	$ 362,447	$ 294,578	$ 142,865
Net income applicable to common shares	$ 355,696	$ 291,350	$ 139,028
Earnings per share	$ 3.00	$ 2.45	$ 1.13
Weighted average common and common equivalent shares outstanding	$119,807,495	$122,473,707	$123,092,962

See Notes to Consolidated Financial Statements.

Functional Expense Classification

A functional classification groups all expenses that accomplish a particular operating function. All manufacturing wages, manufacturing depreciation, and manufacturing energy costs are shown as a single total, "Manufacturing Costs." All selling salaries and wages, sales depreciation, and sales energy costs are "Sales Costs." Typical functional expense categories might be as in the following example. This income statement and the statement illustrating natural classification are different only in the way the $85,000 in expenses is classified.

CLASSIFICATION COMPANY INCOME STATEMENT
For Year Ended December 31, 19XX

Revenues		$100,000
Less Expenses:		
Manufacturing	$25,000	
Selling	40,000	
Administration	10,000	
Financing	5,000	
Taxes	5,000	85,000
Net Income		$ 15,000

Exhibit 7-2 shows the income statement of Trinity Industries, Inc. The statement uses a single step format and a functional expense classification.

EXHIBIT 7-2 SINGLE STEP INCOME STATEMENT WITH FUNCTIONAL EXPENSE CLASSIFICATION— TRINITY INDUSTRIES, INC.

		Year Ended March 31	
(in millions except per share data)	1993	1992 (Restated)	1991 (Restated)
Revenues	$1,540.0	$1,273.3	$1,348.1
Operating costs:			
Cost of revenues	$1,333.7	1,118.0	1,182.0
Selling, engineering and administrative expenses	93.4	77.5	74.1
Interest expense of Leasing Subsidiaries	28.1	25.4	24.9
Retirement plans expense	10.2	9.0	8.0
	$1,465.4	$1,229.9	$1,289.0
Operating profit	74.6	43.4	59.1
Other (income) expenses:			
Interest income	(1.2)	(1.2)	(0.6)
Interest expense—excluding Leasing Subsidiaries	4.5	7.6	10.0
Other, net	(0.8)	(2.7)	(1.8)
	2.5	3.7	7.6
Income before income taxes	72.1	39.7	51.5
Provision for income taxes:			
Current	25.7	20.4	17.6
Deferred	1.4	(5.0)	(1.9)
	27.1	15.4	19.5
Net income	$ 45.0	$ 24.3	$ 32.0
Net income per common and common equivalent share	$ 1.91	$ 1.07	$ 1.40
Weighted average number of common and common equivalent shares outstanding	23.6	22.8	22.9

See accompanying notes to consolidated financial statements.

The Multiple Step Income Statement

A multiple step income statement contains a series of components and subtotals that accountants and financial statement readers have found useful. Multiple step income statements almost always classify expenses by function. Typical components and subtotals that appear in a multiple step income statement are discussed in the following paragraphs.

Revenues

The first section of the multiple step income statement contains all operating revenues, such as sales, services, and rental revenues. Sales are shown, less any discounts taken by customers for early payment and returns made by customers of defective merchandise. Occasionally a company will grant an allowance, or price reduction, when the customer receives defective, but usable, merchandise. In such cases, total sales minus "discounts" and "returns and allowances" equals net sales. Small companies might show "sales" and the amounts subtracted to get "net sales" as follows. Large companies show only net sales.

Sales	$200,000	
Less Discounts, Returns, and Allowances	30,000	$170,000

Minus Cost of Goods Sold

Cost of goods sold is the purchase or manufacturing cost of inventory sold. This expense is found only in the income statements of merchandising or manufacturing companies; companies that provide only services do not have this expense.

Equals Gross Profit

Gross profit is the difference between net sales and cost of goods sold. Gross profit is sometimes called *gross marqin*. (Most service companies do not have a gross profit or gross margin.)

Minus Operating Expenses

Operating expenses include selling, general, and administrative expenses.

Equals Operating Net Income

Operating net income is the earnings generated by a company's normal, continuing operations. A company's pattern of operating income is usually the best predictor of its ability to earn profits in the future. Other revenues and expenses are frequently more erratic than operating net income.

Plus Other Revenues or Gains

Other revenues or gains are items generated by activities other than normal, continuing operations. This category might include incidental investment earnings or gains on the occasional sale of used office furniture.

Minus Other Expenses or Losses

Other expenses or losses are related to activities other than normal, continuing operations. This category might include the interest expense on loans or losses on the occasional sale of used office furniture.

Equals Pretax Income from Continuing Operations

This subtotal is the income before tax generated from all revenues and expenses related to the continuing activities of the company.

Minus Income Tax Expense

Income tax expense is the tax on income from continuing operations.

Equals Income from Continuing Operations

This subtotal is the income after tax generated from all revenues and expenses related to the continuing activities of the company. This is a company's net income.

Earnings per Share

A publicly traded company must show its earnings per share (EPS) on published financial statements. Although EPS is a deceptively simple concept, it is actually a complicated ratio, as explained in Chapter 15. Basically, earnings per share is income divided by the average number of common shares outstanding.

Chapter 14 discusses income statement items that might appear below income from continuing operation. Exhibits 7-3 and 7-4 are multiple step income statements for Tyson Foods, Inc. and Kelly Services, Inc. and Subsidiaries. Tyson Foods sells inventory and shows cost of goods sold (cost of sales) and gross profit (unlabled). Kelly Services is a service company and calculates gross profit on services. Many service companies are not able to calculate a gross profit subtotal.

EXHIBIT 7-3 MULTIPLE STEP INCOME STATEMENT FOR A MANUFACTURER—TYSON FOODS, INC.

Three Years Ended October 2, 1993   (In thousands except per share data)

	1993	1992	1991
Sales	$4,707,396	$4,168,840	$3,922,054
Cost of Sales	3,796,539	3,390,343	3,147,475
	910,857	778,497	774,579
Operating Expenses:			
Selling	397,361	322,221	303,338
General and administrative	107,201	95,102	108,840
Amortization	30,753	29,502	29,201
	535,315	446,825	441,379
Operating Income	375,542	331,672	333,200
Other Expense (Income):			
Interest	72,811	76,887	95,459
Other	(6,904)	(6,254)	(4,782)
	65,907	70,633	90,677
Income Before Taxes on Income	309,635	261,039	242,523
Provision for Income Taxes	129,301	100,505	97,025
Net Income	$ 180,334	$ 160,534	$ 145,498
Earnings Per Share	$ 1.22	$ 1.16	$ 1.05
Average Shares Outstanding	148,341	138,392	138,037

See accompanying notes.

EXHIBIT 7-4 MULTIPLE STEP INCOME STATEMENT FOR A SERVICE COMPANY— KELLY SERVICES, INC. AND SUBSIDIARIES

	1992[1]	1991	1990
	(In thousands of dollars except per share items)		
Sales of services	$1,722,526	$1,437,884	$1,470,524
Cost of services	1,372,387	1,115,635	1,098,557
Gross profit	350,139	322,249	371,967
Selling, general and administrative expenses	298,114	262,000	258,958
Earnings before income taxes	61,025	60,249	113,009
Income taxes:			
Federal	16,840	16,605	33,565
State and other	4,960	5,025	8,250
Total income taxes	21,800	21,630	41,815
Net earnings	$ 39,225	$ 38,619	$ 71,194
Earnings per share	$1.30	$1.28	$2.37
Dividends per share	$ 73	$ 72	$ 66
Average shares outstanding (thousands)	30,134	30,093	30,069

See accompanying Notes to Financial Statements.
[1] Fiscal year included 53 weeks.

8

OPERATING REVENUES

A revenue is the source of an asset, produced by doing business. Revenues can be derived from sales, services, fees, commissions, rentals, or any other business activity. The asset produced is most commonly either cash paid by a customer or a promise by the customer to pay cash. Customer promises to pay are called accounts receivable.

Operating revenues are sources of assets produced by the company's primary business activities. A hardware store is in business to sell hardware, and Hardware Sales is the store's operating revenue. If the store allows a few customers to finance items and pay over time, the interest customers pay is a nonoperating revenue, Interest Earned. (However, if credit business grows until it is a significant part of the store's business activity, Interest Earned will be a second operating revenue.)

Exhibit 8-1 shows the income statement of Centex Corporation. Centex lists four different operating revenues.

EXHIBIT 8-1 MULTIPLE OPERATING REVENUES— CENTEX CORPORATION

	For the Years Ended March 31,		
	1993	1992	1991
	(Dollars in thousands, except per share data)		
Revenues			
Home Building and Mortgage Banking	**$1,561,012**	$1,137,913	$1,078,818
Contracting and Construction Services	**783,222**	865,009	965,826
Construction Products	**141,164**	135,676	149,633
Savings and Loan	**17,294**	27,109	49,559
	$2,502,692	$2,165,707	$2,243,836
Costs And Expenses			
Home Building and Mortgage Banking	**1,437,597**	1,064,109	997,172
Contracting and Construction Services	**787,325**	861,267	954,257
Construction Products	**136,516**	134,538	147,973
Savings and Loan	**14,267**	24,994	48,305
Corporate General and Administrative	**13,120**	12,807	12,124
Interest	**22,108**	22,140	27,423
	$2,410,933	$2,119,855	$2,187,254
Earnings Before Income Taxes	**91,759**	45,852	56,582
Income Taxes	**30,721**	11,295	12,977
Net Earnings	**$ 61,038**	$ 34,557	$ 43,605
Earnings Per Share	**$ 1.91**	$ 1.11	$ 1.42

See notes to consolidated financial statements.

Net Operating Revenues

Companies generally allow customers to return unsatisfactory merchandise for a refund or credit. Alternately, customers may keep unsatisfactory merchandise but receive an allowance or reduction in price. Refunds or allowances may also be made when the customer claims to have received unsatisfactory service. A customer may, for instance, complain that a rented tool performed poorly on the job; as a result, the rental company might offer the customer an allowance or a reduction in the amount owed. Exhibit 8-2 contains the revenue recognition note to the financial statements of American Greetings. (American Greetings estimates returns of seasonal greeting cards.)

EXHIBIT 8-2   ESTIMATES OF RETURNS— AMERICAN GREETINGS

NOTE

Revenue Recognition: Sales and related costs are recorded by the Corporation upon shipment of products to non-related retailers and upon the sale of products at Corporation-owned retail locations. Seasonal cards are sold with the right of return on unsold merchandise. The Corporation provides for estimated returns of seasonal cards when those products are shipped to retailers.

Many companies offer discounts if a customer pays within a certain discount period, often 10 to 30 days after the sale. If the customer does not pay within this period, the full amount must be paid. For example, a company might sell a $1,000 item with terms 2/10, n/30, meaning "take a 2% discount if you pay in 10 days; otherwise pay the net (entire) amount in 30 days." The customer can pay $980 during the 10-day discount period, or $1,000 from day 11 to day 30.

Amounts of returns, allowances, and discounts are accumulated separately so management can monitor performance and credit terms. Returns, allowances, and discounts are subtracted from operating revenues to determine net operating revenues for the period. Total operating revenues, returns, allowances, and discounts are all used in the income statement to determine net income, but in practice it is unusual to see discounts, returns, and allowances on the face of the income statement. The income statement usually shows only net operating revenue, which is total operating revenues less any returns, allowances, and discounts.

When Is a Revenue Created?

With potential discounts to be taken, returns and allowances to be made, and receivables that might not be collected, you might wonder how accountants and managers know when they have created a revenue. There can, in fact, be a problem. Accountants use two criteria to decide whether a company has produced revenue that should be shown in the income statement: First, the earnings process must be complete; second, there must be a reliable measure of the worth of the goods or services provided. These criteria tell accountants (1) when they should record revenue and (2) how much revenue they should record.

Completion of the earnings process generally occurs when a company has produced and sold a completed product or service. A reliable measure of worth occurs when the selling price is known with certainty and any events that might affect the price (such as a return or a bad debt) can be reasonably estimated. So long as customers may seek a return or allowance, or fail to pay, the worth of the goods or services transferred may not reliably determined.

So how do accountants recognize revenue before cash is collected? They estimate the returns, allowances, and bad debts that might occur. In most companies, potential returns and allowances are not a large enough percentage of operating revenues to cause concern. The great uncertainty is the amount of bad debts, and this is estimated based on experience, current and projected economic trends, and company credit policy. Bad debts are estimated as a percentage of revenues, as a percentage of the balance in receivables, or as an amount determined by an examination of the actual accounts receivable. The examination of accounts is called an *aging of accounts receivable*.

Instead of using a percentage of total accounts receivable to estimate uncollectible accounts expense, many companies arrange accounts according to how many days each has been outstanding and apply different percentages to each age group. The assumption is that the older an account is, the less the probability that it will be collected. Exhibit 8-3 shows how an aging schedule might look.

EXHIBIT 8-3   ACCOUNTS RECEIVABLE AGING SCHEDULE
December 31, 19XX

Customer	Balance	Not Yet Due	1–30	31–60	61–90	Over 180
				Number of Days Past Due		
K. Smith	$ 90,000		$90,000			
F. Harmon	$160,000	$150,000	$ 5,000	$ 5,000		
G. Wilikers	$ 3,000			$ 3,000		
T. Hoyt	$ 40,000		$30,000	$ 5,000	$ 4,000	$ 1,000
T. Button	$ 12,000					$12,000
L. Woo	$ 35,000	$ 35,000				
V. Estavez	$ 88,000			$ 88,000		
Totals	$428,000	$185,000	$125,000	$101,000	$ 4,000	$13,000
Estimated Uncollectible Percentage		1%	4%	10%	20%	50%
Amount Estimated Uncollectible		$ 1,850	$ 5,000	$ 10,100	$ 800	$ 6,500

Total Estimated Uncollectible $ 24,250

Exceptions to the Rule

Like most rules, the general rule that recognizes revenue at the point of sale has exceptions, and the recognition may be advanced or delayed. Under certain circumstances, operating revenue may be recognized in the income statement during production of an item to be sold, at the completion of production, or after the sale when cash is finally collected.

Revenue Recognized During Production

Because each step in producing and selling a product is part of an earnings process, some accounting theorists believe that revenue should be continuously recognized as value is created, instead of all at the point of sale. This would make revenue recognition rather arbitrary, because revenue can generally be measured objectively only at the point of sale. Still, this approach is useful in the income statements of companies involved in long-term construction projects.

Construction of highways, dams, buildings, and other large projects may take several years. If a company shows no profit for three years while constructing a highway, then reports all the profit of the project in the year the project is completed (called the *completed contract method*), its income statements will be very misleading. Income statements will be more informative if the *percentage of completion method* is used and profit (revenue and expenses) recognized ratably during production. Accountants use this approach to measure the progress made toward completion each period by determining the percentage of completion of the project, then recognizing the profit associated with the progress made.

In general, if a project that will generate $2,000,000 in profit is 20% complete at the end of its first year, $400,000 in profit will be recognized ($2,000,000 × 20%). If the project is 50% complete at the end of year two (30% additional progress toward completion), a $600,000 profit will be reported in that year.

$2,000,000	contract profit
× 50%	complete at end of year two
$1,000,000	profit through year two
−$400,000	profit in year one
$600,000	profit in year two

There are several methods used to determine the extent of progress toward completion, but it is not necessary to understand these methods to understand how the percentage of completion method works.

Revenue Recognized on Completion of Production

Some things don't have to be sold to have a reliable worth. Precious metals, such as gold and silver, and certain agricultural products, such as corn and soybeans, normally have a ready market at established prices. For items of this type, if there are no significant marketing or delivery costs, the completion of production is the culmination of the earnings process. At that point, the earnings process is complete, the amount of revenue can be objectively measured, and revenue can be recognized.

This is called the *completed production basis* of revenue recognition. The logic is that the selling price and costs of production are known and performance by the producer has been completed. The only uncertainties are receipt of the selling price and recovery of delivery expense. These costs are as accurately estimated as when revenue is recognized at the point of sale. In practice, the production method is not widely used because of recent volatility in the prices of precious metals and agricultural products.

Revenue Recognized When Cash Is Collected

When collection of a receivable is uncertain, revenue (and profit) are not recorded until cash is collected. This is called the *collection basis* of revenue recognition. There are two methods of collection basis revenue accounting: (1) the cost recovery method and (2) the installment sales method.

The collection basis is appropriate in those few instances when revenue cannot be accurately determined at the point of sale because collectibility of the asset cannot be assumed. This might occur in a situation in which installment sales are made to individuals with poor credit histories. The collection basis is also used by dealers of heavy equipment and in land development sales, in which payments are made over an extended period.

The cost recovery method assumes that the first cash received is a recovery of the cost of the product sold. After the total cost is recovered, any additional collections are profit. The cost recovery method is used for franchise and real estate sales because of the uncertainty regarding collection of receivables. If a company sold for $2,000 land that had cost $1,000, collection of four $500 payments would be recorded as follows.

Payment	Cost Recovery	Profit
$ 500	$ 500	
$ 500	$ 500	
$ 500		$ 500
$ 500	____	$ 500
$2,000	$1,000	$1,000

Cost is recovered in the first two payments, profit in the last two.

When the installment sales method is used, each dollar collected is part return of cost and part profit. If, as above, a company sold for $2,000 land that had cost $1,000, each collection of four $500 payments would be 50% cost recovery and 50% profit.

Payment	Cost Recovery	Profit
$ 500	$ 250	$ 250
$ 500	$ 250	$ 250
$ 500	$ 250	$ 250
$ 500	$ 250	$ 250
$2,000	$1,000	$1,000

Disclosure of Revenue Recognition in the Notes

The footnotes to the financial statements disclose any revenue recognition methods that differ from the point-of-sale general rule. Exhibit 8-4 shows the revenue recognition footnote of Sun Microsystems, Inc. Sun recognizes some revenues when goods are shipped, some when services are rendered. In Exhibit 8-5 Southwest Airlines explains that it recognizes revenue when passengers fly, not when tickets are sold. Readers of income statements should be aware of the alternative methods of revenue recognition and understand their effect on net income.

**EXHIBIT 8-4   REVENUE RECOGNITION NOTE—
SUN MICROSYSTEMS, INC.**

NOTE: **Revenue Recognition**—Sun generally recognizes revenues from hardware and software sales at the time of shipment. Service revenues are recognized ratably over the contractual period or as the services are provided.

**EXHIBIT 8-5   REVENUE RECOGNITION NOTE—
SOUTHWEST AIRLINES CO.**

NOTE: *Revenue recognition*—Passenger revenue is recognized when transportation is provided. Tickets sold but not yet used are included in "Air traffic liability."

9

COST OF GOODS SOLD AND OPERATING EXPENSES

The income statement matches effort with the benefit it produces. Expenses (the effort) are the costs of producing sales of products or services. Expenses are matched against the revenues (benefits) they produce. Costs directly associated with producing specific revenues are expensed in the same period that the specific revenues are earned.

For example, the warranty is part of the reason a customer purchases a particular refrigerator. If there is no warranty, there is no sale. Thus, the cost of a two-year warranty is expensed in the year the refrigerator is sold and the revenue earned, not later when warranty work is performed and service personnel paid. In this case, because no one can foresee the future, an educated estimate of warranty costs is expensed. Still, expensing an uncertain cost matched correctly to revenues is more informative than expensing an actual, certain amount later.

The net benefit in year one of selling, on the last day of the year, a $900 refrigerator that cost $300 to produce and that will cost an estimated $100 to service under its two-year warranty, is $500 ($900 − $300 − $100) in year one. The benefit is not $600 ($900 sales price − $300 cost) in year one and negative $50 ($100 warranty/2 years) in each of the following years. Failing to see the net benefit of the sale as associated with the obligation to service the refrigerator under its warranty overstates earnings in year one and understates earnings in the following two years.

Most companies do not disclose the detailed components of their operating expenses. When detail is disclosed, the components will vary with the company and the nature of its business. Exhibit 9-1 shows the operating expenses of Pacific Gas and Electric Company. Pacific Gas and Electric lists expense components such as Cost of electric energy, Distribution, and Transmission—costs you would not expect to find in the income statement of a company not in the energy business.

**EXHIBIT 9-1   OPERATING EXPENSES—
PACIFIC GAS AND ELECTRIC COMPANY**

Year ended December 31, (in thousands, except per share amounts)	1993	1992	1991
Operating Revenues			
Electric	$ 7,866,043	$ 7,747,492	$7,368,640
Gas	2,716,365	2,548,596	2,409,479
Total operating revenues	10,582,408	10,296,088	9,778,119
Operating Expenses			
Cost of electric energy	2,250,209	2,416,554	2,318,179
Cost of gas	1,092,055	1,062,879	960,208
Distribution	226,975	219,082	208,881
Transmission	166,539	184,165	195,642
Customer accounts and services	403,560	421,990	372,088
Maintenance	442,939	484,751	525,220
Depreciation and decommissioning	1,315,524	1,221,490	1,140,877
Administrative and general	1,041,453	927,316	875,878
Workforce reduction costs	190,200	—	—
Income taxes	1,006,774	906,845	863,089
Property and other taxes	297,495	295,164	288,610
Other	385,755	322,411	316,368
Total operating expenses	8,819,478	8,462,647	$8,065,040
Operating Income	1,762,930	1,833,441	$1,713,079

Operating costs are, generally, the costs of buying, producing, and selling inventory or a service in the company's normal course of business. Operating costs include the costs of consuming long-lived productive assets, as well as other operating activities, such as selling and administrative costs. This chapter discusses (1) expenses resulting from items that are inventoried and (2) selling and administrative expenses. Manufacturing costs and the consumption of long-lived assets are covered in Chapters 10–12 and 13, respectively.

Expenses from Inventoried Items

Supplies Expense

The cost of all supplies purchased during an accounting period is generally accumulated in a supplies inventory account. The cost of supplies consumed each day is generally not recorded. Instead, when financial statements are prepared at the end of the period, the supplies still on hand are counted and an adjustment is made to record the supplies expense for the period.

If a supplies account has a beginning balance of $1,000 and $5,000 worth of supplies is purchased, the supplies account will have a balance of $6,000 before adjustment. If a count of supplies at the end of the period found $2,000 worth still on hand, the account would be adjusted to show a supplies expense of $4,000 ($6,000 − $2,000).

Cost of Goods Sold for a Retailer

Cost of goods sold, sometimes called cost of sales, is frequently the largest expense in the income statement. The basic method used to determine supplies expense (in the preceding paragraph) is also used to determine cost of goods sold in a retail company. When this method is used to account for an inventory of merchandise, it is called the *periodic inventory method*.

The procedure is essentially the same as that used for supplies, but is modified slightly because of the large dollar amounts that flow through merchandise inventory. One change results from the need to maintain a separate record of the merchandise purchased each period.

Basic Cost of Goods Sold Using Periodic Inventory

Inventory, beginning balance	$1,000
Plus purchases (for the period)	5,000
Total goods available for sale	$6,000
Less ending inventory balance, by count	2,000
Cost of goods sold (for the period)	$4,000

Three other factors cause accounting for inventory to differ from accounting for supplies: a company may (1) pay a separate bill for freight-in*; (2) return inventory to a supplier for credit or rebate of a portion of the purchase cost because of damage or unsuitability; or (3) pay promptly and receive a discount. A schedule of cost of goods sold including freight-in, purchase returns and allowances, and purchase discounts follows.

Complete Schedule of Cost of Goods Sold

Inventory, beginning the balance		$1,000
Plus purchases (for the period)	5,000	
Plus freight-in	700	
Less purchase returns and allowances	(300)	
Purchase discounts taken	(94)	
Net delivered cost of purchases		$5,306
Total goods available for sale		$6,306
Less inventory, ending balance by count		2,000
Cost of goods sold (for the period)		$4,306

*Whether included in the purchase cost of inventory, or paid as a separate charge, freight-in is the cost of having inventory shipped to the company and has future benefit. Because of this, freight-in is an asset, is carried in inventory as part of the cost of inventory, and is charged to cost of goods sold only when the inventory is sold.

The periodic inventory method is simple and requires only a minimum of bookkeeping because no effort is made to track individual units or maintain a current book value for inventory or the cost of goods sold. Cost of goods sold is determined only when financial statements are prepared and inventory units on hand are counted. However, while simple, the method provides only minimum information. Between income statement dates managers have no record of the cost of inventory on hand, or of goods sold since the last inventory count. There is no information about losses from theft or spoilage.

Companies use the periodic method when the cost of additional records is greater than the benefit of the added information obtained. The periodic method is often best when units are inexpensive and not unique (such as costume jewelry).

If a company wants more information, it can maintain a perpetual balance for inventory and the cost of goods sold, recording each increase or decrease in inventory (from purchase, sale, or return to supplier) as it occurs. This is the *perpetual inventory method*. The perpetual method is used when units are expensive or unique (such as diamond jewelry). A perpetual inventory for a diamond merchant might appear as follows.

Inventory at Cost

1/1 Beginning balance	$500,000
1/12 Sale	(12,000)
Subtotal	488,000
1/19 Sale	(30,000)
Subtotal	450,000
1/25 Purchase	65,000
Subtotal	515,000
1/30 Customer return	5,000
Subtotal	520,000

Cost of Goods Sold

1/12 Sale	$12,000
1/19 Sale	30,000
Subtotal	42,000
1/30 Return	(5,000)
Subtotal	37,000

Theft Expense

When perpetual inventory records are kept, the end-of-period inventory count is compared with the calculated ending balance in the account. A difference between the balance in the inventory account and the quantity actually on hand is often presumed to be the result of theft.

If a count found only $515,000 in inventory on hand at year end, but records showed $520,000, management could recognize a theft expense of $5,000. Small companies might show the cost of theft as a separate expense in the income statement; large companies probably would show this cost as part of cost of goods sold.

Other Operating Costs

Except for cost of goods sold, operating expenses are reported on the income statement after gross profit. The most frequent and basic components of operating expenses are often selling expenses and administrative expenses. Managers responsible for controlling operating costs function in one of three types of environment, generally called cost centers, profit centers, and investment centers.

The manager of an investment center is somewhat like the manager of a separate company: the manager has an investment base, consisting of the assets employed in the center, and manages an activity that generates both sales revenues and operating expenses. Investment center profit can be determined (revenue minus expenses) separately from the rest of the company. Evaluating the profitability of an investment center is similar to evaluating the profitability of a separate company.

Profit center managers have no investment base. These managers manage both revenues and operating expenses, however, and their contribution to profitability is easy to measure in a separate income statement showing only the accomplishments of their segment. Income statements prepared for investment or profit centers are intended for internal, management use only.

Evaluating a cost center as to its effect on profitability is not as easy. Cost center managers control only operating expenses. They generate no revenues and control no investment base.

To contribute to profits, cost center managers must provide efficient, effective output of product for minimum cost. Cost center managers must continually try to increase output or reduce cost. Often cost center managers argue that all costs incurred in their operations are necessary and should be passed along to the next department. But if small inefficiencies are passed on, department to department, the total cost may be so high that the marketing department cannot generate an acceptable profit margin. Sales will fall as fewer and fewer customers are willing to pay for the high cost of inefficient operations.

Exhibit 9-2 illustrates the effect of inefficiencies on costs by showing three departments with efficient production costs, and three with costs inefficiently 5% higher.

EXHIBIT 9-2 THE EFFECT OF A 5% INEFFICIENCY ON PRODUCTION COST

Case A

	Efficient Operation		
	Cost Added	Prior Dept. Cost	Transferred Out
Department 1	$100.00	0	$100.00
Department 2	$200.00	$100.00	$300.00
Department 3	$150.00	$300.00	$450.00
Total cost charged to units manufactured			$450.00

Case B

	Inefficiencies of 5%		
	Cost Added	Prior Dept. Cost	Transferred Out
Department 1	$105.00	0	$105.00
Department 2	$210.00	$105.00	$315.00
Department 3	$157.50	$315.00	$472.50
Total cost charged to units manufactured			$472.50

Selling and Administrative Costs

Selling expenses are the costs incurred to generate and maintain sales revenues, such as salaries and commissions, compensation-related payroll taxes and pension costs, travel and entertainment, advertising and promotion, delivery or shipping costs, and sales office support, such as telephone, equipment, and supplies.

Administrative expenses are the costs of managing the company, such as salaries of officers and staff, compensation-related payroll taxes and pension costs, accounting, legal, and data processing services, research and development, utilities, insurance, depreciation, and administrative office support, such as telephone, equipment, and supplies.

Controlling Operating Costs by Metering

Costs are sometimes allocated even when there is no direct relationship between the costs and the activity or product to which they are assigned. When there is no direct relationship, how do accountants apportion costs to the cost objects? The answer is: arbitrarily, but rationally.

We must realize that even when there is no direct relationship between a cost and the activities to which the cost is charged (such as averaging the cost of warranties over all appliances manufactured, not just those that break down), the activities (warranty repairs) do cause these costs to be incurred. Operating managers can frequently cause more or less of a cost to be incurred. Finally, we must realize managers try to control only those costs they feel responsible for incurring. They do not try to control costs they do not feel responsible for incurring.

When an operating manager cannot affect the total amount spent on a cost, part of which is allocated to the manager's department, do not hold the manager responsible for any portion of the cost; allocate the cost for accounting purposes only. However, when a manager can affect the total amount of the cost that is allocated, as, for example, a regional motor pool supervisor can (to some extent) affect the pool maintenance costs, meter or charge the cost to the department in small increments based on activity. Do not simply divide maintenance costs by the number of departments receiving the service. Instead, meter the cost by allocating maintenance costs based on work orders, time cards, or some other measure of activity, thus metering the cost to the departments based on use of the service.

10

MANUFACTURING COSTS

A merchandising company has a simple flow of product costs to cost of goods sold. The company buys merchandise and holds the costs as assets in inventory. When the goods are sold, the cost of the merchandise is removed from inventory and charged to cost of goods sold.

A manufacturing company's procedure is not so simple. A manufacturer buys raw materials and components and places these as assets in raw materials inventory. When the manufacturer pays workers to manufacture products and incurs the overhead costs (such as energy, supervision, and facilities costs) necessary to support the efforts of the workers, the manufacturer accumulates costs in a work-in-process inventory until production is completed.

When production is complete, all the production costs (raw materials, labor, and overhead) are transferred to finished goods inventory. At this point, all the costs necessary to manufacture the product are still assets. Finally, when the product is sold to a customer, the costs of the products produced (and sold) become expenses and are charged to cost of goods sold, an expense in the income statement. The flow of costs in a manufacturing operation parallels the physical flow of goods: materials are put into process, labor and overhead are added, and the raw materials are formed into finished products, which are sold.

Exhibit 10-1 shows a statement of cost of goods manufactured and sold. This statement is much like the basic cost of goods sold calculation for a retail company; it is used only inside the company.

EXHIBIT 10-1   STATEMENT OF COST OF GOODS MANUFACTURED AND SOLD

(in thousands)

Beginning inventory of materials	$ 450,100	
Plus purchases	1,340,000	
Total available for use	1,790,100	
Less ending materials	600,000	
Material used in production		$1,190,100
Direct labor		290,500
Factory overhead		3,560,750
Total manufacturing costs		$5,041,350
Plus beginning work in process		340,000
Total costs in process		5,381,350
Less ending work in process		500,450
Cost of goods manufactured		4,880,900
Plus beginning finished goods		520,000
Cost of goods available for sale		5,400,900
Less ending finished goods		300,500
Cost of goods sold		$5,100,400

Generally, only the cost of goods sold for a period is shown in the income statement. Other components are not shown because they are not expenses. Merchandise inventory at the end of the period will be in the balance sheet, and sometimes the notes to the financial statements will show the ending amounts in the other inventory accounts (supplies, raw materials, and work in process).

Job-Order Costing

Some companies rarely, if ever, make the same product twice. These companies use job-order costing. An example is a construction company that builds custom houses designed by the buyer, or an automobile body repair shop that never fixes the same wreck twice.

Because each job is different, job-order companies must charge material, labor, and overhead costs separately to each job. Tracing and charging materials and labor costs to specific jobs is simple because certain materials and labor can be observed going directly to individual jobs. Typically, workers record the time worked and materials used on each job and report them to management on appropriate forms. Overhead costs, however, cannot be traced to individual jobs.

All costs other than materials and labor directly traceable to units produced are included in manufacturing overhead. A schedule of overhead costs is shown in Exhibit 10-2.

EXHIBIT 10-2 SCHEDULE OF FACTORY OVERHEAD INCURRED

For the Month Ended June 30

Data processing	$ 15,500
Depreciation on equipment	22,500
Engineering	2,300
Insurance on factory	700
Janitorial	11,800
Maintenance of equipment	7,000
Property tax	21,250
Rent on factory	6,500
Security	2,100
Set-up of equipment	47,750
Supervision	53,100
Supplies used	7,500
Utilities	2,000
Total	$200,000

Overhead is assigned to jobs by calculating an overhead application rate. The rate is determined by dividing total overhead cost for the period by some measure of manufacturing activity. Frequently used measures of manufacturing activity are labor dollars, labor hours, or machine hours. The rate can be determined using actual or budgeted amounts.

$$\text{Overhead Rate} = \frac{\text{Total Manufacturing Overhead}}{\text{Total Manufacturing Activity}}$$

If a job-order company actually incurs $200,000 total overhead costs, as in Exhibit 10-2, and works 4,000 assembly labor hours, the actual costing rate for June is $50 per assembly labor hour.

$$\text{Overhead Rate} = \frac{\$200,000}{4,000 \text{ hours}} = \$50/\text{hour}$$

Assume that a certain job—Job 1024—requires $340 in materials and 30 assembly labor hours at $25 per hour to complete. Labor cost is $750 ($25 × 30 hours) and, like materials, easily traceable to Job 1024. Using the rate calculated from actual overhead and actual assembly labor activity in June, $1500 in overhead is charged to Job 1024.

Cost Schedule
Job 1024
(Actual Overhead; Manufactured in June)

Materials	$ 340
Labor	750
Overhead ($50 × 30 hours)	1,500
Total cost	$2,590

As you can see, actual costing is simple. But actual costing is seldom used because it results in after-the-fact costing. The company must wait until month or year end to determine the overhead rate and individual job costs. The company might not know job costs until well after products have been produced, priced, and sold. The cost of Job 1024 is determined only after all invoices are received for resources used during June. If Job 1024 is manufactured the first week in June, total June overhead might not be known until late July when bills for supplies and electricity are received.

Even more worrisome, actual costing often results in overhead rates that change from month to month. The property tax shown in the June overhead costs is a once-a-year cost and may drive up the overhead rate for June relative to other months. Likewise, manufacturing activity may change from month to month, whereas some costs may not: factory rent is $6,500 per month, but manufacturing activity may range from 2,000 to 5,000 hours per month. The component of the overhead rate that relates to factory rent will thus range from $3.25 to $1.30 per hour.

Conversely, some costs may change from month to month throughout the year even if manufacturing activity remains constant. For example, when the heat is turned on, total energy usage in a northern winter might be significantly higher than in summer, even though production activity remains essentially unchanged. Add the cost of snow removal during a harsh January, and overhead rates may thus be significantly higher than summer rates. Exhibit 10-3 shows overhead in January.

Exhibit 10-3 lacks the property tax paid once per year in June, but includes additional costs for snow removal and heat that increase overhead 10% (from $200,000 to $220,000).

Overhead per hour is increased to $55 per hour ($220,000/4,000 hours), and overhead for Job 1024 is $150 higher in January than in June.

EXHIBIT 10-3 SCHEDULE OF FACTORY OVERHEAD INCURRED

For the Month Ended January 30

Data Processing	$ 15,500
Depreciation on Equipment	22,500
Engineering	2,300
Insurance on Factory	700
Janitorial	11,800
Snow Removal	12,750
Maintenance of Equipment	7,000
Rent on Factory	6,500
Security	2,100
Set-up of Equipment	47,750
Supervision	53,100
Supplies Used	7,500
Utilities	30,500
Total	$220,000

(Note increased utilities and snow removal versus June overhead.)

Cost Schedule
Job 1024
(Actual Overhead; Manufactured in January)

Materials	$ 340
Labor	750
Overhead ($55 × 30 hours)	1,650
Total cost	$2,740

Fluctuations in actual overhead rates can mislead managers who use the data to analyze profitability or to set prices. If companies bid on jobs, pricing is very important. A northern company that set its bid using June overhead costs could sell at a loss (or at least a reduced profit) if the job is bid in June and manufactured in January.

In practice, a company usually uses the same overhead rate throughout the year and determines the rate in advance using budgeted or predetermined costs and activities, not actual results. Predetermined overhead rates are developed to minimize fluctuations in the overhead rate and to provide more timely cost data for products.

$$\text{Predetermined Overhead Rate} = \frac{\text{Budgeted Manufacturing Overhead for the Year}}{\text{Budgeted Production Activity for the Year}}$$

If, instead of monthly costs, the company uses an annualized predetermined overhead rate, the overhead application rate can be very different. If budgeted overhead for the year is $2,400,000 and budgeted assembly labor use for the year is 40,000 hours, the predetermined rate is $60 per assembly labor hour. Job 1024 is now charged with overhead of $1,800.

Cost Schedule
Job 1024
(Predetermined Annual Overhead Rate)

Materials	$ 340
Labor	750
Overhead ($60 × 30 hours)	1,800
Total cost	$2,890

Departctmental Overhead Rates

When companies determine predetermined overhead rates, it is generally believed that more rates, related to smaller groups of activities, are better. For example, if a manufacturer has five departments performing different manufacturing functions, it is better to have five departmental rates, rather than one plantwide rate, if possible.

There are several reasons for this. First, different departments might have different ratios of overhead cost and manufacturing activity. For instance, consider the five departments of a particular plant. The plantwide overhead rate is $6.40 per machine hour.

Department	Overhead Cost	Manufacturing Activity
		(in labor hours)
Assembly	$300,000	20,000
Fabrication	40,000	40,000
Machining	100,000	25,000
Grinding	75,000	5,000
Painting	125,000	10,000
Totals	$640,000	100,000

Plantwide rate = $640,000/100,000 hours = 6.40/labor hour

If Job 198 requires 25 labor hours, total, for all departments, 25 hours × $20/hour = $160 in overhead will be charged to the job. (The schedule calculating the overhead rate and the cost schedule are both for internal use only.)

Job 198
Cost Schedule
(Plantwide Overhead Rate)

Materials	$2,000.00
Paint	50.00
Labor (25 hours × $20/hour)	500.00
Overhead (25 hours × $6.40/hour)	160.00
Total	$2,710.00

If, however, we calculate rates for the individual departments, we find that departmental overhead rates vary from $0.67 to $15 per labor hour, as in the following table.

Department	Overhead Cost (in labor hours)	Manufacturing Activity (per labor hour)	Departmental Rate (cost/activity)
Assembly	$300,000	20,000	$15.00
Fabrication	40,000	40,000	1.00
Machining	100,000	25,000	4.00
Grinding	75,000	5,000	15.00
Painting	125,000	10,000	12.50
Totals	$640,000	100,000	

Plantwide rate = $640,000/100,000 hours = $6.40/labor hour

At the $6.40 plantwide overhead rate, management is over-estimating the cost of manufacturing activity in two departments (fabrication and machining) and undercosting in three (assembly, grinding, and painting). If this company is a job-cost company and competes with other companies in bidding jobs, it will bid too low on jobs requiring assembly, grinding, or painting. Management believes it costs $6.40 per labor hour for overhead in grinding, for instance, when a departmental rate tells us it costs $15. Likewise, managers will overprice jobs that require fabrication or machining. This can be disastrous: the company will tend to lose jobs that require the activities that it does inexpensively, and get the ones for which it underprices its services.

Using departmental rates, the cost of Job 198 is considerably changed.

Job 198
Cost Schedule
(Departmental Overhead Rates, Based on Labor Hours)

Materials			$2,000.00
Paint			50.00
Labor	(25 hours × $20/hour)		500.00
Overhead in each department:			
Assembly	(25 hours × $15.00/hour)	$375.00	
Fabrication	(25 hours × 1.00/hour)	25.00	
Machining	(25 hours × 4.00/hour)	100.00	
Grinding	(25 hours × 15.00/hour)	375.00	
Painting	(25 hours × 12.50/hour)	312.50	1,187.50
Total			$3,737.50

Additional support for using departmental rates stems from the notion that each department might have costs that are better traced using different measures of activity. If the most appropriate activity measure is used for each department, we might find that costs in assembly, machining, and painting are best traced by activities other than labor hours, as in the following table.

Department	Overhead Cost	Manufacturing Activity	Departmental Rate (per activity unit)
Assembly	$300,000	10,000 machine hours	$30.00
Fabrication	40,000	30,000 work orders	1.33
Machining	100,000	5,000 units processed	20.00
Grinding	75,000	5,000 labor hours	15.00
Painting	125,000	50,000 drying hours	2.50
Totals	$640,000	100,000	

Assuming use levels for each activity, the cost of Job 198 is again changed.

Job 198
Cost Schedule
(Departmental Rates, Based on Different Activities)

Materials			$2,000.00
Paint			50.00
Labor	(25 hours × $20/hour)		500.00

Overhead in each department:

Assembly	(1 machine hour	× $30.00/hour)	$ 30.00	
Fabrication	(10 work orders	× 1.33/order)	13.30	
Machining	(6 units processed	× 20.00/unit)	120.00	
Grinding	(25 labor hours	× 15.00/hour)	375.00	
Painting	(7 drying hours	× 2.50/hour)	17.50	555.80
Total				$3,105.80

11

PROCESS COSTS AND STANDARD COSTS

When job-order costing is used (as in the preceding chapter), the focus in calculating the cost of items produced is the individual job. The cost of units as assets in inventory and as cost of goods sold expense is determined by tracking the costs of units in individual jobs. Because individual units in a job-order costing environment are unique in some way (color, finish, options), units in each job have a different cost. But when companies manufacture a single, homogeneous product in a more or less continuous process, every unit of product is essentially the same as every other and there are no individual jobs. This type of environment uses process costing, as typified by a petroleum company or a sugar refinery. With process costing, the focus in calculating the cost of items produced (gallons of gasoline, pounds of sugar) is the average unit. Such companies can calculate unit costs by dividing production costs by the number of units produced.

Chapter 10 describes the way companies treat manufacturing costs when units are unique and manufactured in separate jobs. This chapter considers a manufacturing environment with essentially identical units and explains how a company can use process costing or standard costing to determine the cost of individual units manufactured.

Process Costing

We cannot simply divide total costs by the number of units completed during a period, because some units will be only partially completed. The cost of these partial units is kept in work-in-process inventory. Work-in-process inventory contains units on which some, but not all, work has been done and the measure of production must include work done on partially complete units. Thus, the division must be by the *equivalent* units of work done, not the actual units completed.

$$\text{Unit Cost} = \frac{\text{Total Cost}}{\text{Equivalent Unit Production}}$$

Suppose a company begins a month with no inventories, starts 10,000 units on its assembly line, but completes only 8,000 units and does 40% of the work on the other 2,000 units that remain in process. It has done the *equivalent* of 8,800 units of work.

8,000 units begun
  and completed   = 8,000 equivalent units of production
2,000 units begun
  and .40 completed = 800 equivalent units of production
Total production is   8,800 equivalent units of production

If the total cost incurred during the period is $52,800, the cost per equivalent unit of production is $6 ($52,800/8,800 equivalent units). This $6 per equivalent unit is used to transfer the cost of completed units to finished goods inventory.

8,000 units completed × $6/unit =
$48,000 transferred to finished goods

The cost of partially completed units remaining in work-in-process inventory is $4,800, calculated as 800 equivalent units of production × $6/unit.

Companies show cost of goods sold in the income statement and inventory in the balance sheet. Frequently, companies disclose the finished goods, work-in-process, and raw material components in the notes to the financial statements. Exhibit 11-1 shows the note disclosure of inventory components for Interface, Inc. and Subsidiaries in a year when cost of goods sold was $427,321,000 and net income was $13,849,000.

EXHIBIT 11-1 DISCLOSURE OF INVENTORY COMPONENTS—INTERFACE, INC. AND SUBSIDIARIES

NOTE: Inventories are summarized as follows:

(In thousands)	1/2/94	1/3/93
Finished Goods	$ 64,497	$ 55,527
Work-in-Process	20,010	21,882
Raw Materials	31,534	23,981
Total	**$116,041**	**$101,390**

Process costing is not always straightforward. In our example we have only one percentage-of-completion figure, which assumes that units are equally complete as to materials, labor, and overhead. Usually, that is not the case, and partially complete units have different completion percentages for materials and labor or machine time. In such cases, equivalent production and unit costs must be calculated separately for materials, labor, and overhead. Then unit-cost calculations must also be made separately.

Process costing alone is relatively rare. In practice, most companies that process essentially identical units also use standard costs.

Standard Costing

A standard cost is essentially a budget for a unit or batch of product. Whatever the product, its standard cost is determined from the standard or budgeted quantity of an input (labor, materials, or overhead) allowed for a unit and the standard or budgeted cost of the input.

$$\text{Standard Quantity of Inputs} \times \text{Standard Price of Inputs} = \text{Standard Cost of Output}$$

Setting Standard Costs

There are several ways to set standards, among them historical projections, engineering methods, and manager judgment. Frequently, companies use a combination of methods to establish and monitor standard costs.

Historical Projections—Managers sometimes set quantity standards based on previous operating results, adjusted for changes made or anticipated in product design or manufacturing methods. There is a disadvantage in using past results to set quantity standards. Any inefficiencies included in the data on which standards are based will be perpetuated by the standards.

Engineering Methods—Engineering techniques, such as time-and-motion studies, can be used to set labor standards. The characteristics or specifications of a product can often be extended to establish material or processing standards. Engineers may set intervals for equipment maintenance (a part of overhead). Engineering methods have the advantage of not using historical data, but often have the disadvantage of reflecting unattainable engineering ideals.

Manager Judgment—Participative management holds that the managers who are responsible for meeting standards should participate in setting the standards. When managers help set the standards, they are more committed to meeting them. Companies may also benefit by encouraging managers to have their workers participate in setting standards.

Variances from Standard Cost

Only two types of events can cause a difference or variance between budgeted or standard cost of units manufactured and actual cost of units manufactured. These events can occur alone or in combination.

1. There must be either a difference between standard "quantity" of inputs (material, labor, overhead) and actual quantity, or

2. There must be a difference between standard and actual "cost" of inputs.

For example, suppose the standard for a unit allows 10 pounds of raw material at $40 per pound:

Standard Quantity of Inputs		Standard Price of Inputs		Standard Cost of Output
10 lbs.	×	$40	=	$400

Quantity Variance—Actual results will differ from standard if the production process uses a different quantity from the quantity allowed by the standard, say 12 pounds instead of 10.

Actual Quantity of Inputs		Standard Price of Inputs		Actual Cost of Output
12 lbs.	×	$40	=	$480

The quantity variance is $80 unfavorable ($400 − $480).

Price Variance—Actual results will also differ from standard if the purchasing department pays a different price from the price allowed by the standard, say $41 rather than $40, and actual quantity remains at standard of 10 lbs.

Actual Quantity of Inputs		Actual Price of Inputs		Actual Cost of Output
10 lbs.	×	$41	=	$410

The price variance is $10 unfavorable ($400 − $410).

Combined Price and Quantity Variance—Actual results will also differ from standard if there is a combination of price and quantity variances.

Actual Quantity of Inputs		Actual Price of Inputs		Actual Cost of Output
12 lbs.	×	$41	=	$492

The total variance is $92 unfavorable ($400 − $492).

Price and quantity variances alone are easy to calculate. When there is a combined price and quantity variance, the total variances are also easy to calculate. But how are individual price and quantity variances calculated when both occur?

To see the calculation clearly, we can focus separately on the (1) purchase and (2) use of the raw material in our illustration. When the raw material was purchased, the purchasing agent paid $1 per pound above the standard price per pound of $40. One dollar per pound unfavorable variance for the 12 pounds in our example is a total unfavorable price variance of $12.

Later, when the raw material is used in production, the production supervisor uses 2 pounds more than the quantity allowed by standard. As we have seen earlier in the example, 2 pounds excess material results in an $80 unfavorable quantity variance when price variance is not considered. The new $12 price variance plus the new $80 quantity variance equals (and explains) the $92 total variance.

The price variance is	$12 unfavorable.
The quantity variance is	$80 unfavorable.
The total variance is	$92 unfavorable.

The price and quantity variances for materials, labor, and the component of overhead that varies with production volume are all calculated the same way. They are, however, often called by several different names, as follows.

Price variance	Quantity variance
Rate variance	Usage variance
Spending variance	Efficiency variance

Investigating Variances

Variances do not tell managers why there is a difference between standard cost and actual results. Calculating price and quantity variances is only a first step in evaluating performance. Knowing that production used more or less than the standard amount of materials does not explain why it did. It could be simply an inaccurate or out-of-date standard. (Remember we said that standards based on engineering ideals might be unrealistic?)

In addition, a variance in one department might be caused by poor work done in another department. For instance, a purchasing manager who buys low-quality materials at a price below standard will generate a favorable material price vari-ance. Difficulty in using the low-quality materials in production, however, may increase both material and labor required to produce good units and result in unfavorable material and labor quantity variances.

Shortcuts taken in one department on the quantity or quality of labor or materials used will often have undesirable consequences in the next department. To avoid such unintentional interactions between departments, management should investigate all significant variances, favorable and unfavorable.

But there are other reasons to investigate favorable variances: failing to investigate favorable variances allows inaccurate standards (permitting excess labor or materials) to continue; and, failing to investigate such variances may mean ignoring cost-cutting techniques that might be used in other areas.

Causes of Variances

Once managers have calculated price and quantity variances, they must still investigate to see why the variances occurred. Separating total variances into price and quantity components helps managers know where to begin their investigation. The list in Exhibit 11-2 gives examples of a few possible causes for the material and labor price and quantity variances.

EXHIBIT 11-2   CAUSES OF MATERIALS AND LABOR VARIANCES

MATERIAL PRICE VARIANCES MAY BE CAUSED BY:

Change in market price

Change in supplier

Change in quantity purchased

Change in quality

Change in shipping

Change in packaging

MATERIALS QUANTITY VARIANCES MAY BE CAUSED BY:

Poorly maintained machines

Poorly trained workers

Shoddy work

Inaccurate materials measurement

Change in materials quality

Change in manufacturing specifications (but not standards)

LABOR PRICE VARIANCES MAY BE CAUSED BY:

Renegotiated union contract

Raises given to individual workers

Changes in work flow to use different workers

Absenteeism causing worker substitution

Use of trainees or interns

LABOR QUANTITY VARIANCES MAY BE CAUSED BY:

Change in work flow

Use of poorly trained workers

Change in raw material quality

Poorly maintained machines

Absenteeism causing worker substitution

Use of trainees or interns

Overhead Variances

In general, favorable variances, which are signs of efficient, effective operation, increase net income. Unfavorable variances, conversely, are generally indicative of inefficient, ineffective operations and reduce net income. This is true for items for which total cost varies directly with production volume, such as the cost of labor, materials, and a component of overhead called variable overhead. There is, however, another component of overhead cost that does not vary in total with production volume, called fixed overhead. The total of fixed overhead cost remains constant or "fixed" despite changes in production activity.

Because fixed overhead cannot be linked directly to individual units or jobs in the way labor, materials, and variable overhead can, it is applied to products in a somewhat arbitrary way. If, at the beginning of the year, a company budgets $800,000 in fixed overhead for production of 100,000 units, fixed overhead is charged to production at the rate of $8 per unit ($800,000 divided by 100,000 units).

If the company actually spends more or less than was budgeted for fixed overhead, the company calculates an unfavorable or favorable budget variance. Budget variances are not confusing: as stated in regard to variances generally, favorable variances are signs of efficient, effective overhead management and increase net income. Unfavorable variances, conversely, are generally indicative of inefficient, ineffective management and reduce net income.

If, however, a market downturn slows sales and the company produces 10,000 units less than planned, only $720,000 ($8/unit × 90,000 units) in fixed overhead will be charged to units produced. The remaining $80,000 ($800,000 − $720,000) in fixed overhead becomes an unfavorable volume variance, and, like an expense, reduces net income. An unfavorable volume variance is caused by the company failing to produce at its planned volume. Failing to use production capacity to the extent planned is bad practice.

The fixed overhead volume variance is also called the idle capacity variance, denominator variance, or application variance. This variance is the most difficult to interpret, does not relate directly to efficiency or effectiveness, and is the hardest for managers to control.

Standard Costs in the Income Statement

When standard costs are used, cost of goods sold is valued at standard cost (actual quantity sold × standard cost per unit). Variances from standard production costs appear on the income statement as expenses (if unfavorable) or negative expenses (if favorable). Large and medium-sized manufacturers use standard costing more than actual costing because standard costing integrates standard costs and variances into the accounts, isolating variances as soon as possible, so action can be taken. This method is also simpler to use for repetitive or processing operations.

Exhibit 11-3 shows how standard costs and an unfavorable variance might be shown in the multiple step income statement of a small company. Large companies do not generally show the detailed effect of variances on gross margin.

EXHIBIT 11-3   STANDARD COSTS IN THE INCOME STATEMENT

ABC COMPANY
Income Statement
for year ended December 31, 19XX

Sales	$4,500,000
Standard cost of goods sold	1,800,000
Standard gross margin	2,700,000
Less variances	50,000
Actual gross margin	2,650,000
Selling expenses	600,000
Administrative expenses	700,000
Operating profit before taxes	$1,350,000
Taxes	500,000
Net income	$ 850,000

12

INVENTORY FLOWS TO COST OF GOODS SOLD

Cost of goods sold is the largest expense for many companies, but because identical units are often purchased at different prices, accountants may not know the cost of units in ending inventory or the cost of units sold. Still, they must determine these amounts. To do so, accountants must choose one of several methods of accounting for inventory, each method the result of making different assumptions about how goods flow through the company or costs through the accounting system.

Flow Assumptions

To illustrate, assume a company has beginning inventory of one unit on January 1st and purchases three more units during the month. The company sells one unit for $25 during January, leaving an ending inventory of three units. If all the units are identical, how does the company calculate ending inventory and cost of goods sold? The calculation is simple if all the units cost $10: inventory is $30 (3 × $10) and cost of goods sold is $10 (1 × $10). But units frequently do not all have the same cost. Costs rise and fall with the business cycle, or new suppliers enter the market and costs change. Assume market pressures cause a company's costs to rise as follows.

Beginning Inventory	1 unit @ $10/unit	$10
Purchases:		
January 10	2 units @ $15/unit	30
January 25	1 unit @ $20/unit	20
Total	4 units	$60

Generally accepted accounting principles (GAAP) allow four main methods of accounting for inventories and cost of goods sold when units do not have the same cost.

1. Specific identification
2. First in–first out (FIFO)
3. Last in–first out (LIFO)
4. Weighted average

Companies can use any of these methods. Companies with several inventories often use several methods. The inventory accounting policy of Avon Products, Inc. is reproduced in Exhibit 12-1. Avon uses LIFO for domestic inventories and FIFO for foreign inventories (many foreign countries do not allow LIFO inventory).

Specific Identification

Under the specific identification method, a merchant can affect income by choosing the unit to be sold. Accountants do not like specific identification because it permits managers to manipulate earnings. Assume the company in our example sells one unit for $25. If the company uses specific identification, it can select the cost it wants to expense and recognize gross profit of $5, $10, or $15.

	Options		
	A	B	C
Income Statement:			
Sales	$25	$25	$25
Cost of Goods Sold	10	15	20
Gross Profit	15	10	5
Balance Sheet:			
Inventory	50	45	40
	(15 + 15 + 20)	(10 + 15 + 20)	(10 + 15 + 15)

Specific identification is used for unique, high-value items such as jewels or automobiles. Using specific identification is easy for a car dealership or jewelry store because each item has unique features and its own invoice. A hardware store purchasing nuts and bolts at different prices has a difficult time identifying units with particular costs.

First In–First Out (FIFO)

The other methods allowed by GAAP give three patterns of flowing costs for cost of goods sold and ending inventory that parallel the options in the preceding illustration. Option A charges the cost of the oldest unit from beginning inventory to the cost of goods sold. The most current costs of the most recent purchases are in ending inventory. This method is called first in–first out (FIFO) and flows costs through the records

the way most merchants flow units of inventory: the oldest units are sold first to rotate stock. FIFO is popular because it follows the normal physical flow of goods.

EXHIBIT 12-1 INVENTORY ACCOUNTING POLICY— AVON PRODUCTS, INC.

NOTE: **Inventories**—Inventories are stated at the lower of cost or market. Cost is determined using the last-in, first-out (LIFO) method for substantially all U.S. inventories and using the first-in, first-out (FIFO) method for all other inventories.

Last In–First Out (LIFO)

The pattern of Option C is called last in–first out (LIFO). LIFO charges the cost of the most recently purchased unit to cost of goods sold and leaves the oldest costs in ending inventory. It is difficult to find situations in which merchants physically flow goods in a LIFO pattern. A coal pile flows coal the way LIFO flows costs. The new coal purchased is dumped on top of the pile. The oldest coal is on the bottom of the pile. When coal is sold, it is taken from the top of the pile, selling the most recently purchased inventory and keeping the oldest.

Weighted Average

Option B uses the weighted-average cost per unit for both cost of goods sold and ending inventory. The weighted-average cost per unit is determined by dividing total cost by the number of units available.

Calculation of Weighted-Average Cost Per Unit

Total cost of units available for sale	$60
Total units available for sale	4
Weighted-average cost per unit	$15

Which Method Is Best?

Think about the effect of each method on the financial statements. How much better off are we after selling one unit in the previous example? Should gross profit be $15, $10, or $5? To decide, let us think: What happens next? If the company continues in business it must replace the unit sold. If the replacement cost is increasing rapidly (as in our example), the next unit will cost $20 or more.

If we sell a unit for $25 and must pay $20 or more to replace it, we are only $5 or less better off. If we pay taxes on the profit created (and we do), we are not $5 better off. LIFO gives results that best show how much better off a company is from having done business.

FIFO reports deceptively high profits when costs are rising. When a company uses FIFO inventory during a period of rising inventory replacement costs, the company charges the cost of old, lower cost inventory to cost of goods sold. Our example charges the old $10 cost to cost of goods sold. This results in a cost of goods sold expense that is less than the cash required to replace the inventory sold. In our example, the cost of units most recently purchased is $20. To replace the unit sold, the company can be expected to spend $20 cash, or more. The weighted-average method gives results that fall between LIFO and FIFO.

But what about the cost of inventory on hand? Under LIFO the cost of the oldest units is in ending inventory. FIFO shows the most recent costs as the cost of ending inventory and the oldest costs as the cost of units sold. FIFO provides better information about the cost of units in ending inventory. Weighted average reports a cost between LIFO and FIFO.

Analysts believe the income statement is more important than the balance sheet. A weak balance sheet can be overlooked if a company has a strong earnings record, but a strong balance sheet will seldom outweigh poor earnings. Because of this, accountants attempt to use the best available information in the income statement, even if balance sheet content is sacrificed. As a result, accountants generally prefer LIFO inventory.

Tax Effect

The Internal Revenue Service (IRS) will allow companies to use LIFO for tax reporting only if they also use it for financial reporting. These companies can, however, report an alternative inventory amount (usually FIFO) in the notes to the financial statements or through the use of a LIFO reserve (discussed later in this chapter). A company does not have the same requirement regarding FIFO or weighted average. For example, a company could use weighted average for taxes and FIFO for financial reporting.

When costs are rising LIFO charges the most current, higher costs against earnings, reducing income and reporting lower earnings than would be obtained using FIFO or weighted average. As a result, the companies pay lower taxes. But if costs are decreasing, the situation is reversed and LIFO charges the most current, lower prices against earnings, increasing income and reporting higher earnings than would be obtained using FIFO or weighted average. Because historically there is more inflation (rising prices) than deflation (falling prices), companies using LIFO tend to pay lower taxes.

It is important to note that a company can use LIFO, FIFO, or weighted average to flow costs through the accounting system, *regardless of the way individual units flow through the company.* The choice of an inventory accounting method is an accounting decision. Selecting procedures to rotate stock is a marketing decision. A company can have a FIFO physical flow of units and still use LIFO to prepare financial statements and pay taxes.

LIFO Reserve

A LIFO reserve is the difference between LIFO cost and the replacement cost of the inventory (usually assumed to be FIFO cost). This difference occurs because LIFO shows inventories at older, often lower costs than if the inventories were shown at their (FIFO) replacement costs. In our example, LIFO inventory is $40, and FIFO inventory is $50. The LIFO reserve is $10, the difference between the two.

Some companies show the LIFO reserve on the balance sheet, some in the notes. Exhibit 12-2 shows the inventory note of Witco Corporation that discloses the LIFO reserve. Exhibit 12-3 shows the balance sheet of Federal Paper Board Company. Federal Paper Board shows the LIFO reserve on the face of its balance sheet.

EXHIBIT 12-2 LIFO RESERVE—WITCO CORPORATION

NOTE
Inventories are classified as follows:

(thousands of dollars)	1992	1991
Raw materials and supplies	$ 89,305	$ 69,382
Finished goods	160,359	93,427
	$249,664	$162,809

Work in progress included above is not significant.

Inventories valued on a LIFO basis, at December 31, 1992 and 1991, amounted to $147,670,000 and $115,985,000, respectively. Inventories would have been $71,023,000 and $74,045,000 higher than reported at December 31, 1992 and 1991 if the FIFO method (which approximates current cost) had been used by the Company for all inventories.

In thousands except per share amounts For Fiscal Year	1993	1992	1991
Net Sales	**$1,386,386**	$1,460,819	$1,435,021
Costs and Expenses:			
Cost of products sold	**1,038,785**	1,034,854	1,008,508
Depreciation, amortization, and cost of timber harvested	**144,087**	146,566	122,695
Selling and administrative expenses	**60,149**	64,769	64,144
Interest expense	**85,474**	85,018	90,243
Other—net	**7,791**	(6,088)	5,231
Total Costs and Expenses	**1,336,286**	$1,325,119	$1,290,821
Income before taxes and cumulative effect of accounting change	**50,100**	135,700	144,200
Provision for income taxes	**29,300**	53,100	61,800
Income before cumulative effect of accounting change	**20,800**	82,600	82,400
Cumulative effect of accounting change	**—**	9,000	—
Net Income	**20,800**	91,600	82,400
Preferred dividend requirements	**6,610**	7,060	8,129
Net income available to common shares	**14,190**	$ 84,540	$ 74,271
Average common shares outstanding:			
Assuming no dilution	**41,995**	41,448	40,540
Assuming full dilution	**42,414**	46,695	46,429

Earnings Per Common Share

	1993	1992	1991
Assuming no dilution:			
Income before cumulative effect of accounting change	**$.34**	$1.82	$1.83
Cumulative effect of accounting change	**—**	.22	—
Net Income	**$.34**	$2.04	$1.83
Assuming full dilution:			
Income before cumulative effect of accounting change	**$.34**	$1.77	$1.77
Cumulative effect of accounting change	**—**	.19	—
Net Income	**$.34**	$1.96	$1.77

See accompanying notes to financial statements.

In thousands At Year End	1993	1992
Assets		
Current Assets:		
Cash	$ 271	$ 280
Accounts and notes receivable, less allowance for doubtful accounts of $1,284 in 1993 and $1,672 in 1992	52,062	88,351
Inventories:		
Raw materials	58,720	59,680
Work in process	15,469	9,404
Finished goods	99,329	87,680
Supplies	51,701	52,485
Subtotal	225,219	209,249
LIFO reserve	(2,819)	(8,257)
Total inventories	222,400	200,992
Deferred tax asset	15,142	11,010
Other current assets	19,818	15,254
Total Current Assets	**309,693**	**315,887**
Property, Plant and Equipment, at Cost:		
Land	16,227	14,990
Buildings, including leasehold improvements	238,859	227,437
Machinery and equipment	2,259,622	2,198,152
Construction in progress	151,715	92,105
Subtotal	2,666,423	2,532,684
Accumulated depreciation and amortization	(769,869)	(654,334)
Property, Plant and Equipment–Net	**1,896,554**	$1,878,350
Timber and Timberlands	189,674	191,840
Goodwill and Other Intangibles	118,418	123,200
Other Assets	55,955	64,222
Total Assets	**$2,570,294**	$2,573,499

See accompanying notes to financial statements.

100   *Inventory flows to cost of goods sold*

When the LIFO reserve is shown, statement readers know the current replacement cost of the inventories and the company receives the tax and other benefits of using LIFO. The LIFO reserve allows readers to compare companies using LIFO with companies using FIFO. Companies often keep their books on a FIFO basis (the way their physical units flow) and convert to LIFO at year end.

Inventory Estimating Methods

When a company sells many different items, all at different prices, it is difficult and time-consuming to count and price inventory to determine the cost of goods sold. This is particularly true of retailers. But because many retailers mark up merchandise by the same percentage each period, the cost of goods sold is often a predictable, continuing percentage of sales. Even retail companies that sell many types of products and mark up each product by a different percentage, still often have relatively constant gross-margin and cost-of-goods-sold percentages.

To consider a simple illustration, assume that a clothing store sells dresses, shoes, and sport clothes and marks up each type of product by a different percentage. Cost and markup calculations follow.

Merchandise	Cost of Goods	× Markup on Cost	= Gross Profit	Selling Price (Cost + Gross Profit)
Dresses	$10,000	100%	$10,000	$ 20,000
Shoes	20,000	50%	10,000	30,000
Sport clothes	40,000	25%	10,000	50,000
Total	$70,000		$30,000	$100,000

The weighted average markup of all sales is gross profit/cost ($30,000/$70,000), or 42.86%. The gross profit percentage is gross profit/selling price ($30,000/$100,000), or 30%. A partial income statement shows the relationship between sales revenue, cost of goods sold, and gross profit.

Sales	$100,000	
Cost of Goods Sold	70,000	70% of sales
Gross Profit	$ 30,000	30% of sales

Sales mix describes the proportions in which merchandise is sold. The mix in the preceding table, based on sales dollars, is 20%, 30%, 50%. As long as the markup on each type of product and the sales mix do not change, the relationship between sales and cost of goods sold (in total) will not change. This allows accountants to estimate cost of goods sold and inventories on hand without counting inventory.

Assume in our illustration that the costs and retail (sales) values of purchases relate to January operations. Beginning inventory at cost was $5,000 and sales (at retail) are $80,000. All of this information is available from the accounting records. If we believe the cost-to-retail ratio of 70% represents a stable relationship for purchases and sales, we can estimate the cost of goods sold as 70% × the January sales of $80,000.

Beginning inventory (at cost)	$ 5,000
Plus second quarter purchases (at cost)	70,000
Total goods available for sale	75,000
Less estimated cost of goods sold (at cost)	
$80,000 sales × 70% cost/retail ratio	(56,000)
Estimated ending inventory	$ 19,000

This approach can be used to make estimates of cost of goods sold and ending inventory quickly and easily from historical data. The disadvantage is that the sales mix and markup percentages don't always remain constant. If either mix or markup percentages change, estimates will not be accurate.

To increase the accuracy of this approach, managers maintain contemporaneous records of the cost of goods purchased, the goods' retail price after markup, and any additional markups or markdowns. This method of estimating inventories is called the retail inventory method. Even though the retail method is an estimating technique, some companies use it to compute inventory for their financial statements. Normally, a company makes physical inventory counts throughout the year to validate the estimated inventory amounts. Exhibit 12-4 gives the footnote disclosure of TJX Companies, a retailer of specialty apparel. TJX uses the retail inventory method and the lower of cost or market.

EXHIBIT 12-4 RETAIL INVENTORY METHOD— TJX COMPANIES

NOTE: **Merchandise Inventories**—Inventories are stated at the lower of cost or market. The Company primarily uses the retail method for valuing inventories on the first-in first-out basis.

Lower of Cost or Market Losses from Devaluing Inventory

The principle of conservatism requires that accountants show inventories in the balance sheet at the lower of cost or market. *Market* here generally means replacement cost, the cost the company would incur to replace or replicate the inventory items. If our clothing store has ending inventory that cost $17,500 but that can be replaced for $16,500, accountants will believe the market for these goods is deteriorating and that the company's selling prices will eventually also fall. To inform income statement readers of this situation, ending inventory will be shown at $16,500 (the lower of cost or market) and the $1,000 devaluation will be shown in the income statement as a loss.

Estimating Theft Loss

The retail inventory method is also used to estimate inventory losses from theft or from other causes. The clothing store in our example might count and find inventory actually on hand, at cost, of only $17,500, yielding an estimate of inventory lost from theft of $1,500.

Inventory estimated from sales	$19,000
Inventory estimated from count	17,500
Estimated loss from theft	$ 1,500

13

DEPRECIATION, DEPLETION, AND AMORTIZATION

Assets are costs that have future benefit to the company (such as prepaid insurance); expenses are costs that have no future benefit. Much of accounting involves recording asset costs and then expensing those costs as their benefits are consumed. With prepaid insurance, there is no problem matching the expiration of benefits (insurance expense) to the period benefited (the term of the insurance) and the revenue generated during that period. For certain long-lived assets—such as plant and equipment, natural resources, or intangibles—matching the expired cost to the period benefited is difficult and arbitrary. This chapter explains the processes of allocating, in a rational and systematic manner, the costs of long-lived assets to the periods benefited.

Depreciation Expense

Depreciation expense is deducted from revenues in determining net income. The amount of accumulated depreciation taken to date is shown in the balance sheet. Accumulated depreciation accumulates charges to depreciation expense over the life of the asset. The difference between the historical cost of the asset and its related accumulated depreciation is its book value. Because the asset is recorded at historical cost and both the scrap or salvage value at the end of the asset's life and the asset's useful life are estimates, the book value of an asset does not indicate its market value.

(Moreover, accumulated depreciation is not cash set aside for replacing the asset. It is merely the cumulative cost of the asset charged against the revenues it helped create in prior periods.)

Estimates and Arbitrary Methods

Depreciation is the allocation of a long-lived asset's cost to the periods or products that receive the benefit of the asset's use. The allocation is arbitrary, because there is no direct link between consuming a productive asset's economic benefit and either the periods when it is used or the products or services created by the asset.

For example, assume a business spends $40,000 on a new computer. The $40,000 represents the cost of a "basket" of benefits that will be consumed over the computer's estimated three-year life. At the end of the first month, 3,000 reports have been generated. How much benefit has been consumed? We can't say—not objectively. We can determine directly the cost of labor to operate the computer (look at the payroll); we can determine directly the cost of paper used (count the remaining paper). But we can only estimate the benefit consumed and the depreciation that should be expensed. And that estimate is arbitrary; different accountants may use different methods and arrive at different amounts.

We can link the expiration of one month's prepaid fire insurance directly to a particular month in a particular year. We can link the cost of raw materials consumed to a specific unit of product or batch of products. But when a productive asset is consumed or rendered economically useless over a period of 10 or 20 years, no particular dollar amount of cost can be linked to any particular month, year, or unit of product. So accountants use several "rational and systematic" methods to spread the cost of the asset to the periods and products benefited.

Depreciation is an estimate based on other estimates. An accountant must make several estimates, regardless of the depreciation method used. Assume a company has just purchased for $24,000 a new car that will be used by the sales manager (a familiar example).

1. The accountant estimates the output of the asset over its life.
   - Assume that the car is expected to be useful for 100,000 miles.

2. The accountant estimates the company's annual need for the asset's output.
   - Assume the sales manager expects to drive the car 20,000 miles per year. Using these two estimates, the accountant calculates that the car will last five years (100,000 miles/20,000 miles per year = 5 years).

3. The accountant estimates the asset's residual or salvage value at the end of its life.
   - Assume the accountant estimates that after 100,000 miles and five years, the car will have a residual value of $4,000. This allows the accountant to calculate the cost that will be consumed over the car's life. In this case, the accountant estimates that $20,000 of the car's cost will be consumed over its life. The $20,000 is called the car's depreciation base.

$24,000 Cost
$$\underline{-\ 4,000}\ \text{Residual value}$$
$20,000 Depreciation base

Sometimes the useful or economic life of an asset is simply a period of time determined by changing technology, as with a computer system, and not by the company's use of benefits. For computer systems and computerized operating systems (such as those used in chemical manufacturing or commercial printing), the physical life of the asset is often much longer than its economic life. In general, the usefulness of an asset falls because of physical wear and tear, obsolescence, and inadequacy. These factors determine estimates of the asset's useful life and its salvage value at the end of its life.

Determining Depreciation Expense

Once an accountant estimates the cost that will be consumed over an asset's life, as in the example of the sales manager's car, the accountant must decide in what pattern the company will consume the asset's benefit. Because there is no direct link between the asset's consumption and the company's activity, this is a subjective decision. The pattern of depreciation expense over the useful life of the asset should reflect the pattern in which its benefits are consumed.

1. When benefits are consumed in the same amount each year, use straight-line depreciation. If a company uses a car to deliver mail and samples between two plants, making the same trip each day, an accountant might decide that the benefit is the same each period; there is no difference between a new and an old car, so long as it makes the trip.

2. When benefits are consumed in the same pattern that utility is provided, use units-of-activity or production-units depreciation. This method might be used to depreciate a taxi, whereby benefit received is directly related to the number of miles driven.

3. When benefits are consumed more in the early years and less in later years of the asset's life, use one of two accelerated methods, sum-of-the-years'-digits or double-declining-balance depreciation. Accelerated methods are used when accountants believe an asset is more useful or productive in its early years, so more benefit is received and more depreciation expensed than in later years. If the car is a limousine, appearance and newness would count and an accelerated depreciation method would be appropriate.

Straight-Line Depreciation

Straight-line depreciation expenses an equal amount of the depreciation base each period of an asset's useful life.

$$\text{Annual Depreciation Expense} = \frac{\text{Depreciation Base}}{\text{Useful Life}}$$

For the sales manager's car, straight-line depreciation divides the depreciation base of $20,000 by its expected five-year life to calculate a $4,000 per year depreciation expense.

Units-of-Activity Depreciation

The units-of-activity method is used when the benefit provided by an asset is closely related to a particular activity (such as the number of units manufactured or services rendered), rather than to the mere passage of time. Annual depreciation expense is the depreciation rate per unit of activity multiplied by the number of activity units consumed during the period. This method is appropriate only for assets whose benefit output is easily measured, such as a car driving a certain number of miles or a machine producing a certain number of units of product.

If the sales manager's car were depreciated using units-of-activity, we would divide the $20,000 depreciation base by the estimated 100,000-mile life to calculate a $0.20 per mile depreciation rate. If the car is driven 21,682 miles during year one, depreciation expense for that year is $4336.40 (21,682 miles × $0.20/mile). Exhibit 13-1 shows part of a financial statement note identifying straight-line and units-of-production as two methods used by the Federal Paper Board Company. (Units-of-production is the same as units-of-activity.)

EXHIBIT 13-1   DEPRECIATION DISCLOSURE— FEDERAL PAPER BOARD COMPANY

NOTE: **Property, Plant and Equipment**—Property, plant and equipment is recorded at cost. Depreciation is computed on the straight-line method based on the estimated useful lives of related assets except for the Augusta, GA paperboard mill, where the units-of-production method is used. Depreciable lives are 20 to 33 years for buildings and 3 to 30 years for machinery and equipment.

Accelerated Depreciation

Accelerated depreciation is used when the benefits received from the asset are greater in the early years and less in the later years of the asset's life. Such a pattern might occur because of technological developments, wear and tear, or increases in repairs and maintenance costs. Accelerated depreciation methods give a pattern of depreciation expense that begins high and declines over the asset's life.

Sum-of-the-Years'-Digits Depreciation—One procedure for calculating an accelerated pattern of depreciation expense is called the sum-of-the-years'-digits method. This procedure depreciates a different fraction of the asset's depreciation base each year. The numerator of the fraction is the number of years remaining in the asset's useful life at the beginning of the year, the denominator the sum of the years' digits.

If the sales manager's car is depreciated using sum-of-the-years'-digits over its five-year life, the sum of the five years' digits is

$$1 + 2 + 3 + 4 + 5 = 15$$

Depreciation in year one is 5/15 times the $20,000 depreciation base, and in year four is 2/15 times the depreciation base. A depreciation schedule for the car is shown in Exhibit 13-2.

EXHIBIT 13-2 ACCELERATED DEPRECIATION—SUM-OF-THE-YEARS'-DIGITS

Year		Depreciation Expense	Accumulated Depreciation	Book Value
				$24,000
1st year	5/15 × $20,000	$ 6,667	$ 6,667	17,333
2nd year	4/15 × $20,000	5,333	12,000	12,000
3rd year	3/15 × $20,000	3,999	15,999	8,001
4th year	2/15 × $20,000	2,667	18,666	5,334
5th year	1/15 × $20,000	1,333	$20,000	4,000
		$20,000		

Double-Declining-Balance Depreciation—The double-declining-balance (DDB) method begins with the straight-line rate (in our example, 1/5 or 20%). To use this method, double the straight-line rate so that an asset with a five-year life and a straight-line rate of 20% has a DDB rate of 40%. (The method is sometimes called double-rate depreciation.) But that rate is applied to the book value of the asset, not to the depreciable base, as with straight-line depreciation. Although the salvage value is ignored in calculating depreciation year-by-year, the asset is depreciated only to its salvage value. Exhibit 13-3 shows the DDB method used to depreciate the $24,000 car to its $4,000 salvage value.

EXHIBIT 13-3 ACCELERATED DEPRECIATION—DOUBLE-DECLINING-BALANCE

Year	[.40× (3)]	Depreciation Expense (1)	Accumulated Depreciation (2)	Book Value (3) = $24,000 − (2)
				$24,000
1st year	[.40 × $24,000]	$9,600	$ 9,600	$14,400
2nd year	[.40 × $14,400]	5,760	15,360	8,640
3rd year	[.40 × $ 8,640]	3,456	18,816	5,184
4th year	[.40 × $33,280]	592*	19,408	4,592
5th year	[.40 × $26,624]	592*	20,000	4,000

*The $592 amounts are necessary in the last two years to limit the amount depreciated to the salvage value of $4,000 (40% × $5,184 = $2,073.60, an amount that would reduce the book value below $4,000).

Other accelerated depreciation procedures include the Accelerated Cost Recovery System (ACRS) and the Modified Accelerated Cost Recovery System (MACRS). These methods are used for tax purposes only, not in financial reporting.

Group and Composite Depreciation

Large companies do not, as a rule, depreciate individual assets, but rather groups of assets combined into classes and depreciated at an average rate. Group depreciation is the depreciation of a collection of similar assets having approximately the same useful lives (such as a fleet of delivery trucks). Composite depreciation is the depreciation of a collection of dissimilar assets (such as all the assets in an office: furniture, fixtures, equipment).

The computation is the same for both methods. An average rate is determined and used each period.

Exhibit 13-4 shows how composite depreciation is calculated for the collection of assets in an office. The composite rate is 16.91%, calculated by dividing total depreciation expense per year by the total depreciation base ($5,750/$34,000). Annual depreciation expense is 16.91% of depreciable cost. The composite life is 5.91 years ($34,000/$5,750). Composite and group depreciation methods save time by not calculating and maintaining separate records for each asset.

Income Taxes and Depreciation

The depreciation method used to determine income for taxes need not be the same as the method used to determine income for financial reporting purposes. As a result, many companies use ACRS or MACRS accelerated depreciation for income taxes and straight-line depreciation for financial reporting. Because these methods yield higher depreciation expense and lower income than the straight-line method in an asset's early years, a company pays less tax in the early years of an asset's life and more in the later years. Income taxes are postponed, and the company has the postponed payment as an interest-free loan until the difference reverses.

Exhibit 13-5 compares straight-line and MACRS accelerated depreciation for the car used in our examples. Here, MACRS corresponds to the DDB depreciation amounts, but ACRS and MACRS annual depreciation amounts are set out in the tax code and differ for different classes of assets. Exhibit 13-6 contains the Property, Plant and Equipment footnote for Upjohn Company. Upjohn's note tells financial statement readers that it uses different depreciation methods for tax and financial reporting.

EXHIBIT 13-4 COMPOSITE DEPRECIATION

Asset	Original Cost	Residual Value	Depreciable Base	Estimated Life (Years)	Depreciation Per Year
Furniture	$20,000	$5,000	$15,000	10	$1,500
Fixtures	10,000	1,000	9,000	4	2,250
Equipment	12,000	2,000	10,000	5	2,000
	$42,000	$8,000	$34,000		$5,750

Composite rate = $5,750/$34,000 = 16.91%

EXHIBIT 13-5 DEPRECIATION AND TAXES— STRAIGHT-LINE DEPRECIATION VERSUS THE MODIFIED ACCELERATED COST RECOVERY SYSTEM (MACRS)

Asset cost:	$24,000
Asset depreciation base	20,000
Asset life	5 years

Year	Straight-line Depreciation	Modified Accelerated Cost Recovery System (MACRS)	Difference
1	$ 4,000	$ 9,600	$ 5,600
2	4,000	5,760	1,760
3	4,000	3,456	− 544
4	4,000	592	− 3,408
5	4,000	592	− 3,408
Total	$20,000	$20,000	−0−

EXHIBIT 13-6 PROPERY, PLANT AND EQUIPMENT— UPJOHN COMPANY

NOTE: **Property, Plant and Equipment**—Property, plant and equipment are carried at cost. Depreciation is computed principally on the straight-line method for financial reporting, while accelerated methods are used for income tax purposes. Maintenance and repair costs are charged to earnings as incurred. Costs of renewals and improvements are capitalized. Upon retirement or other disposition of property, any gain or loss is included in earnings.

ACRS and MACRS permit a faster recovery of an asset's cost and larger tax benefits during the early years of an asset's life. The intent of Congress in enacting legislation creating ACRS and MACRS was to encourage and stimulate capital investment.

Routine Maintenance of Equipment

Companies often spend money on existing assets, so that it is necessary to distinguish between revenue expenditures and capital expenditures, that is, between costs that have no future benefit and are expenses, and costs that have future benefit and are assets.

Expenditures for routine maintenance (such as machine lubrication) and repairs (replacing a broken part) are expensed, because they do not extend an asset's useful life nor help it increase output. Capital expenditures either (1) increase the service quality received from the asset, (2) extend the asset's useful life, or (3) increase the quantity of output produced by the asset. These costs are capitalized as assets. Exhibit 13-7 shows the capitalization policy of Clark Equipment Company as explained in the notes to Clark's statements.

Proper classification of revenue and capital expenditures is important, because misclassification leads to inaccurate income statements covering several accounting periods. Income is over- or understated, and the balance sheet accounts relating to plant assets and stockholders' equity are incorrect.

EXHIBIT 13-7 CAPITALIZATION POLICY—
CLARK EQUIPMENT COMPANY

NOTE: **Depreciation**—Property, plant and equipment are carried at cost. Expenditures for maintenance and repairs are charged to expense as incurred. Expenditures for major renewals and betterments are capitalized. The Company generally uses the straight-line method of depreciation. Depreciation lives generally range from eight to 50 years for land improvements, eight to 50 years for buildings, and three to 25 years for machinery and equipment. Properties retired or sold are removed from the property accounts, with gains or losses on disposal included in income.

The year-end property, plant and equipment balances for the past two years are classified as follows:

	Amounts in millions	
	1992	1991
Land	$ 7.4	$ 13.2
Land improvements	5.9	8.8
Buildings	77.3	126.0
Machinery & equipment	398.4	451.7
	489.0	599.7
Accumulated depreciation	(272.8)	(315.9)
	$ 216.2	$ 283.8

Depletion

Assets such as stands of timber, oil fields, and coal, mineral, and other ore deposits are called natural resources or wasting assets. There are three categories of costs related to natural resources: (1) acquisition cost, (2) exploration costs, and (3) development costs. These assets are consumed through extraction or production. The expensing of the costs of natural resources is called depletion and is similar to depreciation.

Depletion is computed in the same manner as units-of-activity depreciation. For example, assume that a coal deposit is purchased for a total cost of $10,000,000. Exploration and development costs total $5,000,000. The total cost is $15,000,000. We estimate that after the deposit is exhausted and the land reclaimed, we can sell the property as a recreation site for $2,000,000. The company's geologist estimates that the deposit contains 6,000,000 tons of coal. The depletion per ton of coal is then $2.1667 [($15,000,000 − $2,000,000)/6,000,000].

If 200,000 tons are extracted and sold during the year, the depletion cost charged to the coal is $433,340. If other mining costs are $100,000, the cost of coal sold is $533,340.

There is no depletion expense account, because the cost of depletion goes to Inventory of Coal and then to Cost of Coal Sold when the coal is sold. Exhibit 13-8 contains the Chesapeake Corporation income statement showing the cost of timber it harvested.

EXHIBIT 13-8   INCOME STATEMENT: TIMBER DEPLETION—CHESAPEAKE CORPORATION

For the years ended December 31, *(In millions except per share data)*	1992	1991	1990
Income:			
Net sales	**$888.4**	$840.5	841.2
Costs and expenses:			
Cost of products sold	**663.0**	616.8	633.2
Depreciation and cost of timber harvested	**66.5**	62.1	55.8
Selling, general and administrative expenses	**106.7**	103.1	93.3
Income from operations	**52.2**	58.5	58.9
Other income (expense), net	**1.7**	3.0	(.4)
Interest expense	**(31.4)**	(35.4)	(29.4)
Income before taxes and cumulative effect of accounting changes	**22.5**	26.1	29.1
Income taxes	**8.1**	10.7	12.4
Income before cumulative effect of accounting changes	**14.4**	15.4	16.7
Cumulative effect of accounting changes	**(9.7)**	—	—
Net income	**4.7**	15.4	16.7
Per share:			
Earnings before cumulative effect of accounting changes	**$ .63**	$.75	$.81
Cumulative effect of accounting changes	**(.46)**	—	—
Earnings	**.17**	.75	.81
Retained earnings:			
Balance, beginning of year	**$260.3**	$259.7	$257.8
Net income	**4.7**	15.4	16.7
Cash dividends declared, $.72 per share each year	**(16.7)**	(14.8)	(14.8)
Balance, end of year	**$248.3**	$260.3	$259.7

The accompanying Notes to Consolidated Financial Statements are part of the financial statements.

Amortization

Intangible assets are long-lived productive resources that generally have no physical existence. They derive their value from the rights and privileges granted to the firm owning them. Examples include patents, copyrights, trademarks and trade names, franchises, organization costs, leases, leaseholds, leasehold improvements, and goodwill.

Intangible assets are recorded at historical cost. The expensing of an intangible asset is called amortization. With the exception of certain leases, leaseholds, and leasehold improvements, generally accepted accounting principles require straight-line amortization unless a company can demonstrate that another method is more appropriate under the circumstances.

Exhibit 13-9 shows the income statement for Reader's Digest Association, Inc. and its notes for Property, Plant and Equipment and for Intangible Assets. Reader's Digest has a rather summarized income statement with only two operating expenses, but shows the detail of its depreciation and amortization in its notes.

EXHIBIT 13-9 DEPRECIATION AND AMORTIZATION DISCLOSURE—READER'S DIGEST ASSOCIATION, INC.

Dollars in thousands, except per share data	Years ended June 30,		
	1993	1992	1991
Revenues	$2,868,637	$2,613,958	$2,345,068
Cost of sales, fulfillment and distribution expense	1,111,198	1,015,116	915,902
Promotion, selling and administrative expense	1,404,787	$1,268,628	$1,137,164
	2,515,985	2,283,744	2,053,066
Operating profit	352,652	330,214	292,002
Other income, net	67,267	50,897	48,061
Income before provision for income taxes and cumulative effect of changes in accounting principles	419,919	381,111	340,063
Provision for income taxes	161,669	146,728	130,923
Income before cumulative effect of changes in accounting principles	258,250	234,383	209,140
Cumulative effect of changes in accounting principles for:			
Income taxes	2,375	—	—
Postretirement benefits (net of tax benefit of $33,375)	(53,313)	—	—
Net Income	$ 207,312	$ 234,383	$ 209,140
Earnings per share:			
Before cumulative effect of changes in accounting principles	$ 2.16	$ 1.95	$ 1.74
Cumulative effect of changes in accounting principles for:			
Income taxes	.02	—	—
Postretirement benefits	(.44)	—	—
Earnings per share	$ 1.74	$ 1.95	$ 1.74
Average common shares outstanding	118,702	119,800	119,413

See accompanying notes to consolidated financial statements.

NOTES
Property, Plant and Equipment

	1993	1992
Land	$ 17,354	$ 19,705
Buildings and building improvements	193,944	210,808
Printing and fulfillment equipment	147,550	144,109
Furniture, fixtures and equipment	134,233	128,240
Leasehold improvements	23,312	23,476
	$516,393	$526,338
Less: Accumulated depreciation and amortization	281,233	272,672
	$235,160	$253,666

Intangible Assets

	1993	1992
Distribution rights, contracts, subscription lists and other	$ 62,127	$ 58,857
Excess of cost over fair value of net assets of businesses acquired	78,494	80,874
	140,621	139,731
Less: Accumulated amortization	66,856	59,892
	$ 73,765	$ 79,839

14

NONOPERATING REVENUES AND EXPENSES, INCLUDING INCOME TAXES, DISCONTINUED OPERATIONS, EXTRAORDINARY ITEMS, AND ACCOUNTING CHANGES

Chapter 7 states that gross margin (sales less cost of goods sold) minus operating expenses equals income from operations or, as it is sometimes called, operating net income or operating income. Many financial statement users view operating income as one of the best indicators of how successful a company is, because it measures the company's major ongoing activities.

Other Revenues and Expenses

After operating income, the next section of the income statement is "other revenues and expenses." This category reports revenues and expenses arising from activities outside the main operations of the business. Another term for this category is "other income and expense." Examples include gains and losses on the sale of a plant or other assets, as well as gains and losses on such things as lawsuits. Interest revenue and expenses are also included in this category because they arise principally from lending and borrowing money, financial activities external to the major operations of a company.

Other types of accounts that appear in this classification include dividend revenue from investment in another company's stock, and gains and losses from foreign exchange transactions. These gains and losses are caused by the company's exposure to exchange risk when it receives (or pays) foreign currency in settlement of accounts receivable (or payable). Many companies "net" these items and show only one amount on the income statement. This amount is added to, or deducted from, income from operations in arriving at "pretax income from continuing operations." Exhibit 14-1 presents the disclosure

	Years ended June 30		
Dollars in thousands, except per share data	**1993**	1992	1991
Revenues	**$2,868,637**	$2,613,958	$2,345,068
Cost of sales, fulfillment and distribution expense	**1,111,198**	1,015,116	915,902
Promotion, selling and administrative expense	**1,404,787**	1,268,628	1,137,164
	2,515,985	2,283,744	2,053,066
Operating profit	**352,652**	330,214	292,002
Other income, net	**67,267**	50,897	48,061
Income before provision for income taxes and cumulative effect of changes in accounting principles	**419,919**	381,111	340,063
Provision for income taxes	**161,669**	146,728	130,923
Income before cumulative effect of changes in accounting principles	**258,250**	234,383	209,140
Cumulative effect of changes in accounting principles for: Income taxes	**2,375**	—	—
Postretirement benefits (net of tax benefit of $33,375)	**(53,313)**	—	—
Dollars in thousands, except per share data	**1993**	1992	1991
Net Income	**207,312**	234,383	209,140

	Years ended June 30		
Earnings per share:			
Before cumulative effect of changes in accounting principles	**$ 2.16**	$ 1.95	$ 1.74
Cumulative effect of changes in accounting principles for:			
Income taxes	**.02**	—	—
Postretirement benefits	**(.44)**	—	—
Earnings per share	**$ 1.74**	$ 1.95	$ 1.74
Average common shares outstanding	**118,702**	119,800	119,413

See accompanying notes to consolidated financial statements.

ˈNOTE: Other Income, Net

	1993	1992	1991
Interest income	**$51,728**	$52,832	$48,664
Interest expense	**(4,676)**	(2,933)	(4,078)
Gains on the sales of certain investments	**29,398**	20,729	7,118
Loss on foreign exchange	**(1,395)**	(12,975)	(1,093)
Other, net	**(7,788)**	(6,756)	(2,550)
	$67,267	$50,897	$48,061

for "Other income, net" for The Reader's Digest Association, Inc. and Subsidiaries.

Exhibit 14-2 is from the annual report of The Times Mirror Company and Subsidiaries. The income statement contains an item called "Nonrecurring gains (charges)." These gains and charges are explained in the related footnote in Exhibit 14-2.

EXHIBIT 14-2 INCOME STATEMENT: NONRECURRING GAINS (CHARGES)—THE TIMES MIRROR COMPANY AND SUBSIDIARIES

	Year Ended December 31		
(In thousands of dollars except per share amounts)	1993	1992	1991
Revenues	$3,714,158	$3,594,044	$3,519,975
Costs and Expenses			
Costs of sales	2,039,034	1,977,862	1,943,204
Selling, general and administrative expenses	1,299,431	1,266,753	1,251,656
Restructuring charges	80,164	202,700	42,300
	3,418,629	3,447,315	3,237,160
Operating Profit	295,529	146,729	282,815
Interest expense	(85,237)	(74,501)	(77,403)
Nonrecurring gains (charges)	86,799	8,673	(71,503)
Other, net	4,626	4,896	9,977
Income from continuing operations before income taxes	301,717	85,797	143,886
Income taxes	137,604	50,480	75,932
Income from continuing operations	164,113	35,317	67,954
Discontinued operations:			
Income from discontinued operations, net of income taxes	21,344	21,458	14,000
Gain on sale of discontinued operations, net of income taxes	131,702		
Income before cumulative effect of changes in accounting principles	317,159	56,775	81,954
Cumulative effect of changes in accounting principles:			
Postretirement benefits, net of income tax benefit of $84,931		(133,376)	
Income taxes		10,000	
Net Income (Loss)	$ 317,159	$ (66,601)	$ 81,954

	Year Ended December 31		
(In thousands of dollars except per share amounts)	1993	1992	1991
Earnings (loss) per share:			
Continuing operations	$1.27	$ .27	$.53
Discontinued operations:			
Income from operations	.17	.17	$.11
Gain on sale	1.02		
Before cumulative effect of changes in accounting principles	$2.46	$ .44	$.64
Cumulative effect of changes in accounting principles:			
Postretirement benefits		(1.04)	
Income taxes		.08	
Earnings (loss) per share	$2.46	$ (.52)	$.64

See notes to consolidated financial statements.

`NOTE: **Nonrecurring Gains and Charges**—During 1993, the company sold its investment in QVC Network, Inc. common stock for a gain of $75,740,000 and sold a small cable system for a gain of $11,059,000. These gains increased income before income taxes by $86,799,000 or $50,364,000 (39 cents per share) after applicable income taxes.

During 1992, the company sold two of its Texas cable television systems for a gain of $8,673,000 before income taxes or $5,026,000 (4 cents per share) after applicable income taxes.

During 1991, the company sold Broadcasting Publications, Inc. at a loss of $20,614,000 and sold certain assets of its cable television subsidiary for gains of $14,111,000. The company also recorded a $65,000,000 write-down of the note and other assets outstanding from the 1987 sale of *The Denver Post.* These items reduced income before income taxes by $71,503,000 or $43,415,000 (35 cents per share) after applicable income taxes.

Equity in the Earnings of Investee

Another account that might appear in the "other income (or expense)" category is "Equity in the Net Income of Affiliates" or "Equity in the Earnings of Investee." This account is the investor company's proportionate share of the investee's earnings or losses for the period. If the investee company reports net income of $100,000 and the investor company holds 25% of the investee's common stock, the investor recognizes $25,000 of the investee's income in its own income statement. The method used to account for this type of an investment is called the *equity method*. This method is used by the investor company when the investor owns sufficient shares of stock of the affiliate to exercise significant influence over the actions of that company. Accountants assume that a company has *significant influence* when it owns 20% or more of the common stock of an investee company. Because the company recognizes income (or loss) based on the investee's income (or loss), dividends received from the investee are not counted as revenue. Instead, these amounts reduce the carrying value of the investment account. If a company cannot significantly influence the actions of the investee, the company records dividends received as dividend revenue.

Exhibit 14-3 indicates that Southwestern Bell Corporation had $249.7 million of "equity in net income of affiliates" in 1993. The exhibit also presents the footnote disclosure relating to the company's majority-owned subsidiaries; this note explains the accounting policy used by the company to account for these subsidiaries.

Dollars in millions except per share amounts

	1993	1992	1991
Operating Revenues			
Local service	$ 5,187.4	$ 4,668.4	$ 4,228.9
Network access	2,685.4	2,547.8	2,440.8
Long-distance service	977.3	1,011.7	1,026.6
Directory advertising	869.0	847.9	847.7
Other	971.2	939.6	787.9
Total operating revenues	10,690.3	$10,015.4	$..9,331.9
Operating Expenses			
Cost of services and products	3,387.6	3,423.4	3,159.9
Selling, general and administrative	2,916.1	2,552.4	2,273.4
Depreciation and amortization	2,007.0	1,842.2	1,765.0
Total operating expenses	8,310.7	7,818.0	7,198.3
Operating Income	2,379.6	2,197.4	2,133.6
Other Income (Expense)			
Interest expense	(496.2)	(530.0)	(577.7)
*Equity in net income of affiliates	249.7	208.0	94.5
Other expense—net	(72.9)	(5.7)	(6.2)
Total other income (expense)	(319.4)	(327.7)	(469.4)
Income Before Income Taxes, Extraordinary Loss and Cumulative Effect of Changes in Accounting Principles	2,060.2	1,869.7	1,664.2

Dollars in millions except per share amounts

	1993	1992	1991
Income Taxes			
Federal	550.7	488.2	436.2
State and local	74.3	79.8	51.5
Total income taxes	625.0	568.0	487.7
Income Before Extraordinary Loss and Cumulative Effect of Changes in Accounting Principles	1,435.2	1,301.7	1,156.5
Extraordinary Loss on Early Extinguishment of Debt, net of tax	(153.2)	—	(80.7)
Cumulative Effect of Changes in Accounting Principles, net of tax	(2,127.2)	—	—
Net Income (Loss)	$ (845.2)	$ 1,301.7	$ 1,075.8
Earnings Per Common Share:*			
Income Before Extraordinary Loss and Cumulative Effect of Changes in Accounting Principles	$2.39	$2.17	$1.93
Extraordinary Loss on Early Extinguishment of Debt, net of tax	(0.25)	—	(0.14)
Cumulative Effect of Changes in Accounting Principles, net of tax	(3.55)	—	—
Net Income (Loss)	$ (1.41)	$ 2.17	$ 1.79
Weighted Average Number of Common Shares Outstanding (in millions)	599.8	600.2	600.3

*Restated to reflect two-for-one stock split effective May 25, 1993.
The accompanying notes are an integral part of the consolidated financial statements.

*NOTE: **Summary of Significant Accounting Policies Basis of Presentation**—The consolidated financial statements include the accounts of Southwestern Bell Corporation and its majority-owned subsidiaries (Corporation). Southwestern Bell Telephone Company (Telephone Company) is the Corporation's largest subsidiary. All significant intercompany transactions are eliminated in the consolidation process. Investments in partnerships, joint ventures and less than majority-owned subsidiaries are principally accounted for under the equity method. Earnings from foreign investments accounted for under the equity method are included for periods ended within three months of the Corporation's year end. Certain amounts in prior financial statements have been reclassified to conform to the current year's presentation.

The Minority Interest in Income

Another account that might appear in the "other revenue and expense" section of the income statement is the "minority interest in income." When an investor company owns more than 50% of the outstanding common stock of another company, we say that they have a parent-subsidiary relationship, because the parent can *control* the activities of the investee. In almost all cases, generally accepted accounting principles (GAAP) require that the companies combine and prepare "consolidated" financial statements. Consolidated statements present the balance sheets, income statements, and statements of cash flow as if the two companies were one entity.

When the investor company holds less than 100% of the outstanding common stock of the investee company, the remaining shares are held by "minority shareholders." "Minority interest" is the subsidiary's equity that is held by stockholders other than the parent company. The minority interest has an equity in the net assets of the subsidiary, as well as an interest in the net income of the subsidiary. When consolidated statements are prepared, some companies include *all* (that is, 100%) of the income of the subsidiary in the combined income statement. In this case, the minority interest's share of income is subtracted in arriving at income from continuing operations. Sometimes the minority interest in income is stated separately on the income statement, and other times it is combined with other items in the "other income and expense" category. Exhibit 14-4 displays the disclosure of the "minority interest in income" included in "other income" for Scott Paper Company and CSX Corporation. The minority interest in income is presented on the face of the income statement for the Atlantic Richfield Company in Exhibit 14-5.

Scott Paper Company

(In millions, except on a per share basis)	1992	1991[1]	1990[1]
SALES	**$4,886.2**	$4,704.3	$5,168.6
Costs and expenses			
Product costs	**3,626.2**	3,533.7	3,873.6
Marketing and distribution	**623.4**	587.0	585.0
Research, administration and general	**243.3**	248.0	257.8
Other	**(7.9)**	294.8	158.0
	4,485.0	4,663.5	4,874.4
Income from operations	**401.2**	40.8	294.2
Interest expense	**188.8**	221.4	199.4
*Other income and (expense)	**7.9**	59.8	23.3
Income (Loss) before taxes	**220.3**	(120.8)	118.1
Taxes on income	**58.5**	(20.7)	7.9
Income (Loss) before share of earnings of international equity affiliates	**161.8**	(100.1)	110.2
Share of earnings of international equity affiliates	**5.4**	30.2	37.8
NET INCOME (LOSS)	**$ 167.2**	$ (69.9)	$ 148.0
Earnings (Loss) per share	2.26	(.95)	2.01
Dividends per share	.80	.80	.80
Average common shares outstanding	73.9	73.7	73.6

NOTE: **Other Income and (Expense)**

(Millions)	1992	1991	1990
Interest income	$18.5	$23.5	$ 34.6
Equity affiliate dispositions	—	51.1	6.3
Minority interest	(9.1)	(8.9)	(6.6)
Other	(1.5)	(5.9)	(11.0)
	$ 7.9	$59.8	$ 23.3

Interest income includes $1.2 million, $1.3 million and $7.3 million on advances to affiliates during 1992, 1991 and 1990, respectively. Minority interest represents that portion of earnings of the Company's consolidated subsidiaries belonging to minority owners.

EXHIBIT 14-4 *(continued)*

CSX CORPORATION

(Millions of Dollars, Except Per Share Amounts)		Years Ended December 31,		
		1992	1991	1990
Operating Revenue	Transportation	$8,550	$8,419	$7,947
	Non-Transportation	184	217	258
	Total	8,734	8,636	8,205
Operating Expense	Transportation	7,644	7,643	7,195
	Non-Transportation	125	139	142
	Productivity/Restructuring Charge	699	755	53
	Total	$8,468	8,537	7,390
Earnings (Loss)	**Operating Income**	266	99	815
	˙Other Income	3	94	41
	Interest Expense	.276	306	319
	Earnings (Loss) from Continuing Operations before Income Taxes	(7)	(113)	537
	Income Tax Expense (Benefit)	(27)	(37)	172
	Earnings (Loss) from Continuing Operations	20	(76)	365
	Discontinued Operations, Net of Income Taxes	—	—	51
	Earnings (Loss) before Cumulative Effect of Change in Accounting	20	(76)	416
	Cumulative Effect on Years Prior to 1991 of Change in Accounting for Post-retirement Benefits Other than Pensions	—	(196)	—
	Net Earnings (Loss)	$ 20	$ (272)	$ 416

(Millions of Dollars, Except Per Share Amounts)		Years Ended December 31,		
		1992	1991	1990
Per Common Share	**Earnings (Loss) Per Share:**			
	From Continuing Operations	$ .19	$(.75)	$3.63
	From Discontinued Operations	—	—	.52
	Earnings (Loss) Per Share before Cumulative Effect of Change in Accounting	.19	(.75)	4.15
	Cumulative Effect on Years Prior to 1991 of Change in Accounting for Post-retirement Benefits Other than Pensions	—	.(1.95)	—
	Earnings (Loss) Per Share	$ 19	$(2.70)	$4.15
	Average Common Shares Outstanding (Thousands)	102,907	100,489	98,252
	Common Shares Outstanding at End of Year (Thousands)	103,476	102,378	98,540
	Cash Dividends Paid Per Common Share	$1.52	$1.43	$1.40

See accompanying Notes to Consolidated Financial Statements.

Nonoperating revenues and expenses   127

EXHIBIT 14-4 *(continued)*

NOTE: **Other Income**

	1992	1991	1990
Interest Income	**$43**	$72	$76
Net Gain on Investment Transactions[a]	—	49	—
Gain on Sale of RF&P Corporation Stock[b]	—	31	—
Gain on Short-Line Railroad Sales	—	—	20
Discount on Sale of Accounts Receivable	**(17)**	(32)	(44)
*Minority Interest in Earnings of Subsidiaries	**(15)**	(25)	(15)
Miscellaneous	**(8)**	(1)	4
Total	**$ 3**	$94	$41

(a) In June 1991, the company consummated the sale of one-third of its interest in Sea-Land Orient Terminals Ltd., to Ready City Ltd. (a Hong Kong-based consortium). The sale proceeds amounted to $97 million and resulted in a pretax gain of $65 million, $35 million after-tax, or 35 cents per share. The company also recorded a pretax charge of $16 million, $11 million after tax, or 11 cents per share, related to the establishment of valuation reserves for several investments in "non-core business" affiliates.

(b) In a series of transactions consummated in October 1991, the company exchanged its 6.8 million shares of RF&P Corporation (RF&P) stock for the rail assets of RF&P and $106 million in cash. These transactions resulted in a pretax gain of $31 million, before associated minority interest expense of $5 million, or an after-tax gain of $8 million, or 8 cents per share.

EXHIBIT 14.5 INCOME STATEMENT: MINORITY INTEREST IN INCOME—
ATLANTIC RICHFIELD COMPANY

Millions of dollars, except per share amounts	For the year ended December 31		
	1993	1992	1991
Revenues			
Sales and other operating revenues (including excise taxes)	**$18,487**	$18,668	$18,191
Income from equity investments	**40**	22	119
Interest	**164**	182	261
Other revenues	**492**	376	385
	19,183	$19,248	$18,956
Expenses			
Trade purchases	**7,224**	7,263	7,022
Operating expenses	**3,293**	3,174	3,078
Exploration expenses (including undeveloped lease amortization)	**667**	567	593
Selling, general and administrative expenses	**1,828**	1,724	1,763
Taxes other than excise and income taxes	**1,147**	1,203	1,131
Excise taxes	**1,298**	1,165	1,120
Depreciation, depletion and amortization	**1,718**	1,754	1,694
Interest	**715**	762	892
Unusual items	**659**	(271)	503
	18,549	17,341	17,796
Income before income taxes, minority interest and cumulative effect of changes in accounting principles	**634**	1,907	1,160

Expenses	For the year ended December 31		
Millions of dollars, except per share amounts	**1993**	1992	1991
Provision for taxes on income	**327**	678	420
Minority interest in earnings of subsidiaries	**38**	36	31
Income before cumulative effect of changes in accounting principles	**269**	1,193	709
Cumulative effect of changes in accounting principles	**—**	(392)	—
Net income	**$ 269**	$ 801	$ 709
Earned Per Share			
Before cumulative effect of changes in accounting principles	**$ 1.66**	$ 7.39	$ 4.39
Cumulative effect of changes in accounting principles	**—**	(2.43)	—
Net income per share	**$ 1.66**	$ 4.96	$ 4.39
Retained Earnings			
Balance, January 1	**$5,918**	$5,990	$6,837
Net income	**269**	801	709
Cash dividends Preference stock	**(3)**	(3)	(3)
Common stock	**(876)**	(870)	(869)
Cancellation of treasury stock	**—**	—	(684)
Balance, December 31	**$5,308**	$5,918	$5,990

Income Tax Expense

After the "other revenue and expense" category is added to, or deducted from, operating income, in order to arrive at pretax income from continuing operations, applicable local, state, and federal income taxes are deducted. You should note that tax regulations do not always require that a company use the same accounting methods on its tax return that it uses to calculate net income on the income statement. Frequently companies use different depreciation methods and methods of revenue recognition for their books and tax returns. In some instances, the tax laws allow a company to defer revenue recognition and accelerate expense recognition. For example, a company can choose to use the completed contract method of revenue recognition for tax purposes and use the percentage of completion method for financial accounting purposes. This results in recording revenue on the income statement during the time period that the project is in progress, but reporting no revenue for tax purposes until the project is completed. The same total amount of revenue is reported as taxable income and financial revenue over time; the difference is simply a matter of timing. These revenue recognition methods are discussed in Chapter 8.

Another example relates to the choice of depreciation methods. Depreciation methods are discussed in Chapter 13. A company might choose the straight-line method for financial reporting purposes and an accelerated method for tax purposes. This results in higher accounting net income than taxable income in the early years of an asset's life, because more depreciation expense is deducted for tax purposes than for financial accounting purposes. Over time, the same total expense is deducted for financial accounting and tax purposes, because straight-line depreciation increases relative to depreciation using an accelerated method in the later years of an asset's life.

The tax expense shown on the income statement is derived from the revenues and expenses listed on the income statement. In other words, taxes are recorded on the income statement in the same year as the revenues and expenses giving rise to the taxes. (Recall the concept of "matching," discussed in Chapter 6.) However, the taxes actually due in that year (based on tax law) are derived from the figures on the tax return. The difference between the two tax amounts is called "deferred income taxes." Exhibit 14-6 presents the income tax expense for

Interface, Inc. and Subsidiaries. Note that the company reports taxes on income of $7,455,000 but its tax liability at year end is $9,846,000. Footnote number 8 states that the difference between financial accounting income and taxable income is primarily caused by the use of different depreciation methods for book and tax purposes. Another cause of this difference is tax payments that the company made during the year totaling approximately $16,300,000.

EXHIBIT 14-6   INCOME STATEMENT: INCOME TAX EXPENSE—INTERFACE, INC. AND SUBSIDIARIES

(in thousands, except share data)	Fiscal Year Ended		
	1/2/94	1/3/93	12/29/91
Net Sales	$625,067	$594,078	$581,786
Cost of sales	427,321	404,130	393,733
Gross Profit on Sales	197,746	189,948	188,053
Selling, general and administrative expenses	151,576	149,509	150,100
Operating Income	46,170	40,439	37,953
Other expense (income):			
Interest expense	22,840	21,894	23,253
Other	2,026	(16)	370
	24,866	21,878	23,623
Income Before Taxes on Income	21,304	18,561	14,330
Taxes on income	* 7,455	6,311	5,409
Net Income	13,849	12,250	8,921
Preferred stock dividends	913	—	—
Net Income Applicable to Common Shareholders	$ 12,936	$ 12,250	$ 8,921
Primary Earnings Per Common Share	$ 0.75	$ 0.71	$ 0.52

See accompanying notes to consolidated financial statements.

NOTES 6: **Accrued Expenses**

Accrued expenses consisted of the following:

(in thousands)	1/2/94	1/3/93
Income taxes	$ 9,846*	$ 3,741
Compensation	14,209	12,615
Interest	3,437	4,044
Other	$ 25,252	$ 18,242
Total	**$52,744**	**$38,642**

Principal items making up the deferred tax provisions for fiscal 1991 are as follows:

(in thousands)	
Excess of tax over book depreciation	$ 2,560
Other	424
Total	**$2,984**

Cash and cash equivalents consisted of the following:

(in thousands)	1/2/94	1/3/93
Cash	$4,045	$5,549
Cash equivalents	629	275
Total	**$4,674**	**$5,824**

(continued)

EXHIBIT 14-6 *(continued)*

Cash equivalents, carried at costs which approximate market, consist of short-term, highly liquid investments which are readily convertible into cash and have initial maturities of three months or less. The Company does not believe it is exposed to any significant credit risk on cash and cash equivalents.

Under the Company's cash management program, checks in transit are not considered reductions of cash or accounts payable until presented to the bank for payment. At January 2, 1994 and January 3, 1993, checks not yet presented to the bank totalled approximately $9.7 million and $10.6 million, respectively. In accordance with a Workers' Compensation self-insurance arrangement in the State of Maine, the Company is required by state law to maintain a trust account to pay Workers' Compensation claims. At January 2, 1994 and January 3, 1993, the trust account had balances of approximately $4.0 million and $4.4 million, respectively, and was segregated from cash and cash equivalents and reflected as escrowed and restricted funds at January 2, 1994 and January 3, 1993. Cash payments for interest amounted to approximately $23.4 million, $21.1 million and $23.3 million for the years ended January 2, 1994, January 3, 1993 and December 29, 1991, respectively. Income tax payments amounted to approximately $16.3 million, $8.9 million and $11.3 million for the years ended January 2, 1994, January 3, 1993 and December 29, 1991, respectively.

Other Items Appearing on the Income Statement

In arriving at net income, management normally separates revenues and expenses into operating and nonoperating components. Although financial statement users are interested in total net income, they generally focus on operating income, because that component is usually more representative and continuous than income from nonoperating activities, such as dividend revenue from stock owned and interest expense on bonds.

In addition, to make the income statement easier to understand, accountants separate net income (or loss) into two components. The first is operating income (or loss) generated by ongoing, normal operations. The second component is income derived from activities or events that are not expected to be ongoing or are neither normal nor ongoing. Income from continuing operations includes income from only those operations that will be in existence in the following year.

The components of net income not derived from normal operations are shown separately on the income statement. The purpose of presenting these items separately is to bring them to the attention of the reader. These other separate components are discontinued operations, extraordinary items, and changes in accounting principles, as discussed in the following paragraphs. Moreover, earnings per share is normally presented on

the face of the income statement for each income component. Exhibit 14-7 is the partial income statement on a per share basis from the annual report of Pennzoil Company. Notice that the company has reported a loss from discontinued operations, an extraordinary item, and an accounting change.

EXHIBIT 14-7 PARTIAL INCOME STATEMENT PER SHARE BASIS: NET INCOME NOT DERIVED FROM NORMAL OPERATIONS— PENNZOIL COMPANY

	Year Ended December 31		
	1992	1991	1990
Net Income	**$128,164**	$21,042	$93,768
Earnings (Loss) Per Share			
Continuing operations	**$ .43**	$ .99	$2.37
Discontinued operations	**.29**	.74	—
Total before extraordinary item and cumulative effect of change in accounting principle	**.72**	1.73	2.37
Extraordinary item	**(.41)**	—	—
Cumulative effect of change in accounting principle	**2.85**	(1.21)	—
Total	**$3.16**	$ .52	$2.37
Dividends Per Common Share	**$3.00**	$3.00	$3.00

See Notes to Consolidated Financial Statements

Discontinued Operations

A company's selling or abandoning a segment of its operations (resulting in *discontinued* operations) is a very common event in business. Exhibit 14-8 is from the annual report of First Financial Management Corporation. In its income statement the company reported $15,761,000 of income from continuing operations in 1992. Notice the amount of reported income taxes from operations by First Financial. The income taxes are from continuing operations of segments of the company that will be in existence in the next fiscal year. First Financial shows net earnings from discontinued operations of $30,082,000 ($36,900,000 − $6,818,000) in 1992. That year, the company discontinued operations of a financial services subsidiary.

First Financial's income statement section dealing with the discontinued operations is divided into two components: (1) the income or loss from the segment's operations until the date of disposal (income of $36,900,000) and (2) the gain or loss from the disposal of the segment (loss of $6,818,000). This form of presentation is required because the company operated the segment for a portion of the year. The income or loss from discontinued operation and the gain or loss on disposal are each reported net of income taxes. "Net of taxes" means that the amount reported for discontinued operations has been reduced by income taxes (if a gain) or reduced by the income tax savings (if a loss).

Year Ended December 31, *(In thousands, except per share amounts)*	1992	1991	1990	Year Ended December 31, *(In thousands, except per share amounts)*	1992	1991	1990
REVENUES				**EXPENSES** *(continued)*			
Service revenues	$1,296,122	$ 976,928	$759,300	Income from continuing operations	15,761	58,302	$ 47,677
Product sales revenues	92,011	57,274	55,218	Income from discontinued operations, net of taxes	36,900	30,737	25,223
Other income	16,577	1,918	1,750	Loss on sale of discontinued operations, net of taxes	(6,818)		
	1,404,710	1,036,120	816,268	Net Income	$ 45,843	$ 89,039	$ 72,900
EXPENSES				**INCOME PER SHARE–PRIMARY**			
Operating	1,089,878	809,533	623,517	Continuing operations	$0.27	$1.26	$1.17
General and administrative	23,449	20,720	20,061	Discontinued operations	0.52	0.66	0.62
Cost of products sold	58,033	34,596	33,889	Net income	$0.79	$1.92	$1.79
Depreciation and amortization	82,441	58,580	45,152				
Loss in business unit to be sold	79,567			**INCOME PER SHARE–FULLY DILUTED**			
Interest, net	9,440	12,589	$ 14,495	Continuing operations	$0.27	$1.17	$1.10
	$1,342,808	$ 936,018	$737,114	Discontinued operations	0.52	0.62	0.57
Income from continuing operations before Income taxes	61,902	100,102	79,154	Net income	$0.79	$1.79	$1.67
Income taxes	46,141	41,800	$ 31,477	*See notes to consolidated financial statements.*			

NOTES: • **Basis of Presentation—Effect of Discontinued Operations**—During the fourth quarter of 1992, FFMC sold or signed agreements to sell the businesses that comprised its Financial Services business segment (see Note C—Dispositions). For purposes of the consolidated financial statements, net amounts for these businesses have been presented separately as discontinued operations. Continuing operations consist of the Company's remaining businesses which operate in one business segment (Information Services), together with the corporate entity.

The decision to discontinue the Financial Services segment operations resulted in modifications to the Company's financial statement presentation, including the adoption of classified balance sheets and certain reclassifications in its statements of income. In each of the periods presented, interest expense was allocated to the Company's discontinued operations. This allocation was based on the net assets of discontinued operations relative to the sum of consolidated net assets plus long-term debt of continuing operations, none of which was directly attributable to specific operations. As a result of these changes, certain reclassifications were made to the 1991 and 1990 financial statements to conform to the presentations used in 1992, and financial statements for all prior periods have been restated to reflect these businesses as discontinued operations. No adjustments to previously reported cash balances in the consolidated statements of cash flows were required to reflect discontinued operations, as the Financial Services segment had previously been presented separately due to restrictions on the transfer of cash or dividends between FFMC and these businesses.

(continued)

EXHIBIT 14-8   *(continued)*

• **c. Dispositions**—On November 10, 1992, the sale of First Family Financial Services, a regional consumer finance company and a subsidiary of Georgia Federal Bank ("Georgia Federal"), was completed for $248 million in cash. Georgia Federal subsequently paid FFMC a $100 million cash dividend and $50.4 million in cash for the settlement of income tax liabilities related to the sale of First Family. On December 21, 1992, FFMC signed a definitive agreement to sell Georgia Federal, a wholly-owned subsidiary of FFMC and the largest thrift institution in Georgia, for $268 million in cash. The Georgia Federal sale is subject to federal and state regulatory approvals and is expected to close in the second quarter of 1993. These transactions resulted in a net fourth quarter loss of $6.8 million after providing income tax expenses (net of tax benefits) of $40.1 million. The resultant tax rate on these dispositions is significantly higher than the Company's effective tax rate due to the non-deductibility of the majority of the loss on the sale of Georgia Federal and the provision for other tax costs incidental to the sales. Summary financial information for these discontinued operations is as follows:

Year Ended December 31,	1992	1991	1990
(In thousands)			
Income statement data:			
Revenues	$184,470	$173,941	$162,596
Expenses	123,205	120,012	116,706
Allocation of interest expense to discontinued operations	3,878	5,208	6,092
Income before income taxes from discontinued operations	57,387	48,721	39,798
Income tax	20,487	17,984	14,575
Income from discontinued operations	$ 36,900	$ 30,737	$ 25,223

The assets and liabilities of these businesses (previously presented as the Financial Services segment) have been grouped and included in the consolidated balance sheets as net assets of discontinued operations and have been classified as current in both years for consistency. The Company's balance sheets were not previously classified when these businesses were consolidated. The liabilities reflected above include the accrued loss of $49 million at December 31, 1992 in order to reflect the net assets at their net realizable value. Although these businesses have financial instruments included in assets and liabilities, market value information as of December 31, 1992 is not presented, since the net realizable value of the net assets is more relevant in the circumstances.

On December 31, 1992, FFMC entered into a definitive agreement to sell Basis Information Technologies, Inc. ("Basis"), the Company's business unit that provides data processing services to financial institutions. This transaction was concluded in early 1993, and the Company received $96.5 million, 50% in cash and 50% in capital stock of the buyer.

Prior to entering into the stock purchase agreement for the sale of Basis, the Company discontinued software development and wrote off related costs for a major product line in connection with the settlement of litigation with a vendor, the combination of which resulted in the recording of $13.8 million of other income in 1992. Concurrently, the Company decided to explore the sale of Basis. In reviewing the market value of Basis, FFMC's management determined that a write-down of the carrying value of Basis' net assets was appropriate. Accordingly, in 1992 the Company recognized a pretax loss in this business unit to be sold of $79.6 million.

Extraordinary Items

An extraordinary item is one that is material in amount, unusual and infrequent in occurrence, and not expected to recur in the foreseeable future. The item is presented separately, rather than as a component of income from operations. This puts the reader on notice that it is indeed extraordinary and that because of this item, the comparability of the current period's financial statements with those of other periods is affected. Examples of extraordinary items include gains or losses from flood, fire, earthquake, or the expropriation of a company's assets by a foreign government.

Such events are company-specific in that the qualities of unusualness and infrequency must be viewed from the perspective of the reporting company. Management must assess whether the event is unusual and infrequent, given the character of a company's business and its geographic location. For example, a loss by a company in Kansas City, Missouri, resulting from an earthquake would normally be classified as an extraordinary item. However, an earthquake loss in southern California most likely would not, because earthquakes are recurring events in that part of the country. A natural disaster could result in losses for a company, but hurricane losses in southern Florida are not extraordinary items, because hurricanes in that environment are expected and are a cost of doing business. Thus, these two criteria limit the events that are reported as extraordinary items on the income statement.

Certain types of gains or losses are generally not extraordinary:

1. Losses from writedown or writeoff of receivables, inventories, deferred research and development costs, equipment leased to others, deferred or other intangible assets

2. Gains or losses on disposal of a segment of a business

3. Gains or losses relating to the translation of foreign currencies, including those relating to major currency devaluations and revaluations

4. Gains or losses from the sale or abandonment of property, plant, or equipment used in a business

5. The effects of a strike, including those against competitors and major suppliers

6. Adjustment of accruals on long-term contracts

Items 1 and 4 qualify as extraordinary if they are a direct result of a major casualty, such as an earthquake, an expropriation, or a prohibition under a newly enacted law or regulation. Exhibit 14-9, from the annual report of Debrill Brothers, Incorporated, presents an example of a writedown of a receivable from Iraq in 1992 that meets the aforementioned criteria.

EXHIBIT 14-9   INCOME STATEMENT: WRITE-DOWN OF A RECEIVABLE—DEBRILL BROTHERS, INCORPORATED

Years Ended June 30

	1993	1992	1991
Net sales of goods and services	$1,065,438,864	$1,081,088,968	$1,003,022,296
Cost of goods and services sold	915,490,730	936,339,130	880,931,355
	149,948,134	144,749,838	122,090,941
Selling, administrative and general expenses	81,875,359	77,669,965	72,460,355
Operating income	68,072,775	67,079,873	49,630,586
Other income:			
Interest	4,075,918	3,786,746	9,095,673
Sundry	9,832,904	4,082,262	4,536,880
	13,908,822	7,869,008	13,632,553
Other deductions:			
Interest	20,690,697	26,565,746	28,641,027
Sundry	3,031,340	5,136,275	3,319,175
	23,722,037	31,702,021	31,960,202
Income before income taxes, minority interest, equity in net income of investee companies, extraordinary items and cumulative effect of accounting changes	58,259,560	43,246,860	31,302,937
Income taxes	20,085,134	16,623,196	12,418,342
Income before minority interest, equity in net income of investee companies, extraordinary items and cumulative effect of accounting changes	38,174,426	26,623,664	18,884,595
Income applicable to minority interest	486,320	214,419	540,686
Income before equity in net income of investee companies, extraordinary items and cumulative effect of accounting changes	37,688,106	26,409,245	18,343,909
Equity in net income of investee companies (net of U.S. tax expense of $145,697, 1993; $0, 1992; $0, 1991)	590,289	4,205,956	2,816,832

Years Ended June 30

	1993	1992	1991
Income before extraordinary items and cumulative effect of accounting changes	38,278,395	30,615,201	21,160,741
Extraordinary items:			
Reserve on Iraqi receivable (net of applicable income tax benefit of $2,343,000)	—	(3,637,000)	—
Reduction of foreign income tax arising from utilization of prior years' operating losses	—	3,310,400	—
Cumulative effect of accounting changes:			
Postretirement benefit plans, (net of applicable income tax benefit of $4,720,895)	(7,715,605)	—	—
Income taxes	8,785,000	—	—
Net Income	39,347,790	30,288,601	21,160,741

Earnings Per Share, Primary

	1993	1992	1991
Income before extraordinary items and cumulative effect of accounting changes:	2.87	2.31	1.60
Extraordinary items:			
Reserve on Iraqi receivable, net of tax	—	(.27)	—
Reduction of foreign income tax arising from utilization of prior years' operating losses	—	.24	—
Cumulative effect of accounting changes:			
Postretirement benefit plans, net of tax	(.58)	—	—
Income taxes	.66	—	—
Net Income	$2.95	$2.28	$1.60

EXHIBIT 14-9 *(continued)*

Years Ended June 30

	1993	1992	1991
Earnings Per Share, Assuming Full Dilution			
ncome before extraordinary items and cumulative effect of accounting changes:	**$2.54**	$2.07	$1.59
Extraordinary items:			
Reserve on Iraqi receivable, net of tax	—	(.23)	—
Reduction of foreign income tax arising from utilization of prior years' operating losses	—	.21	—
Cumulative effect of accounting changes:			
Postretirement benefit plans, net of tax	**(.48)**	—	—
Income taxes	**.55**	—	—
Net Income	**$2.61**	$2.05	$1.59

See notes to consolidated financial statements

NOTE: **Extraordinary Items**—At June 30, 1991, the Company had a trade receivable due from Iraq's State Enterprise for Tobacco and Cigarettes against letters of credit issued by an Iraqi bank which the Company believed were confirmed by the U.S. agency of a European bank. On March 31, 1992, the United States District Court for the Northern District of Georgia dismissed the lawsuit that had been brought by a subsidiary of the Company against the European bank for damages resulting from the bank's refusal to honor the letters of credit and entered a judgement in favor of the bank. The Company has recorded in 1992 a $3,637,000 extraordinary charge ($5,980,000 less $2,343,000 tax) for the Iraqi receivable.

In 1992 the Company recognized a $3,310,410 extraordinary credit for the foreign tax benefits related to the utilization of prior years' operating losses. See Note F of the Notes to Consolidated Financial Statements.

Material gains and losses from the extinguishment of debt are considered extraordinary even though they might not meet the criteria for treatment as extraordinary items. The accounting profession feels that these types of transactions are so significant and can affect net income so drastically that they should be treated as extraordinary, so that the readers of financial statements can evaluate their impact on such statements. Coltec Industries' annual report, in Exhibit 14-10, provides an example of this type of extraordinary item.

EXHIBIT 14-10 INCOME STATEMENT: EXTINGUISHMENT OF DEBT— COLTEC INDUSTRIES, INC. AND SUBSIDIARIES

	Year ended December 31,		
(in thousands, except per share data)	1993	1992	1991
Net sales	$1,334,829	$1,368,703	$1,372,979
Costs and expenses			
Cost of sales	905,464	944,405	966,791
Selling and administrative	192,437	181,176	177,168
Restructuring charge (Note 3)	25,219	—	—
Total costs and expenses	$1,123,120	$1,125,581	$1,143,959
Operating income	211,709	243,122	229,020
Dividend income	—	—	1,431
Earnings before interest, income taxes and extraordinary item	211,709	243,122	230,451
Interest and debt expense, net	110,190	135,862	199,942
Earnings before income taxes and extraordinary item	101,519	107,260	30,509
Provision for income taxes (Note 5)	36,293	42,577	28,300
Earnings before extraordinary item	65,226	64,683	2,209
Extraordinary item (Note 4)	(17,792)	$ (106,930)	591
Net earnings (loss)	$ 47,434	$ (42,247)	$ 2,800
Earnings (loss) per common share (Note 1)			
Before extraordinary item	$ .94	$ 1.11	$ .09
Extraordinary item	(.26)	(1.83)	.02
Net earnings (loss)	$ .68	$ (.72)	$ .11
Weighted average number of common and common equivalent shares	69,591	58,413	25,000

The accompanying notes to financial statements are an integral part of this statement.

ˈNOTE: **4. Extraordinary Item**—In 1993, Coltec incurred extraordinary charges of $17,792,000, net of a $9,581,000 tax benefit, in connection with debt refinancings and the early retirement of debt, including $14,675,000, net of a $7,902,000 tax benefit, from a debt refinancing completed in January 1994. Reference is made to Note 16 for information on the refinancing.

In 1992, Coltec incurred extraordinary charges of $105,347,000, net of a $28,000,000 tax benefit, in connection with the Recapitalization and extraordinary charges of $1,583,000, net of a $816,000 tax benefit, in connection with a debt refinancing and early retirement of debt. Reference is made to Note 2 for information on the Recapitalization. In 1991, Coltec recognized an extraordinary gain of $591,000, net of taxes of $305,000, in connection with the early retirement of debt.

There is normally a subtotal identifying income before extraordinary items. Extraordinary items are reported net of tax as a separate component of net income. This form of presentation alerts the reader to the fact that although an item is included in the computation of net income, it does not result from normal operations and is unlikely to occur in the foreseeable future.

Accounting Changes

A company may change from one GAAP to another. Examples of such changes include a change from the FIFO method of costing inventories to the LIFO method, or a change from an accelerated depreciation method to the straight-line method. Accounting changes are always disclosed in the notes to the financial statements, because they affect the comparability of a company's financial statements after the change to those of prior periods. In addition, for most types of accounting changes, the effect on the earnings of prior years (called a *cumulative effect*) of adopting a new accounting principle is also disclosed as a separate item following extraordinary items (if any) in the income statement.

In computing the cumulative effect, we might assume that in the third year of an asset's life, a company changed its method of depreciation on its machinery from the double-declining-balance method to the straight-line method of depreciation. The machinery originally cost $300,000 when purchased, had an estimated useful life of five years, and had no salvage value. The machinery had been used in operations for two full years preceding the change. The calculation of the cumulative effect and the reporting of that effect in the financial statements in the year of the change is as follows:

Year	Double-Declining-Balance Depreciation	Straight-Line Depreciation	Excess of Double-Declining over Straight-Line Depreciation
1st	$120,000	$ 60,000	$60,000
2nd	72,000	60,000	12,000
	$192,000	$120,000	$72,000

Note that the excess or cumulative effect relates to the period starting with the purchase date of the asset and ending at the beginning of the current year. In this case straight-line depreciation, the newly adopted principle, is used in the current year and affects the income statement. The cumulative effect of the change on prior years' earnings is interpreted this way: had straight-line depreciation been used instead of double-declining balance in the first and second years of the asset's life, net income would have been greater by $72,000 (ignoring income taxes) for that period of time.

If the tax rate is 30%, and we assume income from operations is $530,000, the following income statement presentation is made.

Income from operations before the cumulative effect of change in accounting principle	$530,000
Cumulative effect on prior years' income of a change from double-declining-balance depreciation to the straight-line depreciation method (less tax effect of $21,600)	50,400
Net income	$580,400

Exhibit 14-11 presents the disclosure relating to an accounting change resulting from a change from directly expensing airframe overhaul costs to capitalizing those costs by Southwest Airlines Company.

EXHIBIT 14-11 INCOME STATEMENT: ACCOUNTING CHANGE—SOUTHWEST AIRLINES COMPANY

	Years ended December 31,		
	1992	1991	1990
Operating revenues:			
Passenger	$1,623,828	$1,267,897	$1,144,421
Freight	33,088	26,428	22,196
Other	28,262	19,280	20,142
Total operating revenues	$1,685,178	$1,313,605	$1,186,759
Operating expenses:			
Salaries, wages and benefits (Note 10)	501,870	407,961	357,357
Fuel and oil	243,543	225,463	242,001
Maintenance materials and repairs	120,578	97,598	82,887
Agency commissions	106,372	81,245	72,084
Aircraft rentals	64,169	49,171	26,085
Landing fees and other rentals	102,717	83,177	61,167
Depreciation	101,188	86,202	79,429
Other operating expenses	262,105	219,852	183,870
Total operating expenses	1,502,542	$1,250,669	$1,104,880
Operating income	182,636	62,936	81,8X9
Other expenses (income):			
Interest expense	58,941	43,939	32,001
Capitalized interest	(15,350)	(15,301)	(13,738)
Interest income	(10,344)	(10,631)	(7,595)
Nonoperating losses (gains), net (Note 11)	2,552	1,089	(3,542)
Total other expenses	35,799	19,096	126

	Years ended December 31,		
	1992	1991	1990
Income before income taxes and cumulative effect of change in accounting principle	146,837	43,840	74,753
Provision for income taxes (Note 12)	55,816	16,921	27,670
Income before cumulative effect of change in accounting principle	91,021	26,919	47,083
Cumulative effect of change in accounting principle (Note 2)	12,538	—	—
Net income	$103,559	$26,919	$..47,083
Per share amounts (Notes 2, 8 and 13); Income before cumulative effect of change in accounting principle	$ .97	$ .31	$ .55
Cumulative effect of change in accounting principle			
Net income	$ 1.10	$ .31	$ .55
Pro forma amounts showing the new method is applied retroactively:			
Net income	$ 91,021	$27,109	$ 47,538
Net income per share	$ .97	$ .32	$ .56

See accompanying notes.

NOTE: **Accounting Changes**—*Change in Accounting Principle.* Prior to January 1, 1992, the Company expensed scheduled airframe overhaul costs as incurred. This practice was adopted at a time when costs were relatively constant from year to year and consistent with the growth of the fleet.

Given the significant growth of the Company's fleet over the past 10 years and the Company's recent modification of its airframe overhaul maintenance program with the Federal Aviation Administration (FAA), Southwest changed its method of accounting for scheduled airframe overhaul costs from the direct expense method to that of capitalizing and amortizing the costs over the periods benefited, currently estimated to be 10 years. At December 31, 1992, amounts capitalized, including the net book value of the aircraft, were below the fair market value of the related aircraft. The Company believes this method is preferable because it results in charges to expense that are consistent with the growth in the fleet; improves financial reporting; and better matches revenues and expenses.

For the years ended December 31, 1991 and 1990, the Company incurred and expensed approximately $3.7 million and $4.2 million, respectively, in scheduled airframe overhaul costs using the direct expense method. Had the Company capitalized and amortized airframe overhaul costs over the periods benefited, the expense recognized would have been approximately $3.4 million in each of years 1991 and 1990. The Company recognized approximately $6.9

million during the year ended December 31, 1992 in amortization of airframe overhaul expense. Had the direct expense method been used to provide for scheduled airframe overhaul costs during the year ended December 31, 1992, income before cumulative effect of accounting change would have been reduced by approximately $9.8 million (net of provision for income taxes and profit sharing of approximately $8.8 million), or approximately $.10 per share.

This change in accounting principle had the effect of a one-time adjustment increasing net income for the year ended December 31, 1992 by approximately $12.5 million (net of provision for income taxes and profit sharing of approximately $11.5 million).

Change in Accounting Estimate. Effective January 1, 1992, the Company revised the estimated useful lives of its 737-200 aircraft from 15 years to 15-19 years. This change was the result of the Company's assessment of the remaining useful lives of its 737-200 aircraft following the recent promulgations of rules by the FAA for the phase out of stage 2 aircraft by December 31, 1999. The effect of this change was to reduce depreciation expense approximately $3,680,000, or $.02 per share, for the year ended December 31, 1992.

15

EARNINGS PER SHARE

Most investors do not buy entire companies, only a number of shares of stock, and are concerned with per share data, not just total earnings. Earnings per share (EPS), sometimes referred to as *net income per share of outstanding stock*, is a separate item appearing at the bottom of the income statement. The ratio measures the income assumed earned by each holder of one share of common stock. EPS is a measure of income divided by an average number of common shares assumed to be outstanding. Normally, companies show income statements for two or more periods, and readers can assess the change in EPS from period to period. In addition, most companies present five- or ten-year summary statistics that include EPS. Exhibit 15-1 shows such information for the current and preceding four years for The Money Store Incorporated and Subsidiaries.

EXHIBIT 15-1 INCOME STATEMENT: EPS INFORMATION—THE MONEY STORE INCORPORATED AND SUBSIDIARIES

Years ended December 31,

Dollars in thousands, except per share data	1992	1991	1990	1989	1988
Volume of loans originated and purchased	$1,007,465	$944,339	$914,026	$835,562	$735,505
Total revenues	157,306	140,254	121,824	109,724	81,688
Net income[1]	15,226	11,352	8,076	15,079	10,091
Net income per share	$1.90	$1.84	$1.40	$2.55	$1.70
Cash dividends per share	$0.05		$0.05		
Weighted average number of common shares outstanding	8,030,000	6,155,479	5,780,230	5,920,344	5,920,344

As of December 31,

Dollars in thousands, except per share data	1992	1991	1990	1989	1988
Total assets[2]	$611,541	$607,877	$567,689	$485,329	$382,649
Subordinated debt	53,000	57,000	55,000	55,000	
Shareholders' equity	126,155	111,331	63,690	61,878	44,314
Book value per share	15.71	13.86	11.58	9.76	7.49
Serviced loan portfolio	2,963,930	2,703,143	2,321,004	1,924,376	1,540,678

[1]For the year ended December 31, 1990 and subsequent periods, gains on sales of receivables are recognized in accordance with EITF 88-11. If the provisions of EITF 88-11 had been applied in 1988 and 1989, the effect would have been a reduction in net income of $2.7 million and $5.3 million in those years, respectively.

[2]Certain amounts relating to 1991 and prior have been reclassified to conform to 1992 presentation.

Earnings per share is the most widely used financial ratio, and is frequently cited in the financial press. Readers of financial statements depend heavily on EPS to assess the performance of companies. Because of the importance attached to EPS, the accounting profession requires that this information be computed and reported in the financial statements of all companies. Accounting Principles Board Opinion No. 15 is the official pronouncement relating to the computation of EPS. The calculation can be very involved and complex. For example, Opinion No. 15 is 35 pages long and contains de-tailed instructions for computing EPS. Because of its complexity, a separate official interpretation of Opinion No. 15 (more than 100 pages long) was issued by the Board to assist accountants in understanding the original pronouncement.

Our discussion does not propose to explain the detailed computations, but to focus on the basic calculation of EPS and the purpose of the ratio. Nonetheless, some technical discussion of Opinion No. 15 is necessary for an appropriate understanding of the EPS figure.

Implications of Simple EPS

In essence, EPS is computed by dividing the earnings of the company by the number of shares of stock outstanding. EPS is the income per share available to the common stockholders and, in its simplest form, is net income divided by the number of shares of common stock outstanding:

$$\text{EPS} = \frac{\text{Net Income Available to Common Stockholders}}{\text{Number of Shares of Common Stock Outstanding}}$$

This formula is valid, however, only for a company with a capital structure that contains only common stock and whose number of shares of stock outstanding during the period remains unchanged. In observing EPS over several years, a reader attempts to determine whether there is a pattern of growth. By using a measure of income per ownership share (as opposed to just focusing on total income), a reader can evaluate a company's success in increasing income for individual stockholders. For example, suppose a company sells 50,000 additional shares of common stock during the year to expand operations to meet increased demand for its product. The company had 200,000 shares of stock outstanding prior to issuing the additional shares. Your normal inclination might be to see an increase in total earnings from the use of the proceeds of the additional investment by the stockholders. Suppose you are right, and as a direct result of this additional investment the company's earnings increased from $400,000 to $460,000. At first glance, the 15% increase in total earnings looks great; however, if you look at the EPS before and after the additional investment, you see that EPS has actually decreased.

$$\text{EPS prior to additional investment} = \frac{\$400,000}{200,000 \text{ shares}} = \$2.00$$

$$\text{EPS after additional investment} = \frac{\$460,000}{250,000 \text{ shares}} = \$1.84$$

The point is that focusing simply on the change in total earnings can be misleading. Monitoring total earnings is important, but a reader should also focus on any change in earnings per share.

EPS Complications

How does the presence of preferred stockholders affect the computation of EPS? In this situation, a portion of the company's net income must be paid as dividends to the preferred stockholders. For EPS purposes, one treats the dividend payments on preferred stock in a manner similar to interest on debt. That is, they are subtracted from net income to arrive at income available to common stockholders. An additional problem occurs if the company issues or reacquires shares of common stock during the period. In this case there is no single number of shares outstanding, and the weighted-average number of shares outstanding must be calculated and used as the denominator. The equation then becomes

$$\text{EPS} = \frac{\text{Net Income} - \text{Preferred Dividends}}{\substack{\text{Weighted-Average Number} \\ \text{of Common Shares Outstanding}}}$$

We illustrate the calculation of EPS when preferred stock is present and there are changes in the number of common shares outstanding during the period, by assuming the following information for the Starnes Corporation.

1. Assume that Starnes Corporation has net income of $163,000.

2. The company paid preferred stock dividends of $20,000 during 19X0.

3. On January 1, 19X0, the company had 10,000 shares of common stock outstanding and also issued an additional 15,000 shares on September 1, 19X0.

4. The company's year-end is December 31.

5. Income available to the common stockholders is $143,000 ($163,000 less dividends of $20,000).

The weighted-average number of common shares outstanding is computed as follows.

Shares Outstanding   **Weighted Average**

10,000 for 12 months	$10,000 \times \dfrac{12 \text{ months}}{12 \text{ months}} =$	10,000
15,000 issued on September 1	$15,000 \times \dfrac{4 \text{ months}}{12 \text{ months}} =$	5,000
Weighted-average number of common shares outstanding		15,000

$$\text{EPS} = \frac{\text{Net Income} - \text{Preferred Dividends}}{\substack{\text{Weighted-Average Number} \\ \text{of Common Shares Outstanding}}}$$

$$\text{EPS} = \frac{\$143,000}{15,000 \text{ shares}}$$

$$\text{EPS} = \$9.53$$

Note that the number of shares *outstanding* at year end is 25,000. To use the number of shares outstanding at year end would significantly reduce EPS to $5.72 ($143,000/25,000). You can see that since the 15,000 shares were outstanding for only four months of the year, each share is equivalent to one-third of one share. Weighting is used because if a share is outstanding for only a portion of the year, then the proceeds received from the sale of that share can be used only for a part of the year to generate earnings.

Dilutive Effect

Thus far, our example assumes a simple capital structure, meaning that the company does not have debt or equity securities that have the potential to dilute or reduce EPS. Sometimes companies issue bonds or preferred stock that are convertible into common stock. This makes the bonds or preferred stock more attractive to investors. *Convertible bonds* and *convertible preferred stock* are examples of items that have a potentially dilutive effect on EPS. Convertible bonds and convertible preferred stock are potentially dilutive if conversion of the bonds or preferred stock into common stock will (1) increase the denominator by increasing the number of common shares outstanding and (2) increase the numerator by eliminating payments of interest or preferred stock dividends. Convertible bonds and preferred stock *are* dilutive when conversion of the bonds or preferred stock into common stock will result in a decrease in earnings per share. Investors are very much interested in the reduction in EPS that might be caused by potentially dilutive securities. Such securities change a simple capital structure to a complex capital structure.

Stock options and warrants can also have a dilutive effect on EPS. Stock options and warrants can increase the denominator, because they give the holder the right to purchase shares at a designated price. When this happens, the company must issue additional shares of common stock. Stock options and warrants increase the number of shares outstanding but do not affect the numerator of the EPS formula.

Financial statements normally present two measures of EPS. The first, called *primary earnings per share*, includes the effects of any potentially dilutive securities that are *reasonably expected* to be converted into common stock. These potentially dilutive securities are called *common stock equivalents*. These securities are essentially shares of common stock, because we assume they will be converted. The second measure of EPS, *fully diluted earnings per share*, is a hypothetical figure that shows the effect of converting *all* potentially dilutive securities. Fully diluted earnings per share is usually less than primary earnings per share. It assumes a worst-case scenario, that assumes all potentially dilutive securities will be converted. Complete details of these calculations and the effect on EPS are beyond the scope of this book. To illustrate the principles involved, we provide a basic example of the effect of dilutive securities on the calculation of EPS.

Assume the following for Wenger Company:

1. The company has earnings of $480,000.

2. Wenger Company has 40,000 weighted-average shares of common stock outstanding.

3. Wenger also has 10,000 shares of preferred stock that can be converted for an equal number of common shares. The preferred stock pays a $4 dividend per share (or $40,000 in total). The preferred stock is a common stock equivalent, because it is reasonably expected that the preferred stock will be converted.

4. The company has bonds outstanding that can be converted into 6,000 shares of common stock. The bonds are not common stock equivalents, because market conditions do not make it likely that the bonds will be converted.

If the preferred stock were not convertible, EPS would be as follows.

$$\text{EPS} = \frac{\text{Net Income} - \text{Preferred Dividends}}{\substack{\text{Weighted-Average Number} \\ \text{of Common Shares Outstanding}}}$$

$$= \frac{(\$480,000 - \$40,000)}{40,000 \text{ shares}}$$

$$= \quad \$11.00$$

If the preferred stock is assumed to be converted, the preferred stock dividends will be removed from the numerator and 10,000 shares of common stock will be added to the denominator. That is the effect of converting the preferred stock to common stock.

$$\text{Primary EPS} = \frac{\$480,000}{(40,000 + 10,000) \text{ shares}} = \$9.60$$

The preferred stock is dilutive because it lowers primary EPS from $11.00 to $9.60.

Wenger Company's bonds outstanding can be converted into 6,000 shares of common stock; however, they were not used in the calculation of primary earnings per share because they were not common stock equivalents. The bonds are potentially dilutive securities, but are not common stock equivalents because market conditions do not make it likely that the bonds will be converted. Interest of $4,000 per year would not be paid if the bonds were converted. To calculate fully diluted EPS, we add the $4,000 bond interest to net income, and the additional 6,000 shares of stock to the denominator. That would be the effect of converting the bonds to common stock.

$$\substack{\text{Fully} \\ \text{diluted EPS}} = \frac{\$480,000 + \$4,000}{(40,000 + 10,000 + 6,000) \text{ shares}} = \$8.64$$

The bonds are dilutive because conversion would lower EPS from $9.60 to $8.64.

Presentation of Earnings per Share

The consolidated statements of operations (income statements) for Advanced Micro Devices, Inc. are presented in Exhibit 15-2. Notice the presentation of the EPS information. Exhibit 15-3 displays the company's balance sheet and the note disclosure relating to EPS. The balance sheet shows that the number of shares outstanding at year-end are not the same as those used in the EPS calculations on the face of the income statements in Exhibit 15-2. This is because the number used in the EPS calculations is the weighted-average number of shares outstanding during the year.

EXHIBIT 15-2   INCOME STATEMENT: EARNINGS PER SHARE—ADVANCED MICRO DEVICES, INC.

Three years ended December 26, 1993, in thousands except per share amounts	1993	1992	1991
Net Sales	$1,648,280	$1,514,489	$1,226,649
Expenses:			
Cost of sales	789,564	746,486	658,824
Research and development	262,802	227,860	213,765
Marketing, general and administrative	290,861	270,198	244,900
	$1,343,227	$1,244,544	$1,117,489
Operating income	305,053	269,945	109,160
Interest and other income	16,490	18,913	57,007
Interest expense	(3,791)	(17,227)	(20,880)
Income before taxes on income	317,752	271,631	145,287
Provision for taxes on income	88,971	.26,620	—

Three years ended December 26, 1993, in thousands except per share amounts	**1993**	1992	1991
Net Income	228,781	245,011	145,287
Preferred stock dividends	10,350	10,350	10,350
Net Income Applicable to Common Shareholders	$ 218,431	$ 234,661	$ 134,937
Net Income Per Common Share			
Primary	$ 2.30	$ 2.57	$ 1.53
Fully diluted	$ 2.24	$ 2.49	$ 1.52
Shares used in per share calculation			
Primary	95,108	91,383	88,196
Fully diluted	102,063	98,475	95,540

See accompanying notes.

EXHIBIT 15-3   BALANCE SHEET: EARNINGS PER SHARE—ADVANCED MICRO DEVICES, INC.

December 26, 1993, and December 27, 1992, *in thousands except share and per share amounts*	1993	1992
Assets		
Current Assets:		
Cash and cash equivalents	$ 60,423	$ 52,027
Temporary cash investments	427,775	279,061
Restricted cash	—	32,695
Total cash, temporary cash investments and restricted cash	488,198	363,783
Accounts receivable, net of allowance for doubtful accounts of $7,492 in 1993, and $6,679 in 1992	263,617	202,072
Inventories:		
Raw materials	15,371	16,793
Work-in-process	56,504	43,572
Finished goods	32,175	25,683
Total inventories	104,050	86,048
Deferred income taxes	77,922	37,199
Prepaid expenses and other current assets	30,399	48,556
Total current assets	964,186	737,658
Property, Plant and Equipment:		
Land	26,272	22,192
Buildings and leasehold improvements	444,299	422,089
Equipment	1,335,251	1,162,558
Construction in progress	192,541	77,526
Total property, plant and equipment	1,998,363	1,684,365
Accumulated depreciation and amortization	(1,094,037)	(991,082)
Net property, plant and equipment	904,326	693,283
Other Assets		
	$ 1,929,231	$ 1,448,095

December 26, 1993, and December 27, 1992, *in thousands except share and per share amounts*	1993	1992
Liabilities and Shareholders' Equity		
Current Liabilities:		
Notes payable to banks	$ 30,994	$ 40,659
Accounts payable	127,151	61,680
Accrued compensation and benefits	81,860	76,922
Accrued liabilities	83,982	69,665
Income tax payable	34,991	8,122
Deferred income on shipments to distributors	74,436	56,717
Long-term debt and capital lease obligations due within one year	21,205	6,084
Litigation judgment liability	—	32,695
Total current liabilities	454,619	352,544
Deferred Income Taxes	42,837	29,135
Long-term Debt and Capital Lease Obligations due after One Year	79,504	19,676
Commitments and contingencies		
Shareholders' Equity:		
Capital stock:		
Serial preferred stock, par value $.10; 1,000,000 shares authorized; 345,000 shares issued and outstanding ($172,500 aggregate liquidation preference)	35	35
Common stock, par value $.01; 250,000,000 shares authorized; 92,443,911 shares issued and outstanding in 1993, and 88,225,587 in 1992	926	885
Capital in excess of par value	619,733	532,674
Retained earnings	731,577	513,146
Total shareholders' equity	1,352,271	1,046,740
	$ 1,929,231	$ 1,448,095

See accompanying notes.

NOTE: **Net Income per Common Share.**—Primary net income per common share is based upon weighted average common and dilutive common equivalent shares outstanding using the treasury stock method. Dilutive common equivalent shares include stock options and restricted stock. Fully diluted net income per common share is computed using the weighted average common and dilutive common equivalent shares outstanding, plus other dilutive shares outstanding which are not common equivalent shares. Other dilutive shares which are not common equivalent shares include convertible preferred stock.

If extraordinary items, accounting changes, or gains or losses from discontinued operations are included in net income for the period, separate EPS figures are presented for income from continuing operations, discontinued operations, extraordinary items, accounting changes, and net income. Exhibit 15-4 shows how Pennzoil Company presented its EPS figures for these items in its annual report.

EXHIBIT 15-4   INCOME STATEMENT: EARNINGS PER SHARE: EXPANDED PRESENTATION—PENNZOIL COMPANY

	Year Ended December 31		
	1992	1991	1990
	(Expressed in thousands except per share amounts)		
Revenues			
Net sales	**$2,222,673**	$2,158,320	$2,179,832
Investment and other income, net	**134,008**	156,519	186,829
	2,356,681	2,314,839	2,366,661
Costs and Expenses			
Cost of sales	**1,488,119**	1,447,148	1,465,042
Selling, general and administrative expenses	**356,137**	306,269	297,710
Depreciation, depletion and amortization	**222,545**	192,553	184,667
Exploration expenses	**13,821**	52,868	37,907
Taxes, other than income	**52,803**	52,467	47,882
Interest charges	**233,360**	253,943	244,194
Interest capitalized	**(8,731)**	(10,447)	(13,321)
Income (Loss) from Continuing Operations Before Income Tax and Equity in Proven Properties Inc.	**(1,373)**	20,038	102,580
Income tax (benefit)	**(18,783)**	(20,060)	7,923
Equity (loss) in net income of Proven Properties Inc.	**—**	—	(889)
Income from Continuing Operations	**17,410**	40,098	93,768
Discontinued Operations (Note 11)			
Income (loss) from operations, net of taxes	**10,208**	(82,118)	(12,964)
Gain on disposition	**1,455**	—	—
(Income) loss from operations previously offset against reserve for estimated loss on disposition	**—**	(3,706)	12,964
Reversal of remaining reserve for estimated loss on disposition	**—**	115,742	—
Income Before Extraordinary Item and Cumulative Effect of Change in Accounting Principle	**29,073**	70,016	93,768
Extraordinary item (Note 3)	**(16,612)**	—	—
Cumulative effect of change in accounting principle (Notes 2 and 6)	**115,703**	(48,974)	—
Net Income	**$ 128,164**	$ 21,042	$ 93,768

	Year Ended December 31					
	1992		1991		1990	
	(Expressed in thousands except per share amounts)					
Earnings (Loss) Per Share						
Continuing operations	$	**.43**	$	.99	$	2.37
Discontinued operations		**.29**		.74		—
Total before extraordinary item and cumulative effect of change in accounting principle		**.72**		1.73		2.37
Extraordinary item		**(.41)**		—		—
Cumulative effect of change in accounting principle		**2.85**		(1.21)		—
Total	$	**3.16**	$	52	$	2.37
Dividends Per Common Share	$	**3.00**	$	3.00	$	3.00

See Notes to Consolidated Financial Statements.

156   *Earnings per share*

16

THE INCOME STATEMENT, OWNERS' EQUITY, AND RETAINED EARNINGS

The basic accounting equation discussed in Chapter 1 is

$$\text{Assets} = \text{Liabilities} + \text{Owners' Equity}$$

All equity or property right claims to a company's assets are held by either creditors or owners. Owners' equity in a corporation is sometimes called stockholders' equity because the owners hold shares of stock representing their ownership interests. Stockholders' equity in a balance sheet shows amounts for both the investment of owners and the cumulative amount of company earnings not withdrawn by owners. Stockholders' equity is thus divided into two components: (1) invested or paid-in capital and (2) capital from retained earnings.

Paid-in capital is the amount of investment made by stockholders. Retained earnings is the cumulative total of profits not distributed to owners as dividends. Retained earnings is not cash. It is the amount of owners' property rights that result from allowing earnings to be reinvested in company assets rather than distributed to owners. When the company generates earnings, retained earnings is increased. When earnings are distributed to owners as dividends, retained earnings is decreased.

Limited Liability

We can better understand the division of stockholders' equity into invested and earned components if we understand the legal character of a corporation. A corporation is a legal creation that, somewhat like Dr. Frankenstein's monster, takes on a life of its own.

Because a corporation is a separate legal entity, it can own property, lend or borrow money, enter into contracts, and sue or be sued in its own name, separate from its owners. Because a corporation is liable for its own debts, stockholders are said to have only limited liability for the debts of the corporation, as contrasted to a proprietorship or partnership, in which owners are personally liable for debts of the business.

Stockholders are not personally liable for the debts incurred by the corporation, and their liability is limited to the amounts they invest in stock. If the business fails, creditors cannot take the personal assets of the owners.

This is a true benefit for investors. They are free to invest in ventures that might be risky, or about which they have incomplete knowledge. Limited liability enables large numbers of investors who do not know each other to invest and become co-owners of a business. These same investors might be reluctant to invest in a partnership because, as partners, they would each be individually liable for all debts of the business if it fails.

If a partnership of ten investors fails owing $1 million, creditors can sue any one of the owners for the entire $1 million. That owner must then recover from the other nine. Thus, when an investor joins a partnership, the investor's personal assets are at risk for any debts incurred by the partnership or by the other partners in the name of the partnership.

In contrast, if a corporation with ten stockholders fails owing $1 million, creditors can sue only the corporation; they cannot sue the individual owners. Thus, each stockholder has at risk only the amount invested in the stock of the company. The stockholder's personal assets are safe. The limited liability of stockholders allows corporations to raise large amounts of capital not available to partnerships.

Because owners are liable for only the amount invested in the company, it is important to creditors that owners not be able to remove their investments when the company gets in financial trouble. That's why stockholders' equity is divided into its two components. Creditors must be able to see clearly the amount of invested capital owners have placed at risk, separate from the earned capital that they can withdraw through dividends.

Statement of Retained Earnings

Invested capital (among other things) is important to creditors because it serves as a buffer in the event the company should fail. Earned capital is important to owners because it is the amount of earnings reinvested to make the company grow: the dividend distributions foregone in hopes of greater distributions in the future. Because retained earnings is so significant, many companies prepare a Statement of Retained Earnings that shows all the changes in the account during the period.

Increases and decreases that might occur in retained earnings include those listed in Exhibit 16-1. The Consolidated Statement of Income and Retained Earnings of Chesapeake Corporation is shown in Exhibit 16-2. The changes in retained earnings are shown at the bottom of the income statement and are quite simple, consisting of income and dividend declarations.

EXHIBIT 16-1   CHANGES IN RETAINED EARNINGS

Retained earnings can be increased by:
   Net income
   Prior period adjustment
   Sale of treasury stock at an increased price
   Release of an appropriation

Retained earnings can be decreased by:
   Net loss
   Declaration of dividend
   Prior period adjustment
   Sale of treasury stock at a decreased price
   An appropriation

**EXHIBIT 16-2 CONSOLIDATED STATEMENT OF INCOME
AND RETAINED EARNINGS—
CHESAPEAKE CORPORATION**

For the years ended December 31, *(In millions except per share data)*	1992	1991	1990
Income:			
Net sales	**$888.4**	$840.5	841.2
Costs and expenses:			
Cost of products sold	**663.0**	616.8	633.2
Depreciation and cost of timber harvested	**66.5**	62.1	55.8
Selling, general and administrative expenses	**$106.7**	103.1	93.3
Income from operations	**52.2**	58.5	58.9
Other income (expense), net	**1.7**	3.0	(.4)
Interest expense	**(31.4)**	(35.4)	(29.4)
Income before taxes and cumulative effect of accounting changes	**22.5**	26.1	29.1
Income taxes	**8.1**	10.7	12.4
Income before cumulative effect of accounting changes	**14.4**	15.4	16.7
Cumulative effect of accounting changes	**(9.7)**	—	—
Net income	**$ 4.7**	$ 15.4	$ 16.7
Per share:			
Earnings before cumulative effect of accounting changes	**$ .63**	$ .75	$ .81
Cumulative effect of accounting changes	**(.46)**	—	—
Earnings	**$ .17**	$ .75	$ .81
Retained earnings:			
Balance, beginning of year	**$260.3**	$259.7	$257.8
Net income	**4.7**	15.4	16.7
Cash dividends declared, $.72 per share each year	**(16.7)**	(14.8)	(14.8)
Balance, end of year	**$248.3**	$260.3	$259.7

The accompanying Notes to Consolidated Financial Statements are part of
the financial statements.

160 *The income statement, owners' equity, and retained earnings*

Dividends

Dividends are generally distributions of cash or other assets to owners. Dividends usually reduce total assets and the retained earnings component of owners' equity, but not directly. A dividend proceeds in two steps: (1) the dividend is declared and becomes a liability, reducing retained earnings and increasing liabilities; then (2) the dividend is paid, reducing total assets and reducing to zero the dividend payable liability.

Most dividends are paid in cash, but other types of property can be given, such as samples of units produced (a whiskey distiller did this!) or marketable securities from the company's portfolio. In either case, the effect on the accounts is the same. The illustrations show only the changes in the accounts.

Assets	= Liabilities	+ Owners' Equity	
		Common Stock	+ Retained Earnings
	+ Dividend Payable		− Dividend
	$100		($100)
− Cash, etc.	− Dividend Payable		
($100)	($100)		
($100)	−0−		($100)

However, not all dividends are distributions of assets. Sometimes, if cash or other assets are not available, companies will distribute stock dividends instead. When that happens, no assets are given up. The effect of the dividend is to change a portion of retained earnings from invested to earned capital. The net effect on the accounts is to decrease retained earnings and increase common stock by the amount of the dividend.

Assets	= Liabilities	+ Owners' Equity	
		Common Stock	+ Retained Earnings
		+ Stock	− Dividend
		$100	($100)
−0−	−0−	$100	($100)

Appropriations of Retained Earnings

Companies often limit the payment of dividends for some reason: to comply with a debt covenant, to conserve cash for a contingency, to reduce cash outflows while completing a major construction project, or for other reasons. Companies can disclose the restriction of dividends to financial statement readers as a restriction or appropriation of retained earnings.

An appropriation restricts dividend payments but does not change total retained earnings. Retained earnings is simply separated into two components, the part appropriated and the part not appropriated.

For example, if a company has $5,000,000 in retained earnings and management wishes to restrict dividends while constructing a $3,000,000 plant, management may appropriate part of retained earnings. After the appropriation, retained earnings will appear in the statement of retained earnings and in the balance sheet as follows.

Retained Earnings

| Unappropriated | $2,000,000 | |
| Appropriated for Plant Construction | 3,000,000 | $5,000,000 |

An appropriation of retained earnings does not set aside cash. No cash is involved, no asset is affected. The appropriation is nothing more than an apportioning of retained earnings, a paper procedure. As the plant is constructed, cash is spent and a new asset is created. (The asset cash is, in essence, traded for a new asset, the plant.) When construction is complete and management no longer wishes to restrict dividends, the appropriation can be removed. But where does the appropriation go? The answer is, nowhere. When the appropriation is removed, unappropriated retained earnings is once again $5,000,000.

| Retained Earnings | $5,000,000 |

In practice, restrictions on retained earnings are more frequently disclosed in the notes to the financial statements than by a formal accounting entry appropriating retained earnings.

Treasury Stock

Treasury stock is the company's own stock that it purchased in the market and that it intends to reissue. When a company holds treasury stock, some states limit dividend payments to the amount of retained earnings available for dividends less the balance in the treasury stock account. This restriction can be shown either by an appropriation of retained earnings or in a note to the financial statements.

A company purchases its own stock to satisfy employee stock option plans, to exchange for convertible securities, or for other reasons—but not for speculation. (Speculation by a company in its own stock is a *serious* violation of the rules of the Securities and Exchange Commission.) For this reason, accountants do not show the results of treasury stock transactions as gains or losses in the income statement, but as increases or decreases in owners' equity in the statement of changes in owners' equity or in the statement of changes in retained earnings.

If a company buys 100 shares of its own stock for $90 per share and later reissues the stock for $85 per share, retained earnings are decreased for the $500 (100 shares $\times$ $5 "loss" per share) capital reduction. Exhibit 16-3 shows how treasury stock appears in the American Greetings Corporation balance sheet. American Greetings' invested capital (the common shares Class A and Class B) is reduced by treasury shares the company has repurchased.

Liabilities and Shareholders' Equity	1994	1993
Current Liabilities		
Debt due within one year	$ 132,036	$ 113,986
Accounts payable	127,792	113,684
Payrolls and payroll taxes	53,164	54,099
Retirement plans	20,766	17,409
Dividends payable	9,300	7,837
Income taxes	32,857	23,191
Total current liabilities	375,915	330,206
Long-Term Debt	54,207	169,381
Postretirement Benefit Obligation	19,427	—
Deferred Income Taxes	62,243	96,278

Liabilities and Shareholders' Equity	1994	1993
Shareholders' Equity		
Common shares—par value $1:		
Class A—69,590,011 shares issued		
less 43,886 Treasury shares in 1994		
and 68,714,572 shares issued less 66,472		
Treasury shares in 1993	69,546	34,324
Class B–6,066,096 shares issued		
less 1,493,152 Treasury shares in 1994		
and 6,064,522 shares issued less		
1,810,742 Treasury shares in 1993	4,573	2,127
Capital in excess of par value	249,192	259,093
Treasury stock	(28,240)	(28,152)
Cumulative translation adjustment	(16,421)	(11,580)
Retained earnings	774,792	696,723
Total shareholders' equity	1,053,442	952,535
	$1,565,234	$1,548,400

See notes to consolidated financial statements.

Prior Period Adjustments

From time to time retained earnings must be adjusted for errors made in recording revenues, expenses, or other items in prior years. These corrections of retained earnings for errors are called prior period adjustments. If a prior period adjustment affects the income statement, it does not appear in the statement in the period it is discovered, but is taken directly to the retained earnings account and reported as an adjustment to the beginning balance of retained earnings in the current year.

Assume, for example, that management discovers a mathematical error that had resulted in a $20,000 understatement of depreciation expense two years earlier. The current year's depreciation expense is not affected, but depreciation expense for the prior period was $20,000 too low. Because expenses were low, net income was high and current retained earnings is high. A $20,000 prior period adjustment would be made to beginning retained earnings in the current statement of retained earnings.

Other Changes in Owners' Equity

Changes in owners' equity are explained by changes in its two components, invested capital and retained earnings, but it is also affected by a few items that are simply the result of changes in net assets (assets − liabilities) that don't fit easily into either category. We discuss two here: foreign currency adjustments and unrealized gains and losses on marketable debt and equity securities.

Foreign Currency Adjustment

Most large companies publish consolidated financial statements that contain the financial statements of the company and its subsidiaries, often located around the world. In the annual report, the financial statements of these different companies are combined as if they were all one company (which, in essence, they are). Before the financial statements of a foreign subsidiary can be combined with those of its stateside parent, the foreign currency financial statements must be translated into U.S. dollars.

Exchange rate fluctuations (changes in the values of the foreign and U.S. currencies) often create a difference between the translated values of a subsidiary's net assets and its stockholders' equity that requires an adjustment (a gain or loss) to make assets equal liabilities plus owners' equity. This adjustment is called a foreign-currency translation adjustment, and the cumulative amount necessary over the years is reported in the stockholders' equity section of the balance sheet.

The translation adjustment arises because some of a company's accounts are translated at current exchange rates and other accounts are translated at historical exchange rates. We can give a simple illustration of the foreign-currency translation adjustment by considering the cash flows of a hypothetical subsidiary in Wayoff Land.

The currency units in Wayoff are called "wayoffs," abbreviated as "Wfs." Our subsidiary begins the year with cash of 1,000 Wfs, collects 2,000 Wfs when the exchange rate is 10 Wfs per $1 U.S., and pays 2,000 Wfs when the exchange rate is 12 Wfs per $1 U.S. The exchange rate at the beginning of the year is 8, and at end of the year, 14 Wfs per $1 U.S. Our subsidiary's cash flows, converted to U.S. dollar equivalents, follows.

	Wfs	Rate	U.S. $
Beginning of year	1,000	8	8,000
Collection	+2,000	10	+20,000
Payment	−2,000	12	−24,000
End of year	1,000	14	14,000

But something is wrong. In U.S. dollars, the flows do not explain the growth in cash from $8,000 to $14,000. Reconciling the beginning balance and the flows to the ending balance requires a $10,000 "fudge" factor. That $10,000 fudge is the foreign-currency translation adjustment.

Beginning of year	$ 8,000
Collection	+20,000
Payment	−24,000
Subtotal	$ 4,000
Foreign-currency translation adjustment	$ 10,000
End of year	$ 14,000

Translation adjustments are accumulated and disclosed as a component of stockholders' equity, normally between invested capital and retained earnings. The adjustment is reported as a component of stockholders' equity, but not on the income statement, because (1) the adjustment can have a significant impact on consolidated net income because of large swings in exchange rates and (2) the adjustments are unrealized and thus do not represent changes in asset values (and, in fact, may reverse in later periods).

Exhibit 16-3 shows the cumulative foreign-currency translation adjustment in the owners' equity section of American Greetings' balance sheet.

Unrealized Gains and Losses on Marketable Debt and Equity Securities

When the market value of a company's investment in certain marketable debt or equity securities is different from their cost, the company has an unrealized gain or loss. The gain or loss is unrealized because the securities have not been sold, and in fact may never be realized if the movement in the securities' market value reverses. Some unrealized gains and losses are recognized in the income statement, others are recognized in owners' equity.

17

THE INCOME STATEMENT AND THE STATEMENT OF CASH FLOWS

Profitable businesses often fail to generate enough cash to support operations. Because of this, creditors, investors, and financial analysts always want information on cash flows. Although accrual accounting is better for measuring earnings as an increase in owners' property rights, there may be only a vague relationship between earnings and cash flows. For this reason, generally accepted accounting principles (GAAP) require companies to include a statement of cash flows in published financial statements.

Financial statement readers use the statement of cash flows to study a company's liquidity and solvency. *Liquidity* is a measure of a company's ability to pay its short-term debts. If a company cannot pay its short-term debts, it is not liquid. A company's short-term operating cash receipts and payments help financial statement readers to assess a company's liquidity.

Solvency is a measure of a company's ability to pay all its debts, long and short term. A company's cash flows and capital structure (proportion of debt to equity) help financial statement readers to assess a company's solvency.

Quality of earnings is a measure of a company's ability to generate cash in the earnings process. High-quality earnings ultimately generate increases in cash and cash equivalents that can be distributed to creditors and owners. Quality of earnings is discussed in Chapter 23.

Studying the statement of cash flows helps financial statement readers to estimate the value of the company and, from its value, the value of its stock. Although earnings are important, many financial statement readers feel that the present value of a company is determined by the present value of its future cash flows, rather than by its prospective accounting earnings. Estimates of future cash flows are based on the company's present and past cash flows.

Sources and Uses of Cash

The statement of cash flows shows the change in cash and cash equivalents each period. *Cash* is all amounts available for withdrawal at any time without penalty or advance notice. *Cash equivalents* are liquid short-term investments. Treasury notes, commercial paper, and money market funds can be cash equivalents. The statement of cash flows categorizes all cash flows as relating to operating activities, to investing activities, or to financing activities. Operating activities are the company's primary business activities. Investing activities are those relating to changes in a company's noncurrent assets, and financing activities relate to how it gets its long-term capital. Exhibit 17-1 shows the general format of a statement of cash flows.

EXHIBIT 17-1   FORMAT—STATEMENT OF CASH FLOWS
COMPANY NAME STATEMENT OF CASH FLOWS
for the year ended December 31, 19XX

Cash provided by (or used in):	
Operating Activities	$ 50,000
Investing Activities	40,000
Financing Activities	(10,000)
Increase (or decrease) in cash or cash equivalents	$ 80,000
Cash and cash equivalents, beginning of year	25,000
Cash and cash equivalents, end of year	$105,000

The income statement shows the results of operations for a year in flows of revenues and expenses. Revenue and expense flows related to investing and financing activities are also included. Because of this, you might expect the income statement and the statement of cash flows to be very similar, but that is not the case.

For example, the income statement may contain an "interest expense" that resulted from financing activities, which may (or may not) be the same general amount as "cash paid as interest" in the statement of cash flow, because a company may have paid more or less than the interest due. But the biggest impact caused by debt is borrowing and repaying the principal amount. This cash flow does not affect the income statement, as it is neither a revenue nor an expense. When financing is obtained by issuing stock, neither the receipt of cash when stock is issued nor the payment of cash as dividends affects the income statement. Financial statement readers must also review a statement of cash flows if they are to understand a company's changes in financial position during a year. (How to treat interest, dividends, and other items in the statement of cash flows is illustrated in the next section of this chapter.)

Exhibit 17-2 shows the cash sources (inflows) and uses (out-flows) that a company might have in addition to its operating activities. None of these cash flows are shown on the income statement.

EXHIBIT 17-2   CASH FLOWS THAT DO NOT IMPACT THE INCOME STATEMENT

Sources of Cash	Uses of Cash
Issue Stock	Reacquire Stock
Borrow and Incur Noncurrent Debt	Repay Noncurrent Debt
Sell Noncurrent Assets	Buy Noncurrent Assets
	Pay Dividends

Operating Activities

All cash flows that are not the result of investing or financing activities are operating cash flows. Operating activities relate to the manufacturing and sale of goods or the rendering of services. The cash flows from operating activities are the cash effects of the transactions used to compute net income. Because operating activities include all income statement items except gains and losses, accountants use the phrase "associated with net income" to describe the kinds of activities that should be classified as operating activities in the statement of cash flow.

The financing cost "interest expense" is in the income statement, and thus "associated with" the income statement and included in operating cash flows. Items of investing income received, such as dividends, are revenues used to determine net income, and thus are included in operating cash flows. By the same logic, income taxes paid are operating cash flows.

Exhibit 17–3 shows the cash-from-operations portion of the Lubrizol Corporation statement of cash flows. The flows are related to collections from customers, payments to suppliers, and other items having to do with Lubrizol's operating activities. All are associated with the determination of net income.

EXHIBIT 17-3   CASH FROM OPERATIONS— LUBRIZOL CORPORATION

	Year Ended December 31		
(In Thousands of Dollars)	**1992**	1991	1990
Cash provided from (used for):			
Operating activities:			
Received from customers	**$1,549,848**	$1,480,776	$1,395,667
Paid to suppliers and employees	**(1,361,971)**	(1,265,058)	(1,206,060)
Income taxes paid	**(62,576)**	(55,116)	(87,713)
Interest and dividends received	**12,071**	9,960	10,181
Interest paid	**(5,245)**	(7,129)	(6,058)
Tax refund received, including interest		20,418	
Other-net	**3,036**	8,266	8,302
Total operating activities	**$ 135,163**	$ 192,117	$ 114,319

Investing and Financing Activities

Companies have cash outflows when investments are acquired, and cash inflows when investments are liquidated. Cash flows for short-term investments, such as a three-month Treasury bill, are "associated with" current income because the interest earned is included in earnings. Thus short-term investments are operating cash flows.

Cash flows for making and liquidating noncurrent investments, such as purchasing a new plant, are not associated with current earnings and, thus, are investing activities, not operating activities.

Income (as interest or dividends) from an investment, long or short term, is an income statement item and always an operating cash flow.

The general investing sources of cash are:

Selling long-term assets (such as a building)

Selling or collecting noncurrent loans (such as a mortgage receivable)

Selling a noncurrent investment (such as stocks or bonds)

The general investing uses of cash are:

Purchasing long-term assets (such as a building)

Making noncurrent loans (such as a mortgage receivable)

Long-term investing (such as in stocks or bonds)

With one exception, financing activities are cash transactions between a company and its stockholders and long-term creditors. Acquiring and repaying long-term debt and equity capital are financing activities. The general financing sources of cash are:

Issuing stock
Long-term borrowing

The general financing uses of cash are:

Reacquiring the company's own stock issued earlier
Repaying loans
Paying cash dividends

The cost of long-term capital is paid as either interest (to creditors) or dividends (to stockholders). Interest is an income statement item, and thus an operating cash flow, but dividends are distributions of income to owners, not an operating cost of doing business. Therefore, dividends are not income statement items, but are financing outflows. Exhibit 17-4 shows the cash flow statement of West One Bancorp. The statement includes its financing activities, both those involving cash flows as discussed here, and those not involving cash, discussed in the following section of this chapter.

EXHIBIT 17-4   FINANCING CASH FLOWS—WEST ONE BANCORP

Dollars in thousands for the year ended December 31,	1993	1992	1991
Cash flows from operating activities			
Net income	$ 83,187	$ 63,372	$ 41,199
Adjustments to reconcile net income to net cash provided by operating activities:			
Equity in undistributed earnings of subsidiaries	(51,475)	(36,404)	(19,400)
Depreciation and amortization	10,296	7,623	6,064
Changes in other assets and liabilities	(7,094)	(107)	(297)
Net cash provided by operating activities	34,914	34,484	27,566
Cash flows from investing activities			
Change in other short-term investments, maturities less than 90 days	(15,878)	9,567	(4,848)
Purchase of securities held to maturity	(3,416)	(54,643)	(20,147)
Maturity of securities held to maturity	6,139	51,053	2,744
Sale of securities	—	17,894	—
Change in loans to subsidiaries	(23,950)	(9,279)	(20,861)
Change in loans to nonaffiliates	320	4,582	252
Other	(3,432)	(3,429)	(2,800)
Capitalization of subsidiaries	(6,685)	(114,211)	(11,157)
Net cash used by investing activities	(46,902)	(98,466)	(56,817)

Dollars in thousands for the year ended December 31,	1993	1992	1991
Cash flows from financing activities			
Change in short-term borrowings, maturities less than 90 days	(1,416)	14,259	(347)
Proceeds from short-term borrowings	13,200	—	—
Payments on short-term borrowings	(7,000)	—	—
Additions to long-term debt	—	—	50,000
Payments on long-term debt	(27,566)	(4,189)	(12,362)
Proceeds from issuance of common stock	54,526	67,922	5,664
Cash dividends paid	(19,392)	(15,130)	(12,783)
Net cash provided by financing activities	12,352	62,862	30,172
Net increase (decrease) in cash and due from banks	364	(1,120)	921
Cash and due from banks—January 1	66	1,186	265
Cash and due from banks—December 31	$ 430	$ 66	$ 1,186
Supplemental information			
Interest paid	$ 8,737	$ 9,936	$...8,044
Income taxes paid	36,260	19,325	11,253
Noncash activities			
Additions to investment in subsidiaries	3,041	11,512—	
Capital lease for computer equipment	—	10,857	—
Termination of capital lease for computer equipment	—	6,460	—
Tax benefit of stock options exercised	596	812	832
Dividends declared not paid	6,249	9,220	3,367

Investing and Financing Without Cash

Investing and financing activities do not always involve a cash payment or receipt. A company can issue a mortgage note for $10,000,000 instead of paying cash for a new building. By itself, issuing debt for cash is a financing activity. Purchasing a long-term asset for cash is an investing activity. Both activities appear in the statement of cash flows.

However, when debt is exchanged for a building, there is no cash flow and, by definition, this activity is not included in the statement of cash flows. To avoid misleading financial statement readers, generally accepted accounting principles require companies to show noncash investing and financing activities in either a supplementary schedule to the statement of cash flows or in the financial statement notes.

Noncash investing and financing activities include the following (all asset, debt, and equity items listed are noncurrent).

Issuing stock in exchange for debt

Issuing debt in exchange for stock

Trading assets for other assets

Issuing debt to retire other debt

Issuing one class of stock to retire another

Exchanging stock or debt for assets other than cash

Exchanging assets for debt or stock

Exhibit 17-4 shows the disclosure of noncash investing and financing activities in the financial statements of West One Bancorp. Exhibit 17-5 shows the same disclosure in the note to the statement of cash flows of Vulcan Materials Company.

NOTE: **Supplemental Cash Flow Information**—Supplemental information referable to the Consolidated Statements of Cash Flows is summarized below (amounts in thousands):

	1993	1992	1991
Cash payments:			
Interest (exclusive of amount			
capitalized)	$ 9,198	$10,073	$11,632
Income taxes	41,393	45,413	34,205
Noncash investing and financing activities:			
Amounts referable to business acquisitions:			
Other liabilities assumed	—	213	54
Debt issued in purchase of property, plant and equipment	—	191	40

Cash Flows from Operations

There are two ways to determine cash flow from operations, the *direct* and *indirect* methods. The direct method is essentially a cash basis income statement. The Financial Accounting Standards Board (FASB) encourages use of the direct method and, as a result, it is much more commonly seen than the indirect method.

Direct Method

Exhibit 17-6 shows the cash flow statement of AST Research, Inc. with cash from operations determined using the direct method. Note also the classification of flows as operating, investing, and financing.

EXHIBIT 17-6   CASH FROM OPERATIONS USING THE DIRECT METHOD—AST RESEARCH

In thousands	Fiscal Year		
	1992	1991	1990
Cash flows from operating activities:			
Cash received from customers	$906,319	$649,015	$527,030
Cash paid to suppliers and employees	(846,023)	(591,312)	(433,877)
Interest received	6,388	8,531	4,399
Interest paid, net of amounts capitalized	(2,610)	(3,651)	(6,545)
Income tax refund received	—	—	11,056
Income taxes paid	(29,405)	(18,022)	(10,361)
Other cash paid	(2,476)	(510)	(1,207)
Net cash provided by operating activities	32,193	44,051	90,495
Cash flows from investing activities:			
Short-term investments	(52,831)	—	—
Capital expenditures, net	(15,888)	(8,928)	(11,148)
Acquisition of other assets	(381)	(399)	(1,576)
Net cash used in investing activities	(69,100)	(9,327)	(12,724)
Cash flows from financing activities:			
Short-term borrowings	—	678	704
Net proceeds (repayments) of long-term debt	(28,430)	133	(5,119)
Proceeds from issuance of common stock	2,777	50,419	2,688
Repurchase and retirement of common stock	—	(27,658)	—
Net cash provided by (used in) financing activities	(25,653)	23,572	(1,727)
Effect of exchange rate changes on cash	(2,871)	2,757	(2,274)
Net increase (decrease) in cash and cash equivalents	(65,431)	61,053	73,770
Cash and cash equivalents at beginning of year	153,305	92,252	18,482
Cash and cash equivalents at end of year	$ 87,874	$153,305	$ 92,252

See accompanying notes.

In thousands	Fiscal Year		
	1992	1991	1990
Reconciliation of net income to net cash provided by operating activities:			
Net income	$ 68,504	$ 64,724	$ 35,067
Adjustments to reconcile net income to net cash provided by operating activities:			
Depreciation and amortization	11,793	11,279	11,313
Provision (benefit) for deferred income taxes	1,499	(365)	1,881
Increase in accounts receivable	(37,164)	(41,405)	(4,557)
Decrease (increase) in inventories	(54,367)	(54,680)	18,188
Decrease in income taxes receivable	—	—	10,621
Increase in other current assets	(4,985)	(2,538)	(843)
Increase in accounts payable and accrued liabilities	42,862	48,858	14,365
Increase (decrease) in income taxes payable	(7,757)	15,962	3,682
Increase in other current liabilities	9,850	2,430	1,334
Exchange loss (gain)	1,958	(214)	(556)
Net cash provided by operating activities	$ 32,193	$ 44,051	$ 90,495
Supplemental schedule of noncash investing and financing activities:			
Tax benefit of employee stock options	$ 9,042	$ 544	$ 879
Equipment leases capitalized	391	—	276
Purchase of property and equipment through use of restricted cash	—	—	10,778
Conversion of subordinated debentures to common stock, net of debt discount of $1,595	—	—	45,905

See accompanying notes.

EXHIBIT 17-6 *(continued)*

In thousands except per share amounts	Fiscal Year		
	1992	1991	1990
Net sales	$944,079	$688,477	$533,814
Cost of sales	650,819	440,130	360,439
Gross profit	293,260	248,347	173,375
Selling and marketing expenses	120,072	91,289	71,596
General and administrative expenses	45,201	36,328	28,911
Engineering and development expenses	30,461	26,647	18,441
Total operating expenses	195,734	154,264	118,948
Operating income	97,526	94,083	54,427
Interest income	7,009	8,199	4,804
Interest expense	(2,439)	(3,665)	(5,966)
Other expense, net	(1,812)	(241)	(1,694)
Income before provision for income taxes	100,284	98,376	51,571
Provision for income taxes	31,780	33,652	16,504
Net income	$ 68,504	$ 64,724	$ 35,067
Net income per share:			
Primary	$ 2.16	$ 2.13	$ 1.43
Fully diluted	*	*	$ 1.21
Weighted average common and common equivalent shares outstanding:			
Primary	31,758	30,413	24,530
Fully diluted	*	*	30,960

Fully diluted earnings per share were anti-dilutive or not materially different from primary earnings per share.

See accompanying notes.

The direct method determines operating cash receipts and payments by adjusting accrual-based revenue or expense accounts for changes in the related asset and liability accounts. For example, cash inflow from sales is determined by adjusting sales revenue in the income statement for changes in the related accounts receivable. Because the AST Research statement of cash flows contains a section that reconciles net income to net cash from operations, we can see how this works.

AST Research had sales revenue of $944,079,000. The reconciliation shows accounts receivable increased $37,164,000. AST Research therefore collected $37,164,000 less than the amount of sales.

Schedule of Cash from Sales

Sales revenue	$944,079,000
Less increase in Accounts Receivable	37,164,000
Cash collected from customers	$906,915,000

Cash received from customers is $906,319,000 in the statement of cash flows, or $596,000 less than our calculation. This difference is probably due to accounts receivable being net of an allowance for bad debts, which changes year to year.

Cash flows for operating costs are calculated using similar logic, but we do not have enough detailed information to make calculations from AST Research's statements. In general, an operating expense is more or less than the related cash payment because management may pay an invoice from last year in this year and an invoice for items received this year may not be paid until next year. For example, if insurance expense is $20,000, but Prepaid Insurance went up from $3,000 at the beginning of the year to $5,000 at year end, we know that management paid more than one year's insurance.

Management must have paid all the $20,000 required for insurance this year, plus prepaying an additional $2,000, or $22,000 total.

Insurance Expense	$20,000
Plus increase in Prepaid Insurance	2,000
Cash paid for insurance	$22,000

Indirect Method

The indirect method does not determine the operating cash flows for individual categories of revenues and expenses. Instead, net income is adjusted for changes in the related accounts. The statement of cash flows for Texas Industries, Inc. using the indirect method is shown in Exhibit 17-7. Cash provided by operations is calculated by the following.

1. Net income is increased for changes in the current asset and liability accounts that result in increases in cash from operations. For example, if accounts receivable decreased, the company must have collected cash for sales made last year in addition to collecting cash equal to this year's sales. A decrease in accounts receivable of $2,470,000 is added to Texas Industries' net income in calculating cash from operations in 1993.

2. Net income is decreased for changes that result in decreases in cash from operations. For example, if inventory increased, the company must have used cash to purchase additional inventory for next year in addition to using cash to purchase an amount of inventory equal to the cost of goods sold this year. To calculate cash from operations in 1992, Texas Industries subtracted a $12,719,000 increase in inventory from net income.

EXHIBIT 17-7 CASH FROM OPERATIONS USING THE INDIRECT METHOD—TEXAS INDUSTRIES

In thousands	Year Ended May 31,		
	1993	1992	1991
Operating Activities			
Net income	**$ 1,058**	$ 1,920	$ 22,086
Gain on disposal of assets	**(264)**	($13,805)	(44,141)
Non-cash items			
Depreciation, depletion and amortization	**49,799**	47,495	44,979
Deferred taxes	**(4,284)**	432	7,689
Undistributed minority interest	**(1,528)**	206	2,552
Other–net	**819**	880	4,704
Changes in operating assets and liabilities			
Notes and accounts receivable	**(2,125)**	(3,645)	8,120
Inventories and prepaid expenses	**2,431**	(12,719)	(3,403)
Accounts payable and accrued liabilities	**2,470**	4,575	(5,094)
Real estate and investments	**985**	878	(14)
Net cash provided by continuing operations	**49,361**	26,217	37,478
Net cash used by discontinued operations	**—**	—	(3,224)
Net cash provided by operations	**49,361**	26,217	34,254
Investing Activities			
Capital expenditures	**(17,212)**	(21,621)	(98,386)
Proceeds from disposition of assets	**497**	21,794	98,496
Purchase of temporary investments	**(4,660)**	(6,528)	—
Proceeds from temporary investments	**4,816**	—	—
Final payment for Chaparral acquisition	**—**	—	(49,968)
Cash surrender value–insurance	**5,554**	(1,840)	(1,440)
Commissioning costs and other–net	**(375)**	(8,412)	(2,948)
Net cash used by investing	**(11,380)**	(16,607)	(54,246)

In thousands	Year Ended May 31,		
	1993	1992	1991
Financing Activities			
Proceeds of long-term borrowing	**600**	20,337	58,226
Proceeds of short-term borrowing	**—**	—	10,000
Debt retirements	**(22,290)**	(35,351)	(63,888)
Dividends paid	**(2,228)**	(2,213)	(2,152)
Other–net	**(1,439)**	(1,451)	(1,326)
Net cash (used) provided by financing	**(25,357)**	(18,678)	860
Increase (decrease) in cash	**12,624**	(9,068)	(19,132)
Cash at beginning of year	**14,132**	23,200	42,332
Cash at end of year	**26,756**	14,132	23,200
Temporary investments	**6,333**	6,528	—
Cash and temporary investments at end of year	**$ 33,089**	$ 20,660	$23,200

See notes to consolidated financial statements.

Items Not Consuming Cash

The indirect method also adjusts net income for items that do not use or provide cash. Depreciation, amortization, and depletion are operating expenses that do not require cash outflows each year. Cash is used to purchase the asset but in later years the expense is only an allocation of the original cost to the period benefited. No additional cash is involved. Because depreciation and amortization expenses reduce earnings without consuming cash, they are added back to net income to determine cash from operations.

Texas Industries adds back depreciation, amortization, and depletion to net income in each year it calculates cash from operations.

Gains and Losses

Gains and losses are created by activities that are not normally operating activities, such as a $10,000 gain from selling scrapped equipment at the end of its useful life. In addition, the amount of the gain or loss in the income statement does not tell income statement readers anything about the cash flow involved. Did the company receive $100,000 cash for equipment with a book value of $90,000? Or did the company receive $20,000 for equipment with a book value of $10,000? Both cases produce a $10,000 gain.

Gains are subtracted and losses are added back to net income. In the sale of scrapped equipment, the cash flow (whatever it was) is an investing flow generated by selling a noncurrent asset. Texas Industries subtracted from net income a $264,000 gain on the disposal of assets and included a $497,000 investing cash inflow as "proceeds from disposition of assets."

18

MERGERS AND CONSOLIDATED INCOME STATEMENTS

A merger is any combining of two companies into one. When companies merge, they generally must publish consolidated financial statements. The purpose of consolidated financial statements is to present as one economic unit the financial position, cash flows, and earnings of the affiliated companies. Understanding consolidated statements is important because most income statements of large companies are combinations of the income statements of several affiliated companies.

Companies affiliate or combine for many reasons. Companies may combine to strengthen their business position, as defense against a takeover, for tax advantages, or for other reasons. A company may combine with another company within the same industry to strengthen its market position. Nations Bank, headquartered in North Carolina, has purchased banks in Texas, Virginia, South Carolina, Georgia, and Maryland. A company can combine with its suppliers or customers to gain the advantages of vertical integration. Clark Equipment Company, in one year, purchased a distributor/manufacturer in Italy and disposed of previously acquired finance affiliates in France and the Netherlands. Exhibit 18-1 shows the financial statement discussion by American Financial Corporation of its merger activities over six years.

EXHIBIT 18-1 MERGER ACTIVITIES— AMERICAN FINANCIAL CORPORATION

American Financial Corporation is a holding company operating through wholly-owned and majority-owned subsidiaries and other companies in which it holds significant minority ownership interests. These companies operate in a variety of financial businesses, including property and casualty insurance, annuities, and portfolio investing. In non-financial areas, these companies have substantial operations in the food products industry, television and radio station operations, filmed entertainment production and distribution, systems engineering and industrial manufacturing.

Generally, companies have been included in AFC's consolidated financial statements when AFC's ownership of voting securities has exceeded 50%; for investments below that level but above 20%, AFC has treated the investments as investees. The following shows AFC's percentage ownership of voting securities of the significant companies over the past several years:

Ownership at December 31,	1992	1991	1990	1989	1988	1987
Great American Insurance Group	100%	100%	100%	100%	100%	100%
Great American Life Insurance Company	—	100%	100%	100%	100%	100%
American Annuity Group	82%	39%	32%	32%	32%	26%
The Penn Central Corporation	51%	50%	42%	34%	31%	31%
Chiquita Brands International, Inc.	46%	48%	54%	82%	83%	87%
Spelling Entertainment Group Inc. (formerly The Charter Company)	48%	53%	53%	51%	51%	51%
Spelling Entertainment Inc.	—	85%	45%	45%	—	—
Great American Communications Company	40%	40%	65%	62%	60%	65%
General Cable Corporation	45%	—	—	—	—	—
Hunter Savings Association	—	—	100%	100%	100%	100%

A company can acquire another company by purchasing all its assets and assuming its liabilities, paying in cash or stock. In this case, the purchased company is left a hollow shell and ceases to exist. Its separate assets and liabilities are absorbed at their market values onto the purchasing company's balance sheet just as any purchased assets and related liabilities.

Alternatively, rather than buying the assets of another company, the purchasing company can buy control of the other company (and its assets) by purchasing its stock. When this happens, the purchaser does not record the separate assets and liabilities (it does not own them) but instead records its "Investment in Affiliate," the stock in the other company which it does own. The acquired company maintains its separate existence, its separate accounting records, and may publish separate financial statements. It is this type of acquisition that results in consolidated financial statements, the main topic of this chapter.

Pooling of Interests

Mergers normally occur when one company buys another, but companies can also combine through a pooling of interests, whereby stock of one company is exchanged for substantially all the voting common stock of another company, and the businesses are pooled as one entity. To create financial statements for pooled companies, the accounts of the companies are simply added together at book value. In the balance sheet, assets are added to assets, liabilities to liabilities, and owners' equity to owners' equity. Accounts are not restated to market value, as is the case in financial statements of combinations formed by a purchase.

Likewise, in a pooling of interests, income statements are added together. The effects of any business activity between the combined companies (such as sales, lending, or rentals) must be removed from revenues and expenses. The elimination of internal revenue-and-expense-generating activities is explained in the discussion of combinations resulting from one company purchasing another.

In the year companies undertake a pooling of interests, the income statements are combined for the whole year, regardless of when the pooling takes place. By contrast, in the year of a purchase acquisition, the income of the acquired company is combined with the purchasing company's income only from the date of the purchase forward. If the combination is not affected at the beginning of the year, this gives an advantage to pooling over purchase by recognizing higher earnings in the first year of the combination. Exhibit 18-2 shows the income statement and related acquisition footnote of Jostens, Inc. and Subsidiaries in the year it acquired Wicat Systems, Inc. Notice that the note dates the acquisition as August of 1992 (year end is June 30) and shows how net sales and earnings of the two companies for the preceding years are added together to obtain the reported net sales and earnings of the combined entity.

In thousands, except per share data	Years ended June 30,		
	1993	**1992**	**1991**
Net Sales	**$914,848**	$924,167	$908,844
Cost of products sold	**489,475**	486,200	477,621
	425,373	437,967	431,223
Selling and administrative expenses	**353,881**	331,251	318,308
Restructuring charges	**70,581**	—	—
Operating Income	**911**	106,716	112,915
Interest expense	**5,652**	8,449	10,043
	(4,741)	98,267	102,872
Income taxes	**3,206**	36,293	37,957
Income (Loss) Before Change In Accounting Principle	**(7,947)**	61,974	64,915
Cumulative effect of change in accounting principle, net of taxes	**(4,150)**	—	—
Net Income (Loss)	**$ (12,097)**	$ 61,974	$ 64,915
Earnings (Loss) Per Common Share			
Before change in accounting principle	**$ (0.18)**	$ 1.38	$ 1.46
Cumulative effect of change in accounting principle	**(0.09)**	—	—
Net Income (Loss)	**$ (0.27)**	$ 1.38	$ 1.46

NOTE: **Acquisitions**

In August 1992, the Company acquired Wicat Systems, Inc. (Wicat), a provider of technology-based learning systems for the education and aviation markets. The transaction was effected through the exchange of approximately 4.1 million common shares of the Company for all of the issued and outstanding shares of Wicat. The merger has been accounted for as a pooling of interests and accordingly, all financial data for periods prior to the merger have been restated to include the results of Wicat.

Net sales, net income and earnings per share for the two fiscal years preceding the merger were as follows:

	Net Sales	Net Income	Earnings Per Share
1992			
Jostens	$876,395	$61,413	
Wicat	47,772	561	$1.50
Combined	$924,167	$61,974	$1.38
1991			
Jostens	$859,878	$64,164	
Wicat	48,966	751	$1.58
Combined	$908,844	$64,915	$1.46

Another advantage of pooling, relative to purchasing, is that pooling keeps all assets at historical cost. Because of this, the assets of the combined companies have lower depreciation charges than if the combination were accomplished by a purchase and assets increased to their fair market values. In addition, if pooled assets are sold, the combined companies may recognize a gain that would not exist if the assets of a purchased company were adjusted to their fair market value.

Despite their advantages, pooled combinations are not as common as purchased combinations, because generally accepted accounting principles (GAAP) require that a combination meet very specific criteria to qualify as a pooling of interests. A pooling is viewed somewhat as a marriage: a mutual attraction culminating in the voluntary combining of two equals. A purchase is viewed as a big company growing desirous of an attractive smaller company and proceeding to take control. Most combinations are, in fact, takeovers, not marriages.

Because the advantages of pooling over purchase combinations all relate to higher reported net income, financial statement readers should be alert for overstated earnings when analyzing a combination formed by pooling.

Joint Venture

A joint venture is a temporary joining of two or more companies to undertake a project. Two companies may combine to construct a military weapons system, for instance. The companies would work together on the project but would not combine income statements.

Consolidation by Stock Purchase

Business combinations are most frequently accomplished by the purchase of one company's stock by another. A company buys all or part of another company's common stock. When this happens, the acquiring company can either negotiate with the management of the other company or make a public tender offer directly to the stockholders of the other company. A *tender offer* is an offer to buy common stock at a set price, usually in an attempt to take control of a company. If a company buys 5% of the common stock of another company in a takeover, the purchasing company must make a series of disclosures about its activities to the Securities and Exchange Commission (SEC), the target company, and affected stockholders.

Consolidated Financial Statements

When ABC Company acquires XYZ Company by buying all of XYZ's outstanding stock, ABC gives up the asset "Cash," and acquires the asset "Investment in XYZ Company." ABC's cash is reduced, and an account, Investment in XYZ Company, is increased by the same amount. There is no change in total assets, liabilities, or owners' equity, and no increase in revenues or expenses.

After a stock purchase acquisition, the acquired company (XYZ) continues as a separate legal entity, but controlled by ABC.

When a company invests in the stock of another company, a decision must be made on how the investment will be classified. The classification depends on the length of time management intends to hold the investment. If management intends to hold the investment one year or longer, the investment is classified "noncurrent." The investor company will vote its stock and participate in the management of the investee company.

Terminology

If an investor company owns more than 50% of the outstanding common stock of the investee, it has a controlling interest and is called the *parent*. The investee is called the *subsidiary*. When the parent owns 100% of the stock of the subsidiary, it is "wholly owned." The business interests of the parent and subsidiary are combined, and the financial statements of the two companies are *consolidated* and shown as if the two companies were one. The process of combining the financial statements of the two companies is called *consolidation*, and the resulting statements are called *consolidated financial statements*. The parent and its subsidiary are *affiliated* companies.

The parent and its subsidiary are each separate legal entities and separate *economic entities*, for which separate accounting records are kept and separate financial statements are issued. Each company in an affiliated group (parent or subsidiary) will often issue its own financial statements for regulatory agencies or for special purposes such as obtaining financing or credit from suppliers.

However, inasmuch as stockholders control the parent and, through the parent, control the subsidiary, these two economic entities have common control. Because of this common control, the combined companies are also an economic entity, and stockholders, creditors, and others must see financial statements for the combined entity in order to understand the relationship between the companies and its economic implications. Consolidated statements for a parent and its subsidiaries are required by the SEC.

This requirement reflects the concept of *substance over form*. The affiliated companies are legally separate companies, but, in substance, one economic entity. Virtually all large companies issue consolidated statements.

A Simple Consolidation

We now consider how consolidated statements are prepared using the parent, ABC Company, and its subsidiary, XYZ Company. Assume that the book value and fair value of XYZ's owners' equity are equal and that the balance sheet equation for XYZ is as follows.

$$\text{Assets} = \text{Liabilities} + \text{Owners' Equity}$$
$$\$100,000 = \$50,000 + \$50,000$$

Suppose ABC buys 100% of the stock of XYZ for the book value of its owners' equity or net assets. ABC will pay $50,000 (decreasing cash) and will record an investment (an asset) of $50,000.

But what has ABC actually purchased?

ABC now owns every asset that XYZ owns and owes every debt that XYZ owes. Because the fair market value and book value of the XYZ owners' equity (net assets) are both $50,000, ABC has purchased these property rights. If financial statements of ABC simply show only an investment of $50,000, the true nature of the relationship with XYZ is not disclosed. To disclose the economic substance of the purchase, ABC must show every asset owned and liability owed by XYZ.

Let the balance sheet of ABC before the purchase of XYZ stock be as follows.

$$\text{Assets} = \text{Liabilities} + \text{Owners' Equity}$$
$$\$800,000 = \$500,000 + \$300,000$$

Total assets for ABC are the same before and after the investment in XYZ. (Investment in XYZ is increased, but cash is decreased.)

To prepare consolidated financial statements, ABC must remove the $50,000 investment in XYZ and replace it with the individual assets and liabilities of XYZ. ABC's total owners' equity is the same before and after consolidation.

	Assets	=	Liabilities	+	Owners' Equity
ABC before consolidation	$800,000	=	$500,000	+	$300,000
Less: Investment in XYZ	(50,000)				
Plus: the assets and liabilities of XYZ	100,000		50,000		
ABC consolidated balance sheet	$850,000	=	$550,000	+	$300,000

Exhibit 18-3 shows in worksheet format how the account by account consolidation of ABC and XYZ is accomplished. The $50,000 investment is eliminated against the owners' equity accounts of the subsidiary to avoid double accounting: it is the net assets that ABC has bought.

EXHIBIT 18-3 SIMPLE CONSOLIDATION (PARENT OWNS 100% OF SUBSIDIARY STOCK, NO INTERCOMPANY BUSINESS ACTIVITY)

	ABC (Parent)	XYZ (Subsidiary)	Eliminations	Consolidated Statements
INCOME STATEMENT				
Sales	$100,000	$ 60,000		$ 160,000
Cost of Goods Sold	80,000	30,000		110,000
Gross Profit	20,000	30,000		50,000
Other Expenses	10,000	25,000		35,000
Net Income	$ 10,000	$ 5,000		$ 15,000
BALANCE SHEET				
Assets				
Cash	80,000	$ 10,000		$ 90,000
Inventory	70,000	20,000		90,000
Receivables	100,000	30,000		130,000
Property (net)	500,000	40,000		540,000
Investment in XYZ	$ 50,000	—	(50,000)	
Total Assets	$800,000	$100,000	(50,000)	$ 850,000
Liabilities				
Payables	$200,000	20,000		220,000
Mortgage	300,000	30,000		330,000
Total Liabilities	$500,000	50,000		550,000
Owners' Equity				
Common Stock	150,000	30,000	(30,000)	150,000
Retained Earnings	150,000	20,000	(20,000)	50,000
Total Owners' Equity	300,000	50,000	(50,000)	300,000
Total Equities	$800,000	$100,000	(50,000)	$ 850,000

Complex Consolidations

The simple consolidation shown in Exhibit 18-3 can be complicated in many ways. If, for instance, a parent owns more than 50% but less than 100% of a subsidiary, *minority shareholders* own the remainder. The *minority interest* must be shown in the consolidated income statement and balance sheet. In addition, the net assets of a company might be purchased at a cost greater than or less than book value, causing the carrying values of various assets or liabilities to be increased or decreased to their fair market values when consolidated financial statements are prepared. These "adjustments" to value are made only for the purpose of preparing consolidated financial statements on an accountants' worksheet. There is never any adjustment on the separately maintained books of the subsidiary.

Any excess of the price paid over the fair market value of the assets is called *goodwill*. Goodwill is an intangible asset and is amortized to expense in the income statement over a period not longer than 40 years.

Perhaps most important, the parent company might have business transactions with its subsidiary during the year. Because these transactions are not with entities outside the combined economic entity (the subsidiary is part of the parent), their effects must be eliminated in the consolidated income statement and balance sheet. If these transactions are not eliminated, the assets, liabilities, revenues, and expenses of the combined entity will all be overstated.

Minority Interest and Goodwill—The effects of (1) less than 100% ownership and (2) goodwill are illustrated here.

Parent/subsidiary business activity is illustrated in the next section of this chapter. As in our simple example, let the fair market value of XYZ's assets equal their book value. Suppose that ABC purchases, for $55,000, 90% of XYZ common stock (and, thus, 90% of XYZ's net assets). Ninety percent of XYZ's net assets is $45,000 ($50,000 × 90%). Thus the $55,000 purchase price is $10,000 more than the fair market value of 90% of the XYZ owners' equity. The 10% paid above the fair market value of the net assets is goodwill.

As with the simple case, when ABC prepares consolidated financial statements, it must replace the Investment in XYZ account with the individual assets and liabilities of XYZ. The investment is eliminated against ABC's owners' equity accounts.

But, because ABC owns only 90% of the XYZ owners' equity, the $55,000 investment is eliminated against only 90% of the XYZ owners' equity (common stock and retained earnings). When the investment is eliminated

1. $27,000 is eliminated from common stock ($30,000 × 90%) and

2. $18,000 is eliminated from retained earnings ($20,000 × 90% = $18,000).

3. The $10,000 excess of investment over the fair market value of the net assets of XYZ is shown on the consolidated balance sheet as goodwill.

When $27,000 of stock and $18,000 of retained earnings are eliminated, $3,000 in stock ($30,000 − $27,000) and $2,000 in retained earnings ($20,000 − $18,000) remain. This $5,000 ($3,000 + $2,000) is the equity interest of minority stockholders in the net assets of the subsidiary, and is called "Minority Interest."

In the consolidated income statement, (1) a portion of the goodwill must be expensed and (2) net income for the year must be divided between the minority (10%) and majority (90%) stockholders. The minority interests' share of income is called the "Minority Interest in Income." The amortization of goodwill reduces net income relative to the simple case in which there is no goodwill.

Exhibit 18-4 shows, account by account, how this more complex consolidation of ABC and XYZ is accomplished. Study the consolidated statements to see how each aspect of the consolidation occurred. Most important, be sure to notice how the income statement is affected by a complex consolidation.

EXHIBIT 18-4 COMPLEX CONSOLIDATION (PARENT OWNS 90% OF SUBSIDIARY STOCK, $10,000 GOODWILL FROM PURCHASE, NO INTERCOMPANY BUSINESS ACTIVITY)

	ABC (Parent)	XYZ (Subsidiary)	Eliminations	Consolidated Statements
INCOME STATEMENT				
Sales	$100,000	$ 60,000		$160,000
Cost of Goods Sold	80,000	30,000		110,000
Gross Profit	20,000	30,000		50,000
Goodwill Amortization Expense			500*	500
Other Expenses	10,000	25,000		35,000
Net Income	$ 10,000	$ 5,000		14,500
Minority interest Income				1,450
Majority Net Income				$ 13,050

	ABC (Parent)	XYZ (Subsidiary)	Eliminations	Consolidated Statements
BALANCE SHEET **Assets**				
Cash	$ 75,000	$ 10,000		$ 85,000
Inventory	70,000	20,000		90,000
Receivables	100,000	30,000		130,000
Property (net)	500,000	40,000		540,000
Investment in XYZ	$ 55,000	$	(55,000)	
Goodwill	$	$	10,000	9,500
			(500)*	
Total Assets	$800,000	$100,000	($45,500)	$854,500

Liabilities				
Payables	$200,000	20,000		220,000
Mortgage	300,000	30,000		330,000
Total Liabilities	$500,000	50,000		550,000
Owners' Equity				
Common Stock	150,000	30,000	(27,000)	150,000
			(3,000)	
Retained Earnings	150,000	20,000	(18,000)	149,550
			(2,000)	
			(450)*	
Minority Interest			5,000	4,950
			(50)*	
Total Owners' Equity	300,000	50,000	(45,500)	304,500
Total Equities	$800,000	100,000	(45,500)	$854,500

*Goodwill of $10,000 is amortized over 20 years at $500 per year. The $500 goodwill amortization reduces Goodwill in the balance sheet from $10,000 to $9,500 and reduces earnings by the same $500, shown here (1) in the income statement and (2) as a $450 reduction in consolidated Retained Earnings (90%) and a $50 reduction in Minority Interest (10%). (Operating earnings of the two companies, other than the effect of goodwill, is assumed already in the Retained Earnings of each.)

Intercompany Business Activity—Business between a parent and its subsidiaries is similar to a parent's paying a child to do household chores. Does the payment increase or decrease family income? Of course not. Family income rises or falls only when business is conducted with someone outside the family.

We illustrate by assuming again that ABC buys 100% of the stock of XYZ at its book value. (Again, let fair market value of the net assets equal their book value.) During the year, ABC buys merchandise from XYZ that ABC intends to resell to outside parties. The merchandise is bought by ABC for $30,000 and cost XYZ $20,000. At year end, ABC has not sold the inventory to another company outside the consolidated "family." XYZ records revenue of $30,000, cost of goods sold of $20,000, and profit on the sale of $10,000.

Have the earnings of the consolidated parent and subsidiary risen? Of course not. Consolidated earnings rise only when business is conducted with a company outside the consolidated family.

Exhibit 18-5 shows in worksheet format how the intercompany sale is eliminated in preparing the consolidated income statement. The following items are eliminated: revenues of $30,000, cost of goods sold of $20,000, and consolidated profit of $10,000.

EXHIBIT 18-5 CONSOLIDATION WITH INTERCOMPANY SALES (PARENT OWNS 100% OF SUBSIDIARY STOCK, NO GOODWILL)

	ABC (Parent)	XYZ (Subsidiary)	Eliminations	Consolidated Statements
Sales	$100,000	$60,000	($30,000)	$130,000
Cost of Goods Sold	80,000	30,000	(20,000)	90,000
Gross Profit	20,000	30,000	(10,000)	40,000
Other Expenses	10,000	25,000		35,000
Net Income	$ 10,000	$ 5,000	($10,000)	5,000

Exhibit 18-6 shows the consolidated income statement and related note of Whitman Corporation and Subsidiaries. The statement contains both minority interest and goodwill amortization (as Amortization Expense). Undoubtedly, preparation of the statement required eliminating the effects of intercompany business activities. Exhibit 18-7 contains the principles of consolidation from the notes to the financial statements of Murphy Oil Corporation.

EXHIBIT 18-6 CONSOLIDATED INCOME STATEMENT SHOWING GOODWILL AMORTIZATION AND MINORITY INTEREST—WHITMAN CORPORATION

For the years ended December 31 (in millions)	1993	1992	1991
Sales and revenues	$2,529.7	$2,388.0	$2,393.3
Cost of goods sold	1,625.0	1,545.6	1,555.4
Gross profit	904.7	842.4	837.9
Selling, general and administrative expenses	582.3	550.7	548.4
Amortization expense	17.1	17.3	17.7
Operating income	305.3	274.4	271.8
Interest expense	(96.2)	(97.7)	(128.6)
Interest income	12.8	9.0	14.4
Other income (expense), net	(9.7)	(15.1)	4.1
Income before income taxes	212.2	170.6	161.7
Income tax provision	90.7	68.5	70.3
Income from continuing operations before minority interest	121.5	102.1	91.4
Minority interest	15.1	10.0	11.0
Income from continuing operations	106.4	92.1	80.4
Income from discontinued operations after taxes (Note 2)	—	—	17.2

For the years ended December 31 (in millions)	1993	1992	1991
Loss from dispositions of discontinued operations after taxes (Note 2)	—	(32.3)	—
Extraordinary loss on early debt retirement after taxes (Note 4)	(4.2)	—	—
Cumulative effect of change in accounting principle after taxes (Note 5)	(24.0)	—	—
Net income	$ 78.2	$ 59.8	$ 97.6
Average number of common shares outstanding	107.5	107.2	105.9
Income (Loss) Per Common Share (in Dollars):			
Continuing operations	$ 0.99	$ 0.86	$ 0.76
Discontinued operations	—	(0.30)	0.16
Extraordinary loss on early debt retirement	(0.04)	—	—
Cumulative effect of change in accounting principle	$ (0.22)	—	—
Net income	$ 0.73	$ 0.56	$ 0.92
Cash dividends per common share	$ 0.290	$ 0.255	$ 0.445

NOTE: **Principles of consolidation**—The consolidated financial statements include the accounts of Whitman Corporation and all of its significant subsidiaries (the Company).

EXHIBIT 18-7 PRINCIPLES OF CONSOLIDATION: NOTES TO THE FINANCIAL STATEMENTS— MURPHY OIL CORPORATION

NOTE: The consolidated financial statements include the accounts of Murphy Oil Corporation and all majority-owned subsidiaries. The contract drilling business segment, which was sold effective January 1, 1992, is accounted for as discontinued operations. Information presented in the footnotes is based on continuing operations unless otherwise indicated. Investments in jointly owned companies are accounted for by the equity method. All significant intercompany accounts and transactions have been eliminated.

19

CONTENTS OF THE ANNUAL REPORT

A company's annual report, sometimes called the annual report to shareholders, is the primary direct communication from management to a company's shareholders. The report is management's opportunity to discuss operations of the company in detail. Although companies prepare and disseminate quarterly reports to shareholders and regulatory bodies, these reports are very brief.

It is interesting to note that many companies use the talents of their marketing staff, or retain an outside promotional agency, to give the annual report as much eye appeal as possible. The front and back covers of the report normally carry a very attractive picture directed to the theme of the year's annual report. Or the cover is related to some major aspect of the company's operation. The cost of producing such reports is substantial.

The purpose of this chapter and the next is to describe the sections of the annual report of publicly traded companies.

Inside or Outside the Covers

The last page of an annual report usually includes information such as:

Principal location, subsidiaries, branches or divisions of the company

Names of transfer agents and registrar of the company's stock

Notice that the company's 10-K filing with the Securities and Exchange Commission is available upon request

Principal address of the company

Possibly a brief description of the company

Names of members of the board of directors and officers

The table of contents

Exhibit 19-1 is the last page in the annual report of Perkin-Elmer Corporation and Subsidiaries detailing such information.

Board of Directors

Gaynor N. Kelley
Chairman and
Chief Executive Officer
The Perkin-Elmer Corporation

Joseph F. Abely, Jr.
Retired Chairman and
Chief Executive Officer
Sea-Land Corporation

Richard H. Ayers
Chairman and
Chief Executive Officer
The Stanley Works

Jean-Luc Bélingard
Director General
Diagnostics Division
F. Hoffmann-La Roche Ltd.

Dr. Robert H. Hayes
Professor and Senior Associate Dean
Harvard Business School

Donald R. Melville
Retired Chairman and
Chief Executive Officer
Norton Company

Riccardo Pigliucci
President and
Chief Operating Officer
The Perkin-Elmer Corporation

Burnell R. Roberts
Retired Chairman and
Chief Executive Officer
Mead Corporation

John S. Scott
Chairman
Cambridge Biotech Corporation

Richard F. Tucker
Retired Vice Chairman
Mobil Corporation

Corporate Officers

Gaynor N. Kelley
Chairman and
Chief Executive Officer

Riccardo Pigliucci
President and
Chief Operating Officer

F. Gordon Bitter
Senior Vice President and
President, Metco Division

William F. Emswiler
Vice President, Finance
Chief Financial Officer

Julianne A. Grace
Vice President,
Corporate Relations

Joseph E. Malandrakis
Vice President,
Worldwide Operations

André F. Marion
Vice President and President,
Applied Biosystems Division

John B. McBennett
Corporate Controller

Michael J. McPartland
Vice President,
Human Resources

William B. Sawch
Vice President,
General Counsel and Secretary

Rhonda L. Seegal
Vice President and Treasurer

Corporate Offices

The Perkin-Elmer Corporation
761 Main Avenue
Norwalk, Connecticut 06859-0001
(203) 762-1000

Annual Meeting

The annual meeting of shareholders will be held on October 21, 1993 at 11 a.m. at the Company's offices at 50 Danbury Road, Wilton, Connecticut.

Common Stock

The common stock of Perkin-Elmer is traded on the New York and Pacific Stock Exchanges under the ticker symbol PKN.

Form 10-K

A copy of the annual report to the Securities and Exchange Commission on Form 10-K may be obtained without charge by writing to the Secretary at the Corporate Offices address noted above.

Transfer Agent and Registrar

The First National Bank of Boston
Investor Relations Department
Mail Stop: 45-02-09
P.O. Box 644
Boston, Massachusetts 02102-0644
(617) 575-2900
(800) 442-2001 (outside of Massachusetts)

Perkin-Elmer Information

For additional information, write to the Perkin-Elmer Corporation, Shareholder Communications,
761 Main Avenue, Norwalk, Connecticut 06859-0310, or call (203) 761-5472.

Investor relations contact: Julianne A. Grace,
Vice President, Corporate Relations, (203) 761-5400.

Equal Employment Opportunity and Affirmative Action

Perkin-Elmer has long been committed to Equal Employment Opportunity and Affirmative Action. A policy of positive action is the foundation of this commitment and is typified by activities directed toward responsible community involvement. Support is provided to national and local programs designed to increase opportunities for minorities, women, veterans, and persons with disabilities.

Perkin-Elmer and Metco are registered trademarks of The Perkin-Elmer Corporation.

Pionir and QPCR are trademarks of The Perkin-Elmer Corporation.

GeneAmp is a registered trademark/trademark of Roche Molecular Systems, Inc. licensed to The Perkin-Elmer Corporation. EnviroAmp is a trademark of Roche Molecular Systems, Inc.

Perkin-Elmer is exclusively licensed for the detection of PCR products by electrochemiluminescence, except as applied to diagnostic procedures, under patents or patent applications owned by IGEN, Inc., Rockville, MD.

The GeneAmp PCR process is covered by U.S. patents owned by Hoffmann-La Roche Inc. and issued and pending patents owned by F. Hoffmann-La Roche Ltd.

Design: Jack Hough Associates, Inc. Norwalk CT

Major photography: William Taufic and Jerry Sarapochiello

 Financial Section printed on recycled paper.

Table of Contents

Not every report will contain every item discussed in this model table of contents, nor will a company always present these sections in precisely the same order.

Financial Highlights

Exhibit 19-2 is the Financial Highlights from Emerson Electric Company and Subsidiaries' annual report. This financial summary normally focuses on the information relating to the company's operations for the current and preceding years. Such items as stock performance, ratios, dividends, and whatever else management deems to be important are displayed in this summary. This section may also include assets, sales, net income, and earnings per share for several years. It is not unusual for the summary to contain graphs or tables that display the favorable trends management wants to emphasize.

The primary purpose of the financial highlights, or as it is sometimes called, the financial summary, is to show key numbers, with more details available later in the financial statements themselves. In looking over the summary, the reader can quickly determine whether sales volume and net income have increased or decreased, and review the changes in dividends and earnings per share.

Years ended September 30

(Dollars in millions except per share amounts)

	1992	1991	Percent Increase
Net Sales	$ 7,706.0	7,427.0	3.8%
Net earnings	$ 662.9	631.9	4.9%
Percent of net sales	8.6%	8.5%	
Earnings per common share	$ 2.96	2.83	4.6%
Dividends per common share	$ 1.38	1.32	4.5%
Total assets	$ 6,627.0	6,364.4	4.1%
Stockholders' equity	$ 3,729.8	3,256.9	14.5%
Net debt to net capital	17.7%	25.4%	
Return on average stockholders' equity	19.0%	20.2%	

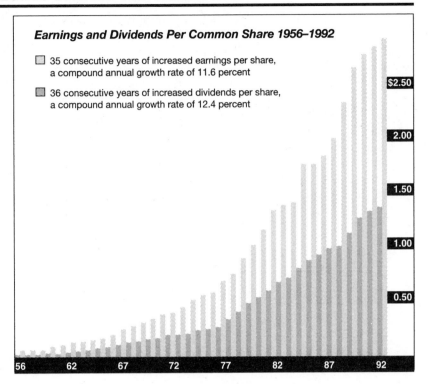

Earnings and Dividends Per Common Share 1956–1992

☐ 35 consecutive years of increased earnings per share, a compound annual growth rate of 11.6 percent

☐ 36 consecutive years of increased dividends per share, a compound annual growth rate of 12.4 percent

Letter to Stockholders

The next section of the annual report commonly begins with the words "To Our Stockholders" and is signed by the president of the company or the chairman of the board. The letter is an opportunity for the president or chairman of the board to express his or her view on what transpired over the preceding year regarding the operations of the company. Sometimes expectations regarding the company's operations are also discussed.

If the company has had a good year, the letter affords an opportunity to boast about the year's accomplishments. On the other hand, if the company has not done well and earnings are down, there is sometimes an effort to gloss over or whitewash the mediocre performance. Generally, however, the letter contains a predictably self-congratulatory, optimistic message. The reader must be cautious, because sometimes the letter may contain vague wording, combined with colorful adjectives and meaningless euphemisms, making the company's message obscure. There are normally a few important comments in the letter and, as a general rule, it is desirable for the reader to skim over the letter and search for significant phrases. The reader should not omit reading this section of the annual report, because it may give valuable insight into the philosophy of management of the company. Exhibit 19-3 is a letter to stockholders from the annual report of Federal Express Corporation.

EXHIBIT 19-3 LETTER TO STOCKHOLDERS—FEDERAL EXPRESS CORPORATION

To Our Stockholders

Our financial performance significantly improved in fiscal 1993. Total revenues increased by $258 million to $7.8 billion. Operating income grew to $377 million. Net income doubled on a year-over-year basis to $110 million, resulting in an earnings per share of $2.01 this year vs. $1.01 in 1992. (This excludes the cumulative effect of a change in accounting for postretirement benefits in 1993 and the European restructuring in 1992.)

As fiscal 1994 begins, you, our stockholders, collectively own the world's fastest, most reliable express transportation company connecting the world's major trading centers. In our core business, the U.S. domestic market, we have widened our lead in market share and continue to improve our service standards and boost customer satisfaction. Our work force is thoroughly trained and highly motivated to meet our customers' needs.

Improving our international and U.S. domestic performances were key to fiscal 1993 results. U.S. domestic per-package costs declined by 4 percent. By year-end, we had cut international losses nearly in half from $359 million in 1992 to $182 million in fiscal 1993 (excluding a $254 million charge in 1992 from restructuring our European operations). It was the first decrease in international losses since our international service began in June of 1985.

Losses in the international market grew each year, especially after the acquisition of Flying Tigers in 1989, as we expanded our global network. The acquisition accelerated international expansion and gave us the route authorities, facilities, equipment and personnel we needed for our intercontinental express network. After acquiring Flying Tigers, however, the air freight market, which is non-time-definite, experienced a cyclical downturn. That, aggravated by overcapacity in the industry, contributed to our international losses.

Some losses were expected, however, because the international network had to be expanded ahead of revenues from global markets. In Europe, the imbalance of resources and market demand became exceptionally costly as we attempted to add intra-regional and intra-country services to our intercontinental services.

At the end of fiscal 1992, we restructured our European operations to focus on intercontinental traffic. In fiscal 1993, this new strategy produced better results than we expected—International Priority Service volumes exceeded our monthly plans. This European network,

together with our extensive operations in Asia and the Pacific, Canada, Latin America and the Caribbean, is the perfect partner for our U.S. domestic operations. Together they give us an intercontinental express delivery system unparalleled in the world.

Today, we are well positioned to serve the global marketplace with a strategic mix of aircraft, geographic coverage and personnel. Our employees provide the best in customer service, speed and reliability in the world's primary trading centers. In regions where low package traffic makes our direct presence less economical, we have carefully selected Global Service Participants to complete deliveries. This allows us to serve 186 countries, which account for virtually all of the world's economic activity.

In the U.S. domestic market, intense competition has steadily reduced our revenue per package. And during the last decade, we have experienced faster growth in our lower-yielding deferred services. In addition, a larger percentage of packages have come from customers who earn increased discounts as their volume increases. We have responded to these trends by continuing to reduce our cost per package in fiscal 1993 and by reducing the rate of yield decline.

While improved productivity has contributed to a better financial picture, so has our strategic use of technology, which has reduced costs. We intend to remain the technology leader, as we have been for 20 years. Deploying new systems to better meet customer needs and improve operating efficiencies is key. In fiscal 1993, we reduced our fleet costs by continuing to deploy McDonnell Douglas MD-11 aircraft, which are more efficient than Boeing 747 freighters for long-distance international routes. The scheduled arrival of new Airbus A300 aircraft in fiscal 1994 will similarly improve the U.S. network.

We are determined to make the most of our strengths in the coming year. We are committed to moving our international operations toward profitability, while building on our leadership position in the United States. As we accomplish these goals, we will strive to balance the needs of our employees, customers and stockholders.

Frederick W. Smith
Chairman, President and
Chief Executive Officer

Review of Operations

The Review of Operations is normally the largest part of an annual report, sometimes representing as much as 50% of the pages in the report. The Review of Operations is a public relations presentation designed to impress the reader. The company may focus on a favorable discussion of its products, services, operations of the company, or its locations in beautiful settings—whatever management and the public relations department decide might be effective in impressing the reader. This represents some of the best work of the marketing department, with glamorous pictures on glossy pages sometimes depicting famous people and places. Most of the photographs and artwork are in this section. Time Warner has full-page, full-color, glossy pictures of guitarist Eric Clapton and actor Clint Eastwood in its annual report, relating to its discussion of the operations of its recording and entertainment divisions. Throughout the rhetoric, which is really a sales pitch, you may sometimes find some useful information. You should enjoy this section of the report, but interpret its message with caution and a certain degree of healthy skepticism.

Financial Statements

The financial statements are the heart of the annual report. They consist of the balance sheet, income statement, the statement of cash flows, and, normally, a statement of stockholders' equity. The numbers reflected in these statements often do not provide enough information to allow their users to make informed decisions. Therefore, narrative and additional disclosures are included in the annual report footnotes and supplementary tables.

The Footnotes—The footnotes are really endnotes, in that they follow the presentation of the financial statements in the annual report. The notes, as they are usually called in the statements themselves, are an integral part of the financial statements and often are as informative as the statements themselves. They contain information that should provide additional insight into the interpretation of the numbers presented in the annual report. Without these disclosures the financial statements might be misleading. There are two types of notes: (1) significant accounting policies and (2) additional disclosures, such as purchase commitments, long-term debt requirements, and pension plan information. Notes to the financial statements are described in detail in Chapter 20, and several company exhibits are presented.

Supplementary Tables—Supplementary tables support information in the current period's financial statements, as well as provide information relating to comparative data for a period of years. In addition, some tables disclose information required by the Financial Accounting Standards Board and the Securities and Exchange Commission (SEC). Supplementary tables are often incorporated in the footnotes rather than presented separately. Chapter 20 also discusses these tables.

Management's Discussion and Analysis

The SEC requires that annual reports contain management's discussion and analysis as part of the financial statements. In this section management discusses summarized income statement, balance sheet, and cash flow data for the past three years. The period of time can be greater than three years if necessary to keep the summary from being misleading.

Management is required to focus on the financial statements as a whole, rather than on a summary of operations, and must discuss at least three aspects of a company's business—results of operations, capital resources, and liquidity.

The *results of operations* refers to the operating and nonoperating income-generating activities of the company. *Capital resources* relate to the acquisition and financing of long-lived productive assets, and the discussion of *liquidity* focuses on the availability of cash from operations and existing credit arrangements.

Within each area of discussion, management is required to discuss favorable and unfavorable trends and to identify and emphasize significant events or uncertainties. The discussion should also include a narrative of the effects of inflation and changing prices on a company's sales and revenues, and on income from continuing operations.

Exhibit 19-4 is Management's Discussion and Analysis from the annual report of Genuine Parts Company and Subsidiaries.

Results of Operations:

Net sales in 1992 increased for the 43rd consecutive year to a record high of $3.7 billion. This was an increase of 7% over the prior year and compares with increases of 3% in 1991, and 5% in 1990. Fundamentals for the automotive aftermarket remain sound and the automotive segment had an increase in sales of 6% in 1992. The industrial segment posted an increase of 6% in 1992 versus an increase of 2% in 1991. Continued geographic and product line expansion allowed the office products segment to end the year with an increase in sales of 11% in 1992 compared with an increase of 6% in 1991.

Consolidated net income in 1992 increased 6% over 1991 net income. Net income in 1991 increased 1% over 1990.

Cost of goods sold improved slightly as a percentage of net sales in each of the past two years. Selling, administrative and other expenses increased each year, and the percentage to net sales has increased slightly each year, due primarily to increased salaries and wages and employee benefits. The effective income tax rate was 37.9% in 1992, and 38% in 1991 and 1990.

In December 1990, the Financial Accounting Standards Board issued new rules that require the projected future cost of providing postretirement benefits, such as health care and life insurance, be recognized as an expense as employees render service instead of when the benefits are paid. The Company will adopt the new rules in the first quarter of 1993. The adoption of these rules will not have a material impact on the Company's financial position or results of operations.

In February 1992, the Financial Accounting Standards Board issued Statement of Financial Accounting Standards No. 109, "Accounting for Income Taxes." The Company will adopt the new method of accounting for income taxes in the first quarter of 1993. The adoption of Statement 109 will not have a material impact on the Company's financial position or results of operations.

Liquidity and Sources of Capital:

The ratio of current assets to current liabilities was 4.1 at the close of 1992 with current assets amounting to 80% of total assets. Trade accounts receivable and inventories increased 10% and 12% respectively, while working capital increased 9%. The increase in working capital has been financed principally from the Company's cash flow generated by operations.

Current financial resources and anticipated funds from operations are expected to meet requirements for working capital in 1993. Capital expenditures during 1992 amounted to $31 million compared with $28 million in 1991 and $45 million in 1990. The decrease in 1991 and 1992 compared to 1990 was primarily the result of the Company's response to the difficult business environment and the overall economy. The Company intends to continue to review capital expenditures in conjunction with the recovery of the economy. It is anticipated that capital expenditures in 1993 will be slightly more than 1992.

On June 30, 1992, the Company acquired all of the outstanding common stock of Davis & Wilmar, Inc., an automotive parts distributor, for $32 million. The acquisition has been recorded using the purchase method of accounting. Results of operations, which are included since the date of acquisition, are not significant to the operations of the Company.

On January 29, 1993, the Company completed its merger of Berry Bearing Company and certain affiliated companies into the Company. The Berry Companies distribute industrial replacement parts and related supplies throughout the Midwestern United States. The Company issued approximately 9,500,000 shares of common stock in exchange for all of the outstanding common stock of the Berry Companies. This transaction will be accounted for as a pooling of interests.

Management Comments on Inflation:

Price increases in the Automotive Parts Group were approximately 2% in 1992 as sales increased 6%. The Industrial Parts Group had a sales increase of 6% and price increases of approximately 2%. The Office Products Group had a sales increase of 11% and price increases of less than 1%.

Price increases in the Automotive Parts Group were approximately 2% in 1991 as sales increased 3%. The Industrial Parts Group had a sales increase of 2% and price increases of approximately 3%. The Office Products Group had a sales increase of 6% and price increases of less than 1%.

The charges to operations for depreciation represent the allocation of historical costs incurred over past years and are significantly less than if they were based on the current cost of productive capacity being consumed. Assets acquired in prior years will, of course, be replaced at higher costs but this will take place over many years.

EXHIBIT 19-4 *(continued)*

Present tax laws do not allow deductions for adjustments for the impact of inflation. Thus, taxes are levied on the Company at rates which, in real terms, exceed established statutory rates. In general, during periods of inflation, this tax policy results in a tax on shareholders' investment in the Company.

Quarterly Results of Operations:

Miscellaneous year-end adjustments resulted in increasing net income during the fourth quarter of 1992 and 1991 by approximately $13,155,000 ($.11 per share) and $11,235,000 ($.10 per share), respectively.

The following is a summary of the quarterly results of operations for the years ended December 31, 1992 and 1991.

	Three Months Ended			
	March 31, 1992	June 30, 1992	Sept. 30, 1992	Dec. 31, 1992
	(in thousands except per share data)			
Net Sales	$873,248	$926,626	$960,923	$908,017
Gross Profit	262,457	274,529	291,460	311,619
Net Income	46,819	54,819	55,626	62,524
Net Income per Common Share	.41	.48	.49	.55

	Three Months Ended			
	March 31, 1991	June 30, 1991	Sept. 30, 1991	Dec. 31, 1991
	(in thousands except per share data)			
Net Sales	$809,177	$884,926	$897,774	$842,765
Gross Profit	243,852	260,517	273,167	283,563
Net Income	43,113	51,912	53,009	59,643
Net Income per Common Share	.38	.45	.46	.52

Report of Management

Normally preceding or appearing on the same page as the auditor's report (see the next paragraph) is the report of management. This report explains the extent of management's responsibility, as contrasted with that of the auditor, for the financial statements of the company. It generally explains how management establishes policies and procedures in fulfilling its duty to fairly report the company's financial position and results of operations. Exhibit 19-5 shows the report of management from Time Warner Inc.

EXHIBIT 19-5   REPORT OF MANAGEMENT— TIME WARNER INC.

The accompanying consolidated financial statements have been prepared by management in conformity with generally accepted accounting principles, and necessarily include some amounts that are based on management's best estimates and judgments.

Time Warner maintains a system of internal accounting controls designed to provide management with reasonable assurance that assets are safeguarded against loss from unauthorized use or disposition, and that transactions are executed in accordance with management's authorization and recorded properly. The concept of reasonable assurance is based on the recognition that the cost of a system of internal control should not exceed the benefits derived and that the evaluation of those factors requires estimates and judgments by management. Further, because of inherent limitations in any system of internal accounting control, errors or irregularities may occur and not be detected. Nevertheless, management believes that a high level of internal control is maintained by Time Warner through the selection and training of qualified personnel, the establishment and communication of accounting and business policies, and its internal audit program.

The Audit Committee of the Board of Directors, composed solely of directors who are not employees of Time Warner, meets periodically with management and with Time Warner's internal auditors and independent auditors to review matters relating to the quality of financial reporting and internal accounting control, and the nature, extent and results of their audits. Time Warner's internal auditors and independent auditors have free access to the Audit Committee.

Gerald M. Levin
Chairman and
Chief Executive Officer

Bert W. Wasserman
Executive Vice President and
Chief Financial Officer

The Auditor's Report

Published annual reports are audited by independent Certified Public Accountants (CPAs). The CPA expresses an opinion on the financial statements prepared by management. The report is short and is addressed to the stockholders and board of directors of the company.

The auditor can give one of three opinions on a company's financial statements or may disclaim an opinion. When an auditor disclaims an opinion, the auditor is saying that he is unable to satisfy himself that the financial statements are presented fairly. The three types of audit opinion are:

1. *Unqualified or "Clean" Opinion.* When expressing this type of opinion, the auditor believes that the financial statements are "fair" representations of the company's financial position, results of operations, and cash flows, in conformity with generally accepted accounting principles (GAAP). This is the most commonly given type of opinion.

2. *Qualified Opinion.* When expressing this type of opinion, the auditor takes exception to the "fair presentation" of a particular financial statement item or disclosure in conformity with GAAP. A qualified opinion contains the words "except for" preceding the item that the auditor is taking exception to. In a qualified opinion the auditor believes that the rest of the statements are "fairly presented."

3. *Adverse Opinion.* When expressing an adverse opinion, the auditor believes that the statements are not "fairly presented" in conformity with GAAP. An adverse opinion is given by the auditor when the departure from GAAP is so pervasive as to make the financial statements misleading to users of those statements.

Exhibit 19-6 is the auditor's report containing an unqualified audit opinion of KPMG Peat Marwick, an international accounting firm, on the financial statements of Peoples Heritage Financial Group, Inc.

EXHIBIT 19-6 AUDITOR'S REPORT—PEOPLES HERITAGE FINANCIAL GROUP, INC.

The Board of Directors
Peoples Heritage Financial Group, Inc.:

We have audited the accompanying consolidated balance sheets of Peoples Heritage Financial Group, Inc. and subsidiaries as of December 31, 1992 and 1991, and the related consolidated statements of operations, changes in shareholders' equity, and cash flows for the three-year period ended December 31, 1992. These consolidated financial statements are the responsibility of the Company's management. Our responsibility is to express an opinion on these consolidated financial statements based on our audits.

We conducted our audits in accordance with generally accepted auditing standards. Those standards require that we plan and perform the audit to obtain reasonable assurance about whether the financial statements are free of material misstatement. An audit includes examining, on a test basis, evidence supporting the amounts and disclosures in the financial statements. An audit also includes assessing the accounting principles used and significant estimates made by management, as well as evaluating the overall financial statement presentation. We believe that our audits provide a reasonable basis for our opinion.

In our opinion, the consolidated financial statements referred to above present fairly, in all material respects, the financial position of Peoples Heritage Financial Group, Inc. and subsidiaries as of December 31, 1992 and 1991, and the results of their operations and their cash flows for each of the years in the three-year period ended December 31, 1992 in conformity with generally accepted accounting principles.

January 19, 1993
Portland, Maine   KPMG Peat Marwick

Notice that the first paragraph of the auditor's report points out that the financial statements are the responsibility of management, not the auditors.

The second paragraph of the report explains what an audit is and that the auditor tests the accounting records and supporting documentation to support the opinion rendered. This is important for the reader, because some users are under the mistaken impression that the auditor checks every transaction that occurred during the year.

The third paragraph contains the auditor's opinion and states that the financial statements are presented fairly in accordance with GAAP.

20

CONTENT OF THE ANNUAL REPORT— FOOTNOTES AND SUPPLEMENTARY INFORMATION

An annual report contains more than the financial statements of a company. Supplemental tables and information appear after the basic financial statements. Supplemental tables may appear in the footnotes (notes) or may be presented separately. A particular financial statement may make direct reference to the footnotes, as the income statement of Dr. Pepper/Seven-Up Companies does in Exhibit 20-1. Or no reference may be made to the notes on the face of the statements. In either case, the footnotes are an essential part of the overall story conveyed by the company in its annual report. They are so important that the basic financial statements contain a reminder saying, "Notes to the financial statements are an integral part of this statement" or "See the accompanying notes to financial statements." A detailed review of footnotes is absolutely essential to understand a company's financial statements. The purpose of this chapter is to acquaint you with some of the note disclosures you might find in a typical company annual report.

Consolidated Statements of Operations

Three years ended December 31, 1992 (In thousands, except per share data)	1992	1991	1990
Net sales (note 12)	$ 658,718	600,941	540,368
Cost of sales	126,002	118,757	109,857
Gross profit	532,716	482,184	430,511
Operating expenses:			
Marketing	329,706	302,192	264,147
General and administrative	27,312	26,621	27,969
Amortization of intangible assets	15,112	15,155	15,142
Total operating expenses	372,130	343,968	307,258
Operating profit	160,586	138,216	123,253
Other income (expense):			
Interest expense	(150,245)	(147,957)	(146,481)
Interest income	4,443	2,729	823
Preferred stock dividends of subsidiaries	(17,538)	(12,294)	(8,974)
Recapitalization charge (note 1)	(6,026)	—	—
Other, net	184	445	(593)
Total other income (expense)	(169,182)	(157,077)	(155,225)
Loss before income taxes, extraordinary items and cumulative effect of accounting change	(8,596)	(18,861)	(31,972)
Income tax expense (benefit) (note 5)	(182)	1,100	563
Loss before extraordinary items and cumulative effect of accounting change	(8,414)	(19,961)	(32,535)

(In thousands, except per share data)	1992	1991	1990
Extraordinary items:			
Benefit from utilization of net operating loss carryforwards (note 5)	—	(1,022)	—
Debt restructuring charge (note 1)	56,934	18,566	—
Cumulative effect of accounting change (note 5)	74,800	—	—
Net loss	(140,148)	(37,505)	(32,535)
Preferred stock dividend requirements (note 7)	12,941	11,882	9,744
Net loss attributable to outstanding common stock	$(153,089)	(49,387)	(42,279)
Loss per common share:			
Loss before extraordinary items and cumulative effect of accounting change	$ (.60)	(.90)	(1.19)
Extraordinary items	(1.60)	(.49)	—
Cumulative effect of accounting change	$ (2.11)	—	—
Net loss	$ (4.31)	(1.39)	(1.19)

There are basically two types of footnotes. The first is the disclosure of the company's major accounting policies. This disclosure is important because where there are alternative policies, the user can obtain insight into management's philosophy by the accounting alternative chosen. For instance, does management take a conservative or aggressive approach to recognize revenues and expenses? The second type of footnote provides additional information that is not in the body of the financial statements. Examples include information on a company's pension plan or its long-term debt, such as interest rates and maturity dates. There is no limit to the number of footnotes a company can include in its annual report.

Summary of Significant Accounting Policies

Certain information must be presented in footnotes. Generally accepted accounting principles (GAAP) require disclosure of accounting policies as the first footnote to the financial statements. Accounting policies include items such as the methods chosen for computing depreciation expense and inventory valuation. Exhibit 20-2 is the first footnote from the annual report of Johnson & Johnson and Subsidiaries.

The company reports its policies relating to such items as its principles of consolidation, inventories, depreciation, and income taxes.

EXHIBIT 20-2   FOOTNOTE—JOHNSON & JOHNSON AND SUBSIDIARIES

1 Summary of Significant Accounting Policies

Principles of Consolidation
The consolidated financial statements include the accounts of Johnson & Johnson and subsidiaries. Intercompany accounts and transactions are eliminated.

Cash Equivalents
The Company considers securities with maturities of three months or less, when purchased, to be cash equivalents.

Inventories
Inventories are stated at the lower of cost (determined principally by the first-in, first-out method) or market.

Depreciation of Property
The Company utilizes the straight-line method of depreciation for financial statement purposes for all additions to property, plant and equipment placed in service after January 1, 1989. Depreciation of property, plant and equipment for assets placed in service prior to January 1, 1989 is generally determined using an accelerated method.

Intangible Assets
The excess of the cost over the fair value of net assets of purchased businesses is recorded as goodwill and is amortized on a straight-line basis over periods of 40 years or less. The cost of other acquired intangibles is amortized on a straight-line basis over their estimated useful lives.

Income Taxes
The Company intends to continue to reinvest its undistributed international earnings to expand its international operations; therefore, no tax has been provided to cover the repatriation of such undistributed earnings. At January 2, 1994 and January 3, 1993, the cumulative amount of undistributed international earnings was approximately $3.0 billion and $2.5 billion, respectively.

Net Earnings Per Share
Net earnings per share are calculated using the average number of shares outstanding during each year. Shares issuable under stock option and compensation plans would not materially reduce net earnings per share. All share and per share amounts have been restated to retroactively reflect prior year stock splits.

Annual Closing Date
The Company follows the concept of a fiscal year which ends on the Sunday nearest to the end of the month of December. Normally each fiscal year consists of 52 weeks, but every five or six years, as was the case in 1992, the fiscal year consists of 53 weeks.

Contingent Liabilities

Another item specifically required by the accounting profession is the existence of contingent liabilities. Contingent liabilities to be reported are those that are dependent on a particular future occurrence or event, resulting in a future payment. The settlement of a lawsuit and a tax court ruling stemming from a dispute are examples of situations involving a contingency. These events, if unfavorably resolved, will result in a loss to the company. Exhibit 20-3 is the disclosure of a contingent liability relating to legal proceedings for First Interstate Bancorp.

EXHIBIT 20-3   CONTINGENT LIABILITY—
FIRST INTERSTATE BANCORP

NOTE G: **Contingent Liabilities and Commitments**—The Corporation's banking subsidiaries are required to maintain balances with Federal Reserve Banks based on a percentage of deposit liabilities. Such balances averaged approximately $1.3 billion and $0.9 billion in 1992 and 1991, respectively.

There are presently pending against the Corporation and certain of its subsidiaries a number of legal proceedings. It is the opinion of management, after consulting with counsel, that the resulting liability, if any, from these actions and other pending claims will not materially affect the consolidated financial statements.

Subsequent Events

Subsequent events are events that occur after year-end (the balance sheet date), but before the company issues its financial statements. The company discloses this type of event to inform the reader of the possible effects on income and the reader's evaluation of the financial statements. If these events were material, and not disclosed, the financial statements would be misleading. Examples of subsequent events include settlement of lawsuits and casualty losses after year-end. Exhibit 20-4 is an excerpt from the annual report of Entergy Corporation. The event described in the note relates to losses realized by the utility company owing to an ice storm.

EXHIBIT 20-4   SUBSEQUENT EVENT—ENTERGY CORPORATION AND SUBSIDIARIES

NOTE 12: **Subsequent Event (unaudited)**—In early February 1994, an ice storm left more than 221,000 Entergy customers without electric power across the System's four-state service area. The storm was the most severe natural disaster ever to affect the System, causing damage to transmission and distribution lines, equipment, poles, and facilities in certain areas, primarily in Mississippi. A substantial portion of the related costs, which are estimated to be $110 million to $140 million, are expected to be capitalized. The MPSC acknowledged that there is precedent in Mississippi for recovery of certain costs associated with storms and natural disasters and the restoration of service resulting from such events. MP&L plans to immediately file for rate recovery of the costs related to the ice storm. Estimated construction expenditures (see Note 8) have not yet been updated to reflect the above amounts.

Segment Reporting

Many large companies operate in more than one line of business. This is the case with most large diversified companies having different business segments. A segment is defined as a product line, territory, department, division, or subsidiary company. When a company has many segments, the results of operations of those segments may differ. The accounting profession requires companies to disclose, on a segmented basis, information about sales, operating income, identifiable assets, depreciation, amortization, depletion, and capital expenditures. Exhibit 20-5 provides this information for Ecolab, Inc. and the Walt Disney Company. You can see that Ecolab defines its segments on the basis of geographic regions, whereas Disney defines its segments in terms of different divisions.

EXHIBIT 20-5   SEGMENT REPORTING—ECOLAB, INC. AND WALT DISNEY COMPANY

ECOLAB, INC.

12 Geographic Segments—The company is engaged in the development and marketing of premium products and services for institutional and industrial markets. The company provides cleaning, sanitizing, pest elimination and maintenance products, systems and services to foodservice, lodging, healthcare, commercial and institutional laundries and to farms, dairies and food and beverage processors. International consists of Canadian, Asia Pacific and Latin American operations. Prior to the 1991 formation of the Henkel-Ecolab joint venture, the company also operated in Europe through consolidated subsidiaries.

(thousands)	1993	1992	1991
Net Sales			
United States	$ 812,788	$ 766,902	$ 716,217
International	228,730	237,931	201,738
Total	$1,041,518	$1,004,833	$ 917,955
Operating Income			
United States	$ 116,471	$ 115,033	$ 106,103
International	9,569	8,985	2,002
Europe			7,958
Corporate	(4,250)	(6,526)	(5,750)
Total	$ 121,790	$ 117,492	$ 110,313
Depreciation and Amortization			
United States	$ 48,773	$ 48,703	$ 45,852
International	10,682	10,719	9,129
Total	$ 59,455	$ 59,422	$ 54,981

(thousands)	1993	1992	1991
Capital Expenditures			
United States	$ 50,785	$ 45,632	$ 41,693
International	16,177	11,519	10,273
Total	$ 66,962	$ 57,151	$ 51,966
Identifiable Assets			
United States	$ 368,930	$ 315,417	$306,545
International	131,677	120,580	116,951
Joint Venture	255,804	289,034	296,292
ChemLawn			70,000
Corporate	106,184	$ 107,326	132,144
Total	$ 862,595	$ 832,357	$921,932

   In accordance with company policy, operating expenses incurred at the corporate level totaling $18,037,000 in 1993, $14,277,000 in 1992 and $12,580,000 in 1991 have been allocated to the geographic segments in determining operating income.

EXHIBIT 20-5 *(continued)*

WALT DISNEY COMPANY

12 Business Segments

	1992	1991	1990
Capital Expenditures			
Theme parks and resorts	$ 380.9	$ 790.1	$ 519.8
Filmed entertainment	76.7	50.1	39.5
Consumer products	38.6	35.5	34.3
Corporate	48.2	48.9	122.7
	$ 544.4	$ 924.6	$ 716.3
Depreciation Expense			
Theme parks and resorts	$ 249.8	$ 213.2	$ 177.4
Filmed entertainment	29.5	23.9	12.9
Consumer products	16.8	12.4	5.8
Corporate	21.2	14.0	7.0
	$ 317.3	$ 263.5	$ 203.1
Identifiable Assets			
Theme parks and resorts	$ 5,076.8	$4,694.7	$4,056.4
Filmed entertainment	2,370.9	1,910.5	1,696.8
Consumer products	642.8	448.4	308.5
Corporate	2,231.7	1,903.8	1,596.7
Investment in Euro Disney	539.5	471.1	363.9
	$10,861.7	$9,428.5	$8,022.3
Supplemental Revenue Data			
Theme Parks and Resorts			
Admissions	$ 1,246.6	$1,093.0	$1,179.9
Merchandise, food			
and beverage	1,223.1	1,048.0	1,113.5
Filmed Entertainment			
Theatrical product	2,251.7	1,776.9	1,545.7
Export revenues	1,457.4	1,267.1	938.8

Related Party Transactions

GAAP requires the disclosure by companies of related party transactions. A related party can be an affiliated company, owners of the company, or any other party with which the company deals if one of the parties can influence the management or operating policies of the other. A related party transaction is defined as any transaction between a company and a related party. Common examples include transactions between two companies controlled by the same individual and sales of merchandise from a parent company to its subsidiary. Engelhard Corporation disclosed related party transactions in the footnotes in its annual report. The disclosure appears in Exhibit 20-6.

EXHIBIT 20-6   RELATED PARTY TRANSACTIONS— ENGELHARD CORPORATION

4. **Related party transactions**—The Company, in the ordinary course of business, has raw material supply arrangements with entities in which it is informed Anglo American Corporation of South Africa Limited (Anglo) has a material interest. Anglo indirectly holds a significant minority interest in the common stock of the Company. The Company's purchases from such entities amounted to $254.5 million in 1992, $284.1 million in 1991 and $278.2 million in 1990, and were transacted upon terms no less favorable to the Company than those obtained from other parties. At December 31, 1992 and 1991 amounts due to such entities totaled $16.2 million and $28.9 million, respectively.

Research and Development

Quarterly Financial Information

Many companies do not separately disclose research and development (R&D) expenses on the face of their income statements. In these cases, disclosure regarding R&D is made in the footnotes. Exhibit 20-7 presents the R&D footnote disclosure for EG&G, Inc. For many companies, R&D expense can be a significant expenditure; hence, the separate footnote disclosure.

EXHIBIT 20-7   R&D EXPENSE—EG&G, INC.

Research and Development—During 1993, 1992 and 1991, Company-sponsored research and development expenditures were approximately $34.7 million, $32.1 million and $24.7 million, respectively. Customer-sponsored research and development, primarily for Department of Energy programs, accounted for additional expenditures of approximately $137 million in 1993, $133 million in 1992 and $127 million in 1991.

Some companies provide quarterly information summarizing the changes for the year. Dole Food Company, Inc. presented this information in its annual report, as reproduced in Exhibit 20-8. Although such information is presented in quarterly reports to shareholders, prospective investors may not have this information readily available and, thus, can benefit from its inclusion in the annual report.

EXHIBIT 20-8   QUARTERLY FINANCIAL INFORMATION—DOLE FOOD COMPANY, INC.

Note 14—Quarterly Financial Information (Unaudited)

The following table presents summarized quarterly results.

(in thousands, except per share data)	First Quarter	Second Quarter	Third Quarter	Fourth Quarter	Year
1993					
Revenue	$766,488	$863,653	$1,005,791	$794,589	$3,430,521
Gross margin	131,791	159,307	149,203	109,718	550,019
Net income (loss)	53,258	39,656	5,103	(20,128)	77,889
Earnings (loss) per common share	$ .89	$ .66	$ .09	$ (.34)	$ 1.30
1992					
Revenue	$753,284	$901,753	$ 956,880	$763,575	$3,375,492
Gross margin	120,857	151,673	151,588	88,645	512,763
Income (loss) before cumulative effect of accounting change	26,694	40,064	21,313	(22,858)	65,213
Cumulative effect of accounting change	(49,492)	—	—	—	(49,492)
Net income (loss)	$ (22,798)	$ 40,064	$ 21,313	$ (22,858)	$ 15,721
Earnings (loss) per common share					
Income (loss) before cumulative effect of accounting change	$ .45	$ .67	$ .36	$ (.39)	$ 1.09
Cumulative effect of accounting change	(.83)	—	—	—	(.83)
Net income (loss)	$ (.38)	$ .67	$ .36	$ (.39)	$ .26

Operating results for the fourth quarters of both 1993 and 1992 include a $42.5 million ($26.7 million, net of tax) and a $45.7 million ($27.4 million, net of tax) charge, respectively, for the Company's cost reduction programs.

The first quarter of 1992 has been restated to reflect the adoption of SFAS No. 106. The impact of the adoption was not material in subsequent quarters, which have not been restated. See Note 7 in Notes to Consolidated Financial Statements.

All quarters have 12 weeks, except the third quarters of 1993 and 1992 which have 16 weeks each and the fourth quarter of 1992 which has 13 weeks.

Operating Lease Information

Exhibit 20-9 discloses the rental expense and future minimum rental commitments for Dillard Department Stores, Inc. and Subsidiaries. The information relating to future rental payments is obviously very important to a user in assessing future cash outflows for a company, especially since these amounts are not recorded as liabilities on the balance sheet. Disclosure of this information is required by the accounting profession.

EXHIBIT 20-9   OPERATING LEASE INFORMATION—DILLARD DEPARTMENT STORES, INC. AND SUBSIDIARIES

10. Operating Leases and Commitments

Rental expense consists of the followng (in thousands of dollars):

	Fiscal 1993	Fiscal 1992	Fiscal 1991
Operating leases:			
Buildings:			
Minimum rentals	$33,922	$32,092	$28,918
Contingent rentals	11,796	13,139	11,912
Equipment	18,107	16,319	16,511
	63,825	61,550	57,341
Contingent rentals on capital leases	1,133	1,201	1,174
	$64,958	$62,751	$58,515

Contingent rentals on certain leases are based on a percentage of annual sales in excess of specified amounts. Other contingent rentals are based entirely on a percentage of sales.

The future minimum rental commitments as of January 29, 1994 for all noncancelable operating leases for buildings and equipment are as follows (in thousands):

Fiscal Year	Amount
1994	$ 41,916
1995	36,464
1996	30,383
1997	29,189
1998	27,704
After 1998	236,150
	$401,806

Renewal options from three to 25 years exist on the majority of leased properties. At January 29, 1994, the Company is committed to incur costs of approximately $142 million to complete and equip certain stores.

Significant Customer

A significant customer can be a particular company, the government, or a foreign company or government. To assess the impact of a customer on a company's operations, a financial statement user must be aware of how dependent the company is on that customer. The accounting profession requires disclosure of significant customers when sales to one customer are equal to or greater than 10% of total sales. Georgia Gulf Corporation and Subsidiaries made such a disclosure in their annual report. The disclosure appears in Exhibit 20-10.

**EXHIBIT 20-10   SIGNIFICANT CUSTOMER—
GEORGIA GULF CORPORATION
AND SUBSIDIARIES**

NOTE 10:   **Significant Customer and Export Sales**—The Company has a supply contract, subject to certain limitations, for a substantial percentage of Georgia-Pacific Corporation's requirements for certain chemicals at market prices. This supply contract has various expiration dates (depending on the product) from 1994 through 1999 and may be extended year to year upon expiration. The sales of Georgia-Pacific Corporation under this supply contract for the years ended December 31, 1992, 1991 and 1990 amounted to approximately 14 percent, 15 percent and 16 percent of net sales, respectively. Receivables outstanding from these sales were $10,850,000, $11,077,000 and $15,988,000 at December 31, 1992, 1991 and 1990, respectively.

Export sales were approximately 15 percent, 17 percent and 11 percent of the Company's net sales for the years ended December 31, 1992, 1991 and 1990, respectively. The principal international markets served by the Company include Canada, Mexico, Latin America, Europe and Asia.

Pension Plan

The cost of employee pension plans is quite significant for most companies. The size of the potential liability and the status of assets that will be used to extinguish that liability do not appear in the body of the financial statements, but can be found in the footnotes. This liability is called the "projected benefit obligation," and the assets to be used to pay retirees are called "plan assets at fair value." The intricacies of pension accounting are not important for our purposes, but in looking at Exhibit 20-11, we see that the assets are in excess of the liability for General Mills, Inc. This is good news for stockholders of the company, in that the plan is fully funded and additional cash contributions are not necessary, thus increasing the likelihood that increased dividends can be distributed. This information is essential in assessing a company's cash flow.

EXHIBIT 20-11   PENSION PLAN—GENERAL MILLS, INC. AND SUBSIDIARIES

NOTE TWELVE: **Retirement Plans**—We have defined benefit plans covering most employees. Benefits for salaried employees are based on length of service and final average compensation. The hourly plans include various monthly amounts for each year of credited service. Our funding policy is consistent with the funding requirements of federal law and regulations. Our principal plan covering salaried employees has a provision that any excess pension assets would be vested in plan participants if the plan is terminated within five years of a change in control. Plan assets consist principally of listed equity securities and corporate obligations, and U.S. government securities.

Components of the net pension income are as follows:

(Income) Expense in Millions	Fiscal Year		
	1993	1992	1991
Service cost-benefits earned	$ 14.7	$ 14.2	$ 12.8
Interest cost on projected benefit obligation	52.6	51.2	49.4
Actual return on plan assets	(136.6)	(75.0)	(70.6)
Net amortization and deferral	38.3	(26.1)	(26.1)
Net pension income	$ (31.0)	$(35.7)	$(34.5)

The weighted-average discount rate and rate of increase in future compensation levels used in determining the actuarial present value of the benefit obligations were 8.5% and 5.1% in fiscal 1993, and 9.5% and 6% in fiscal 1992, respectively. The expected long-term rate of return on assets was 10.4% in fiscal 1993 and 11.35% in fiscal 1992.

The funded status of the plans and the amount recognized on the consolidated balance sheets (as determined as of May 31, 1993 and 1992) are as follows:

In Millions	May 30, 1993		May 31, 1992	
	Assets Exceed Accumulated Benefits	Accumulated Benefits Exceed Assets	Assets Exceed Accumulated Benefits	Accumulated Benefits Exceed Assets
Actuarial present value of benefit obligations:				
Vested benefits	$ 545.5	$ 12.1	$ 453.6	$11.3
Nonvested benefits	55.0	2.3	41.7	2.2
Accumulated benefit obligations	600.5	14.4	495.3	13.5
Projected benefit obligation	680.9	18.8	568.3	19.3
Plan assets at fair value	921.6	—	824.8	—
Plan assets in excess of (less than) the projected benefit obligation	240.7	(18.8)	256.5	(19.3)
Unrecognized prior service cost	40.1	.3	28.3	.4
Unrecognized net loss	125.3	6.0	97.9	7.1
Recognition of minimum liability	—	(10.7)	—	(11.4)
Unrecognized transition (asset) liability	(148.7)	8.8	(165.3)	9.7
Prepaid (accrued) pension cost	$ 257.4	$ (14.4)	$ 217.4	$(13.5)

We have defined contribution plans covering salaried and non-union employees. Contributions are determined by matching a percentage of employee contributions. Such plans had net assets of $715.2 million at May 31, 1993. Expense recognized in fiscal 1993, 1992 and 1991 was $9.6 million, $12.7 million and $16.1 million, respectively.

Supplemental Balance Sheet Information

Many times, because of the number of accounts involved, a company will simply provide a total amount of an item on the balance sheet or income statement and refer the reader to a footnote for more detailed information. James River Corpor- ation of Virginia and Subsidiaries presented this type of infor- mation for $616,192,000 of accounts payable and accrued liabil- ities in its annual report. Exhibit 20-12 shows the referent note.

EXHIBIT 20-12 SUPPLEMENTAL BALANCE SHEET INFORMATION—JAMES RIVER CORPORATION OF VIRGINIA AND SUBSIDIARIES

NOTE 9: **Supplemental Balance Sheet Information**—*Short-Term Securities:* Short-term securities, with a cost of $21.4 million as of December 26, 1993 and $374.1 million as of December 27, 1992, consisted primarily of commercial paper, government repurchase agreements, and time deposits. The carrying value of cash and short-term securities approximates fair value because of the short maturity of these instruments.

Accounts Payable and Accrued Liabilities: Accounts payable and accrued liabilities included the following:

(in thousands)	1993	1992
Accounts payable	$252,144	$221,606
Accrued liabilities:		
Compensated absences	73,471	73,878
Employee insurance benefits	63,009	56,790
Interest payable	24,333	33,011
Postretirement benefits other than pensions	28,000	28,000
Advertising and promotion	34,691	26,932

(in thousands)	1993	1992
Accrued premium on early extinguishment of debt		24,200
Salaries and incentive compensation	20,068	22,302
Taxes payable, other than income taxes	30,983	20,693
Dividends payable	20,467	20,398
Other items	69,026	76,957
Total accounts payable and accrued liabilities	$616,192	$604,767

Five-Year Financial Summary of Financial and Statistical Data

Companies prepare five-year and sometimes ten-year summaries of financial and statistical information. This information normally appears in the back of the annual report or may appear in a footnote. The data presented generally consists of such information as total assets, liabilities, operating revenues and expenses, net income, and earnings and dividends per share. However, other types of information are sometimes provided. Exhibit 20-13 is the ten-year summary for Delta Air Lines, Inc. You can see that Delta has also provided passenger information, as well as information regarding mileage and revenues per passenger mile.

EXHIBIT 20-13   TEN-YEAR SUMMARY—DELTA AIR LINES, INC.

Consolidated Summary of Operations

For the years ended June 30

(Dollars in thousands, except per share figures)

	1993	1992	1991	1990	1989	1988	1987	1986	1985	1984	1983
Operating Revenues											
Passenger	$11,075,212	$10,115,185	$8,566,676	$8,042,496	$7,579,716	$6,443,111	$4,921,852	$4,132,284	$4,376,986	$3,963,610	$3,347,014
Cargo	697,437	587,633	475,547	416,168	393,662	349,775	280,271	240,115	235,199	239,649	227,146
Other, net	224,001	133,967	128,390	123,567	116,106	122,491	116,049	87,663	71,930	60,472	42,253
Total operating revenues	11,996,650	10,836,785	9,170,613	8,582,231	8,089,484	6,915,377	5,318,172	4,460,062	4,684,115	4,263,731	3,616,413
Operating expenses	12,572,089	11,511,691	9,620,595	8,162,719	7,411,159	6,418,293	4,913,647	4,425,574	4,318,105	4,052,339	3,823,747
Operating income (loss)	(575,439)	(674,906)	(449,982)	419,512	678,325	497,084	404,525	34,488	366,010	211,392	(207,334)
Interest expense, net[1]	(176,881)	(151,430)	(97,541)	(26,711)	(38,869)	(65,204)	(61,908)	(55,355)	(62,053)	(109,802)	(63,494)
Gain (loss) on disposition of flight equipment	64,843	34,563	16,843	17,906	16,562	(1,016)	96,270	16,526	94,343	129,511	28,229
Miscellaneous income, net	36,193	5,400	30,496	57,205	55,200	24,992	8,312	7,775	6,863	9,114	15,898
Income (loss) before income taxes	(651,284)	(786,373)	(500,184)	467,912	711,218	455,856	447,199	3,434	405,163	240,215	(226,701)
Income taxes credited (provided)	233,609	271,005	162,646	(186,722)	(279,214)	(180,851)	(219,715)	2,228	(186,624)	(102,625)	109,642
Amortization of investment tax credits	2,927	9,050	13,158	21,593	28,914	31,821	36,245	41,624	40,914	38,014	30,329
Net income (loss)	(414,748)	(506,318)	(324,380)	302,783	460,918	306,826	263,729	47,286	259,453	175,604	(86,730)
Preferred stock dividends, net of tax benefits	(110,392)	(18,567)	(18,592)	(18,144)	—	—	—	—	—	—	—
Net income (loss) attributable to common stockholders	(525,140)[2]	(524,885)	(342,972)	284,639	460,918	306,826	263,729	47,286	259,453	175,604	(86,730)
Net income (loss) per share:											
Primary	$(10.54)[2]	$(10.60)	$(7.73)	$5.79	$9.37	$6.30	$5.90	$1.18	$6.50	$4.42	$(2.18)
Fully diluted	$(10.54)[2]	$(10.60)	$(7.73)	$5.28	$9.37	$6.30	$5.90	$1.18	$6.50	$4.42	$(2.18)
Dividends declared on common stock	$ 34,815	$ 59,405	$ 53,844	$ 84,550	$ 59,054	$ 58,546	$ 44,397	$ 40,073	$ 27,938	$ 23,857	$ 39,761
Dividends declared per common share	$0.70	$1.20	$1.20	$1.70	$1.20	$1.20	$1.00	$1.00	$0.70	$0.60	$1.00
[1]Has been reduced by interest capitalized of	$ 61,948	$ 69,445	$ 65,287	$ 57,226	$ 31,778	$ 32,329	$ 32,092	$ 23,758	$ 22,028	$ 18,263	$ 29,398

[2]Excludes cumulative effect of change in accounting standards of $587.1 million ($11.78 per share)

EXHIBIT 20-13 *(continued)*

Other Financial and Statistical Data

For the years ended June 30

(Dollars in thousands)

	1993	1992	1991	1990	1989	1988	1987	1986	1985	1984	1983
Total assets	$11,871,023	$10,161,574	$8,410,679	$7,227,002	$6,483,986	$5,748,355	$5,342,383	$3,785,462	$3,626,840	$3,268,822	$3,246,960
Long-term debt and capital leases	$ 3,716,672	$ 2,832,633	$2,058,595	$1,315,199	$ 703,014	$ 729,493	$1,018,417	$ 868,615	$ 535,159	$ 670,993	$1,089,796
Common stockholders' equity	$ 1,913,105	$ 1,894,068	$2,456,985	$2,595,569	$2,619,707	$2,208,823	$1,937,912	$1,301,946	$1,287,094	$1,048,907	$ 897,160
Shares of common stock outstanding at year end	50,063,841	49,699,098	49,401,779	46,086,110	49,265,884	49,101,271	48,639,469	40,116,383	39,958,467	39,761,154	39,761,154
Revenue passengers enplaned	85,084,733	77,038,029	69,127,249	67,240,233	64,242,212	58,564,507	48,172,626	39,582,232	39,340,850	36,319,567	35,666,116
Available seat miles (000)	132,282,319	123,101,743	104,327,918	96,463,052	90,741,541	85,833,959	69,013,669	53,336,135	51,637,084	50,935,173	47,915,817
Revenue passenger miles (000)	82,405,893	72,692,734	62,086,304	58,986,912	55,903,857	49,009,094	38,415,117	30,123,387	29,061,618	26,099,115	26,096,996
Passenger load factor	62.30%	59.05%	59.51%	61.15%	61.61%	57.10%	55.66%	56.48%	56.28%	51.24%	54.46%
Breakeven load factor	65.53%	62.99%	62.64%	57.96%	56.09%	52.69%	51.09%	56.01%	51.57%	48.51%	57.84%
Available ton miles (000)	18,182,484	16,625,472	13,825,313	12,499,745	11,724,797	11,249,578	8,999,668	6,934,047	6,667,512	6,569,248	6,202,910
Revenue ton miles (000)	9,502,936	8,361,026	7,103,650	6,693,786	6,338,274	5,556,584	4,327,195	3,371,917	3,275,329	2,983,840	2,951,119
Passenger revenue per passenger mile	13.44¢	13.91¢	13.80¢	13.63¢	13.56¢	13.15¢	12.81¢	13.72¢	15.06¢	15.19¢	12.83¢
Operating expenses per available seat mile	9.50¢	9.35¢	9.22¢	8.46¢	8.17¢	7.48¢	7.12¢	8.30¢	8.36¢	7.96¢	7.98¢
Operating expenses per available ton mile	69.14¢	69.24¢	69.59¢	65.30¢	63.21¢	57.05¢	54.60¢	63.82¢	64.76¢	61.69¢	61.64¢

The financial and statistical information presented above reflect the Company's acquisition of Western Air Lines, Inc. on December 18, 1986.

A Caveat Regarding Footnotes

Management prepares the footnotes found in the annual report. Although the auditor's opinion on the financial statements includes the footnotes, readers should be aware that management has a great deal of latitude in footnote preparation and disclosure. Management attempts to balance divulging information that could be competitively detrimental to the company—and a harm to its competitive advantage—and compliance with the accounting doctrine of "full-disclosure." Managers understand that too little disclosure, or vague and unclear wording, may lead to a lawsuit by unhappy investors or creditors. In many instances this results in footnotes that are carefully worded, yet difficult to read and understand by a user. There is a point where management draws the line on what is "fair and full-disclosure." The user of financial statements should understand that this line is not always clear. In addition, the user should be aware that the financial statements do not tell all. Other sources of information regarding a company are available.

21

COMPARATIVE ANALYSIS

The primary purpose of financial analysis is to make judgments about the future. An analyst might want to know whether a company will be able to repay a nine-month bank loan or a twenty-year bond. Will the company's earnings continue to grow, and is its dividend payment likely to rise? In making these judgments, we use historical information and assume, unless there is information to the contrary, that historical trends will continue.

Users of financial statements look for signs that indicate that the future will be different from the past. Some events are beyond the control of a company's management. A strike may result in lost sales. A company's primary product may become obsolete, or a competitor may develop a vastly superior product. The analyst seeks to assess whether management is managing the company efficiently and effec-

tively, because good management is critical to a company's success. Therefore, financial statement analysis focuses not only on financial and quantitative information, but on nonfinancial and qualitative information as well. Other sources of information include the financial press (for example, *The Wall Street Journal*), reports to the Securities and Exchange Commission, and business service publications (such as *Value Line* and *Dun & Bradstreet*). This chapter focuses on financial and quantitative information in a company's financial statements. We apply analytical tools and techniques to the financial statements of Hudson Foods, Inc. to highlight significant relationships and trends. These analytical tools and techniques fall into three groups: horizontal analysis, vertical analysis, and ratio analysis. Ratio analysis is discussed in Chapter 22.

Horizontal Analysis

Horizontal analysis focuses on the changes in accounting information from period to period. This type of analysis can tell us whether a company's sales, gross profit, expenses, and net income are increasing or decreasing over time, as well as what the change was in each of these items from the previous year. Horizontal analysis can also reveal whether cash (or any other financial statement item) has increased or decreased over the last two years. The dollar change from one period to the next in an individual account may not adequately explain the change such that an informed decision can be made regarding that account. Therefore, the use of the percentage change in an account may enhance the user's understanding of the change in that account.

Comparative financial statements present a company's financial statements for two or more successive periods. There are two necessary steps involved in performing horizontal analysis. First, compute the dollar amount of the change from the base year. The *base year* is the year against which you are making the comparison. Second, divide the dollar amount of the change by the base year amount. Exhibits 21-1 and 21-2 contain the comparative financial statements for Hudson Foods, Inc. and Subsidiaries for 1992 and 1993. We use these statements to illustrate horizontal analysis. Exhibits 21-3 and 21-4 present the horizontal analysis of Hudson Foods.

EXHIBIT 21-1 CONSOLIDATED STATEMENTS OF OPERATIONS—HUDSON FOODS, INC. AND SUBSIDIARIES

For the Years Ended (Dollars in thousands except per share data)	October 2, 1993	October 3, 1992	September 28, 1991
Sales	**$920,545**	$809,243	$765,292
Costs and Expenses:			
Cost of sales	**801,178**	732,205	689,493
Selling	**63,926**	49,907	37,135
General and administrative	**20,695**	18,533	16,645
Total costs and expenses	**885,799**	800,645	743,273
Operating Income	**34,746**	8,598	22,019
Other Expense (Income):			
Interest expense	**7,975**	8,476	9,073
Other, net	**530**	(4,342)	(1,406)
Total other expense	**8,505**	4,134	7,667
Income Before Income Taxes	**26,241**	4,464	14,352
Income Tax Expense	**10,336**	2,294	5,810
Net Income	**$ 15,905**	$ 2,170	$ 8,542
Earnings Per Share:			
Primary	**$1.01**	$ .15	$ .58
Fully diluted	**$1.01**	$ .15	$ .58

The accompanying notes are an integral part of the consolidated financial statements.

EXHIBIT 21-2 CONSOLIDATED BALANCE SHEETS—HUDSON FOODS, INC. AND SUBSIDIARIES

(Dollars in thousands)	October 2, 1993	October 3, 1992
Assets		
Current Assets:		
Cash and cash equivalents	$ 3,891	$ 3,949
Receivables:		
Trade	58,441	47,901
Other	219	228
	58,660	48,129
Less allowance for doubtful accounts	1,208	1,344
	57,452	46,785
Inventories	116,497	108,036
Other	7,275	3,944
Total current assets	185,115	162,714
Property, Plant and Equipment, Net	197,379	198,040
Excess Cost of Investment Over Net Assets Acquired, Net	15,807	16,369
Other Assets	9,968	16,008
Total Assets	$408,269	$393,131

(Dollars in thousands)	October 2, 1993	October 3, 1992
Liabilities and Stockholder's Equity		
Current Liabilities:		
Notes payable	$ —	$ 15,000
Current portion of long-term obligations	5,085	5,229
Accounts payable	31,555	30,125
Accrued liabilities	33,198	19,001
Deferred income taxes (Note 7)	13,386	13,185
Total current liabilities	83,224	82,540
Long-Term Obligations	88,985	125,695
Deferred Income Taxes (Note 7) and Deferred Gain (Note 10)	62,158	50,566
Commitments and Contingencies (Note 10)		
Stockholders' Equity:		
Common stock:		
Class A, $.01 par value, issued 8,630,407 and 6,428,947 shares	86	64
Class B, $.01 par value, issued and outstanding 8,502,052 and 8,503,052 shares	85	85
Additional capital	87,638	62,478
Retained earnings	97,727	83,528
	185,536	146,155
Treasury stock, at cost (958,358 and 983,731 Class A shares)	(11,634)	(11,825)
Total stockholders' equity	173,902	134,330
Total Liabilities and Stockholders' Equity	$408,269	$393,131

The accompanying notes are an integral part of the consolidated financial statements.

EXHIBIT 21-3   COMPARATIVE CONSOLIDATED STATEMENTS OF OPERATIONS— HUDSON FOODS, INC. AND SUBSIDIARIES

For the Years Ended October 3, 1992 and October 2, 1993

(Dollars in thousands)	1993	1992	Increase (Decrease) 1993 over 1992 Amount	Percent
Sales	$920,545	$809,243	$111,302	13.8%
Costs and Expenses:				
Cost of Sales	801,178	732,205	68,973	9.4
Selling	63,926	49,907	14,019	28.1
General and Administrative	20,695	18,533	2,162	11.7
Total Costs and Expenses	885,799	800,645	85,154	10.6
Operating Income	34,746	8,598	26,148	304.1
Other Expense (Income):				
Interest Expense	7,975	8,476	(501)	(5.9)
Other, Net	530	(4,342)	4,872	112.2
Total Other Expense	8,505	4,134	4,371	51.4
Income Before Income Taxes	26,241	4,464	21,777	487.8
Income tax expense	10,336	2,294	8,042	350.6
Net income	$ 15,905	$ 2,170	$ 13,735	633.0%

Exhibit 21-3 shows that sales increased by 13.8% during 1993, with cost of goods sold increasing by 9.4%. The gross profit in 1992 was $77,038,000 ($809,243,000 − $732,205,000) and $119,367,000 ($920,545,000 − $801,178,000) in 1993. The dollar amount of the increase is $42,329,000, resulting in a gross profit increase of 55.0%. Selling, general, and administrative expenses increased. It appears that the 633% increase in earnings is attributable to the combination of a larger increase in gross profit than the increase in expenses.

EXHIBIT 21-4   COMPARATIVE CONSOLIDATED BALANCE SHEETS—HUDSON FOODS, INC. AND SUBSIDIARIES
October 3, 1992 and October 2, 1993

(Dollars in thousands)

Assets	1993	1992	Increase (Decrease) 1993 over 1992 Amount	Percent
Current Assets:				
Cash and Cash Equivalents	$ 3,891	$ 3,949	$ (58)	(1.5)%
Receivables:				
Trade	58,441	47,901	10,540	22.0
Other	219	228	(9)	(4.0)
	58,660	48,129	10,531	21.9
Less Allowance for Doubtful Accounts	1,208	1,344	(136)	(10.1)
	57,452	46,785	10,667	22.8
Inventories	116,497	108,036	8,461	7.8
Other	7,275	3,944	3,331	84.5
Total Current Assets	185,115	162,714	22,401	13.8
Property, Plant, and Equipment (net)	197,379	198,040	(661)	(0.3)
Excess Cost of Investment Over Net Assets Acquired (net)	15,807	16,369	(562)	(3.4)
Other Assets	9,968	16,008	(6,040)	(37.7)
Total Assets	$408,269	$393,131	$15,138	3.9%

(Dollars in thousands)

Liabilities and Stockholders' Equity	1993	1992	Increase (Decrease) 1993 over 1992 Amount	Percent
Current Liabilities:				
Notes Payable	$ —	$ 15,000	$(15,000)	(100.0)%
Current Portion of Long-Term Debt	5,085	5,229	(144)	(2.8)
Accounts Payable	31,555	30,125	1,430	4.8
Accrued Liabilities	33,198	19,001	14,197	74.7
Deferred Income Taxes	13,386	13,185	201	1.5
Total Current Liabilities	83,224	82,540	684	0.8
Long-Term Obligations	88,985	125,695	(36,710)	(29.2)
Deferred Income Taxes and Deferred Gain	62,158	50,566	11,592	22.9
Commitments and Contingencies				
Stockholders' equity:				
Common Stock:				
Class A, $.01 par value	86	64	22	34.4
Class B, $.01 par value	85	85	—	—
Additional Capital	87,638	62,478	25,160	40.3
Retained earnings	97,727	83,528	14,199	17.0
	185,536	146,155	39,381	26.9
Treasury Stock, at Cost	(11,634)	(11,825)	(191)	(1.6)
Total Stockholders' Equity	173,902	134,330	39,572	29.5
Total Liabilities and Stockholders' Equity	$408,269	$393,131	$15,138	3.9%

Exhibit 21-4 reveals that the company's current assets and current liabilities rose slightly in 1993. Long-term liabilities were reduced by almost 30%, and stockholders' equity increased. The reduction in debt and the increase in the Common Stock and Additional Capital accounts were primarily the result of the conversion of bonds into stock. This information is obtained from the footnotes in the company's annual report and is not readily apparent in looking solely at the financial statements.

The largest percentage increase in assets was for "other current assets" (84.5%), and its absolute dollar amount is over $3,000,000. A user must always remember that percentage changes should be viewed from the perspective of the item's relative importance to the company's financial statements taken as a whole. Other current assets are only $7,275,000 (1.77% of total assets). On the other hand, property, plant, and equipment decreased by 0.3% (with a dollar amount decrease of $661,000), but these are the company's most significant assets (48.3% of total assets), because they are used in producing the products the company sells.

Trend Analysis

Trend analysis is a form of horizontal analysis that uses comparative financial statements for more than two successive periods. A user selects a base year and compares other years with it. Trend analysis of financial statements over several time periods is useful for two reasons. First, the analysis discloses changes occurring over time. Second, it provides information as to the direction in which a company is moving. Trends are important, because although comparing just one year with another highlights unusual differences, these differences might not indicate a pattern. Users of financial statements are generally interested in an increasing or decreasing trend in sales, gross profit, and net income.

Exhibit 21-5 is a five-year summary of selected financial data from the annual report of Ace Hardware Corporation.

EXHIBIT 21-5 FIVE-YEAR SUMMARY OF SELECTED FINANCIAL DATA—ACE HARDWARE CORPORATION

For the Years Ended December 31,	1992	1991	1990	1989	1988
Net Sales	$1,870,625	$1,704,203	$1,625,029	$1,546,450	$1,382,042
Cost of Sales	1,723,017	1,569,871	1,497,147	1,426,322	1,270,784
Gross Profit	147,608	134,332	127,882	120,128	111,258
Expenses:					
Warehouse and distribution	32,291	28,981	26,796	26,647	22,865
Selling, general and administrative	48,451	44,438	41,260	37,032	35,632
Interest	8,380	7,010	7,822	7,831	5,471
Other income, net	(2,281)	(5,254)	(8,408)	(1,954)	(1,174)
Total expenses	86,841	75,175	67,470	69,556	62,794
Net earnings before cumulative effect of accounting change	$ 60,767	$ 59,157	$ 60,412	$ 50,572	$ 48,464
Cumulative effect of change in method of accounting for inventory costs	—	—	—	—	5,669
Net earnings	$ 60,767	$ 59,157	$ 60,412	$ 50,572	$ 54,133

We can compute trend percentages for the data in Exhibit 21-5 by using 1988 as the base year. Trend percentages for the years 1988 through 1992 follow.

	1992	1991	1990	1989	1988
Net sales	135%	123%	118%	112%	100%
Cost of sales	136	124	118	112	100
Gross profit	133	121	115	108	100
Expenses:					
Warehouse and distribution	141	127	117	117	100
Selling, general and administrative	136	125	116	104	100
Interest	153	128	143	143	100
Other income, net	194	448	716	166	100
Total expenses	138	120	107	111	100
Net earnings before cumulative					
effect of accounting change	125	122	125	104	100
Cumulative effect of change in					
method of accounting for					
inventory costs	—	—	—	—	100
Net earnings	112	109	112	93	100

Net sales have increased steadily from 1988. After declining in 1989, net income (net earnings) has also solidly risen. The company is growing, with net sales and net income increasing by 35% and 12%, respectively, over the five-year period. This is good news for Ace's stockholders.

Trend analysis is not limited to only income statement items, but can be used for any item in the financial statements. Keep in mind that although a percentage change in an item might appear important, the change should be viewed in terms of absolute dollars, as well as in the context of its relationship to other items in the financial statements.

Vertical Analysis

Vertical analysis focuses on the financial relationships in a single period's financial statements rather than on the dollar and percentage changes in the financial statement items over time (as with horizontal analysis). Interestingly, Tandy Company and Subsidiaries presents a vertical analysis of its income statement in its annual report, as illustrated in Exhibit 21-6.

EXHIBIT 21-6   VERTICAL ANALYSIS OF THE INCOME STATEMENT—TANDY COMPANY AND SUBSIDIARIES

	Year Ended June 30,					
	1992		1991		1990	
n thousands, except per share amounts.	Dollars	% of Revenues	Dollars	% of Revenues	Dollars	% of Revenues
Net sales and operating revenues	$4,680,156	100.0%	$4,561,782	100.0%	$4,499,604	100.0%
Cost of products sold	2,701,969	57.7	2,519,309	55.2	2,380,224	52.9
Gross profit	1,978,187	42.3	2,042,473	44.8	2,119,380	47.1
Expenses:						
Selling, general and administrative	1,586,049	33.9	1,615,103	35.4	1,547,387	34.4
Depreciation and amortization	103,281	2.2	99,698	2.2	92,115	2.0
Net interest (income) expense	(11,138)	(.2)	(11,218)	(.2)	5,939	.1
	1,678,192	35.9	1,703,583	37.4	1,645,441	36.5
Income before income taxes	299,995	6.4	338,890	7.4	473,939	10.6
Provision for income taxes	116,148	2.5	132,827	2.9	183,592	4.1
Income before cumulative effect of change in accounting principle	183,847	3.9	206,063	4.5	290,347	6.5
Cumulative effect on prior years of change in accounting principle, net of taxes	—	—	(10,619)	(.2)	—	—
Net income	$ 183,847	3.9%	$ 195,444	4.3%	$ 290,347	6.5%
Net income per average common and common equivalent share:						
Income before cumulative effect of change in accounting principle	$2.24		$2.58		$3.54	
Cumulative effect on prior years of change in accounting principle, net of taxes	—		(.14)		—	
Net income per average common and common equivalent share	$2.24		$2.44		$3.54	
Average common and common equivalent shares outstanding	79,893		78,258		81,943	

The accompanying notes are an integral part of these financial statements.

Exhibit 21-7 illustrates a vertical analysis of Hudson Foods, Inc. and Subsidiaries' income statements for 1993 and 1992. Each of the percentages beside the income statement amounts are calculated by dividing those amounts by the net sales figure for that year. Vertical analysis of the income statement presents each item on the income statement as a percentage of net sales; this results in all the items summing to 100%. The percentage of each financial statement item denotes the relative significance of that item in the determination of net income.

Vertical analysis of the 1992 and 1993 comparative income statements illustrated in Exhibit 21-7 indicates that Hudson's gross profit increased substantially in 1993. Hudson's gross profit for 1992 and 1993 is $77,038,000 ($809,243,000 − $732,205,000) and $119,367,000 ($920,545,000 − $801,178,000), respectively. Gross profit as a percentage of sales for 1992 and 1993 is 9.5% and 13.0%. The increase in net income was accomplished by the increase in sales and partly by reducing operating expenses from 99.0% of sales to 96.2%. You can also see that Hudson's net income as a percentage of sales is significantly higher in 1993 than 1992.

Sometimes users examine the percentage of certain expense amounts to sales to compare the company with a benchmark, such as the average values for an industry. These benchmarks are usually found in industry trade association publications. Company managers find this type of comparison especially useful in assessing the performance of competitors.

EXHIBIT 21-7 COMPARATIVE CONSOLIDATED STATEMENTS OF OPERATIONS— HUDSON FOODS, INC. AND SUBSIDIARIES

For the Years Ended October 3, 1992 and October 2, 1993

(Dollars in thousands)	1993	1992	1993 Percent	1992 Percent
Sales	$920,545	$809,243	100.0%	100.0%
Costs and Expenses:				
Cost of Sales	801,178	732,205	87.0	90.5
Selling	63,926	49,907	6.9	6.2
General and Administrative	20,695	18,533	2.3	2.3
Total Costs and Expenses	885,799	800,645	96.2	99.0
Operating Income	34,746	8,598	3.8	1.0
Other Expense (Income)				
Interest Expense	7,975	8,476	0.9	1.0
Other, Net	530	(4,342)	0.1	(0.5)
Total Other Expense	8,505	4,134	1.0	0.5
Income Before Income Taxes	26,241	4,464	2.8	0.5
Income tax expense	10,336	2,294	1.1	0.3
Net income	$ 15,905	2,170	1.7%	0.2%

(Dollars in thousands)

Assets	1993	1992	1993 Percent	1992 Percent
Current Assets:				
Cash and Cash Equivalents	$ 3,891	$ 3,949	1.0%	1.0%
Receivables:				
Trade	58,441	47,901	14.3	12.2
Other	219	228	0.1	0.1
	58,660	48,129	14.4	12.3
Less Allowance for				
Doubtful Accounts	1,208	1,344	0.3	0.3
	57,452	46,785	14.1	12.0
Inventories	116,497	108,036	28.5	27.5
Other	7,275	3,944	1.8	1.0
Total Current Assets	185,115	162,714	45.4	41.5
Property, Plant, and Equipment (net)	197,379	198,040	48.3	50.4
Excess Cost of Investment Over				
Net Assets Acquired (net)	15,807	16,369	3.9	4.1
Other Assets	9,968	16,008	2.4	4.0
Total Assets	$408,269	$393,131	100.0%	100.0%

(Dollars in thousands)

Liabilities and Stockholders' Equity	1993	1992	1993 Percent	1992 Percent
Current Liabilities:				
Notes Payable	$ —	$ 15,000	—	3.8%
Current Portion of				
Long-Term Debt	5,085	5,229	1.3	1.3
Accounts Payable	31,555	30,125	7.7	7.7
Accrued Liabilities	33,198	19,001	8.1	4.8
Deferred Income Taxes	13,386	13,185	3.3	3.4
Total Current Liabilities	83,224	82,540	20.4	21.0
Long-Term Obligations	88,985	125,695	21.8	32.0
Deferred Income Taxes and				
Deferred Gain	62,158	50,566.	15.2	12.8
Commitments and Contigencies				
Stockholders' equity:				
Commom stock:				
Class A, $.01 par value	86	64	—	—
Class B, $.01 par value	85	85	—	—
Additional Capital	87,638	62,478	21.5	15.9
Retained earnings	97,727	83,528	23.9	21.3
	185,536	146,155	45.4	37.2
Treasury Stock, at Cost	(11,634)	(11,825)	(2.8)	(3.0)
Total Stockholders' Equity	173,902	134,330	42.6	34.2
Total Liabilities & Stockholders' Equity	$408,269	$393,131	100.0%	100.0%

Exhibit 21-8 presents the 1992 and 1993 comparative balance sheets of Hudson Foods, Inc. and Subsidiaries. Each item is expressed as a percentage of total assets or total liabilities and stockholders' equity. You can see that current assets are a larger percentage of total assets in 1993 than in 1992. Hudson also had a smaller percentage of total liabilities to stockholders' equity in 1993 than in 1992. Together, these changes indicate that the company is slightly more liquid in 1993 than in 1992. In addition, the company reduced its percentage of short-term notes payable in 19X1. The footnotes to the financial statements tell us that the increase in accrued liabilities was due primarily to increased selling, insurance, income tax, and bonus expense accruals. Total stockholders' equity increased from 34.2% of total liabilities and stockholders' equity to 42.6%. The footnotes also indicate that this was caused by the issuance of additional common stock from the conversion of long-term debt, issuance of stock under an employee stock purchase plan, and the exercise of stock options. The increase in retained earnings is due to an excess of net income over dividends paid.

A type of vertical analysis presents financial statements that contain only percentages. Each component of a financial statement is shown as a percentage. The method presents every item in the statement as a percentage of the largest item in the statement. These types of statements are called *common-size financial statements*. Common-size financial statements differ from statements prepared under vertical analysis in that they present only percentages, not dollar amounts. All figures on a common-size balance sheet are percentages of total assets or total liabilities and stockholders' equity. Similarly, on a common-size income statement, the items are percentages of net sales. We refer to this type of presentation as "common-size" because the items always add up to 100%.

Common-size statements give the user a better understanding of the relationship between a particular item and sales (on the income statement), or between an item and total assets or total liabilities and stockholders' equity (on the balance sheet) than that achieved by merely looking at absolute dollar amounts. These statements can be compared with industry averages to assess a company's standing in its industry. Common-size financial statements allow comparisons to be made among companies of different sizes. For example, General Motors Corporation is much larger than Chrysler Corporation, making valid comparisons difficult. However, the financial statements of each company could be modified to common-size to facilitate the comparative analysis. Changes in the relative size of the components of the financial statements now become apparent. These changes might be missed by a user if only the absolute dollar amounts are examined. For example, a company's sales might increase from one period to the next, a positive signal. However, a user might not notice that the company's gross margin decreased or that its selling, general, and administrative expenses increased as a percentage of sales. Common-size financial statements reveal both of these types of changes.

Exhibit 21-9 displays consolidated income statements for three years for AMP Incorporated and Subsidiaries. In Exhibit 21-10 we have converted those income statements into a common-size income statement format.

EXHIBIT 21-9 CONSOLIDATED INCOME STATEMENTS FOR AMP INCORPORATED AND SUBSIDIARIES

(dollars in thousands except per share data)	Year Ended December 31,		
	1992	1991	1990
Net Sales	$3,337,145	$3,094,951	$3,043,589
Cost of Sales	2,218,898	2,069,526	2,012,394
Gross income	1,118,247	1,025,425	1,031,195
Selling, General and Administrative Expenses	584,913	555,662	543,437
Income from operations	533,334	469,763	487,758
Interest Expense	(29,489)	(41,561)	(38,321)
Other Income (Deductions), net	(24,737)	(4,608)	12,575
Income before income taxes	479,108	423,594	462,012
Income Taxes	188,770	163,850	174,900
Net Income	$ 290,338	$ 259,744	$ 287,112
Net Income Per Share	$2.75	$2.45	$2.70

**EXHIBIT 21-10   COMMON-SIZE INCOME STATEMENTS—
AMP INCORPORATED AND SUBSIDIARIES**

	Year Ended December 31,		
	1992	1991	1990
Net Sales	100.0%	100.0%	100.0%
Cost of Sales	66.5	66.9	66.1
Gross income	33.5	33.1	33.9
Selling, General and Administrative Expenses	17.5	18.0	17.9
Income from operations	16.0	15.1	16.0
Interest Expense	(0.9)	(1.3)	(1.3)
Other Income (Deductions), net	(0.7)	(0.1)	(0.4)
Income before income taxes	14.4	13.7	15.1
Income Taxes	5.7	5.3	5.7
Net Income	8.7%	8.4%	9.4%

22

RATIO ANALYSIS

What is a ratio? A ratio is a measure of relative size and is calculated by dividing one number by another. A ratio might be 4 divided by 3 resulting in 1.33. Ratios attempt to provide information about the two quantities used to generate the ratio.

Ratios in and of themselves have little information value unless they are compared with norms, such as average ratios for the industry in which a company operates or values for the same company in previous years. Users of financial statements often compare a company's ratios with benchmarks or norms. There are four areas of interest to investors: liquidity, activity, solvency, and profitability. These areas form the basis for categorizing ratios. *Liquidity* relates to the ability to meet short-term liabilities, and *activity* refers to how efficiently a company is using its assets. *Solvency* refers to a company's ability to meet its long-term obligations, and *profitability* is the company's capacity to generate profits.

Computing ratios is only a starting point in analyzing a company. Ratios do not give answers, but they do provide clues as to what might be expected. Moreover, ratios often give conflicting signals. For instance, one might presume that the more cash a company has, the better it is able to pay its debts. But accumulating a lot of cash is not necessarily a good strategy, because idle cash earns little or no return. The company might have higher net income if it instead invested the cash. This type of inconsistency is pervasive throughout financial statement analysis.

Financial statement users make various types of financial decisions. Creditors whose loans are of relatively short duration (less than six months, or perhaps a year) care about the company's current condition and near-term prospects. Banks and vendors are examples of such creditors. They want to know whether the company will be able to pay its obligations in the near future. Mutual funds and individual investors buy bonds. These investors, who make relatively long-term commitments, are much more concerned with the company's long-term solvency than with its short-term perspective. Long-term creditors, such as bondholders, are interested in financial strength and the likelihood of future earnings, and consequently their analysis is normally more difficult than that of the short-term investor.

Stockholders are concerned with profitability, earnings, dividends, and increases in the market price of a company's shares, as well as with liquidity and solvency. This is because a company may pay its short-term obligations, repay its bonds and other long-term loans, and still not earn enough to justify the purchase of its common stock.

Illustrative Financial Statements of Nike, Inc.

Consider the comparative financial statements and additional information about Nike, Inc. for 1993 and 1992, as shown in Exhibits 22-1, 22-2, 22-3, 22-4, and 22-5. All amounts shown in the financial statements and in the textual material are in thousands.

EXHIBIT 22-1   INCOME STATEMENT—NIKE, INC.

(in thousands, except per share data)

Year Ended May 31,	1993	1992	1991
Revenues	$3,930,984	$3,405,211	3,003,610
Costs and expenses:			
Cost of sales	2,386,993	2,089,089	1,850,530
Selling and administrative	922,261	761,498	664,061
Interest (Notes 3, 4 and 5)	25,739	30,665	27,316
Other expense (income) (Notes 9 and 10)	1,475	2,141	(43)
	3,336,468	2,883,393	2,541,864
Income before income taxes	594,516	521,818	461,746
Income taxes (Note 6)	229,500	192,600	174,700
Net income	$ 365,016	$ 329,218	$ 287,046
Net income per common share (Note I)	$ 4.74	$ 4.30	$ 3.77
Average number of common and common equivalent shares (Note 1)	77,063	76,602	77,067

The accompanying notes to consolidated financial statements are an integral part of this statement.

EXHIBIT 22-2   BALANCE SHEET—NIKE, INC.

(in thousands) May 31,	1993	1992
Assets		
Current Assets:		
Cash and equivalents	$ 291,284	$ 260,050
Accounts receivable, less allowance for doubtful accounts of $19,447 and $20,046	667,547	596,018
Inventories (Note 2)	592,986	471,202
Deferred income taxes (Note 6)	26,378	27,511
Prepaid expenses	42,452	32,977
Total current assets	1,620,647	1,387,758
Property, plant and equipment (Notes 3 and 5)	571,032	497,795
Less accumulated depreciation	193,037	151,758
	377,995	346,037
Goodwill (Note 1)	157,894	110,363
Other assets	30,927	28,703
	$2,187,463	$1,872,861

(in thousands) May 31,	1993	1992
Liabilities and Shareholders' Equity		
Current Liabilities:		
Current portion of long-term debt (Note 5)	$ 52,985	$ 3,652
Notes payable (Note 4)	108,165	105,696
Accounts payable (Note 4)	135,701	134,729
Accrued liabilities	138,563	134,089
Income taxes payable	17,150	42,422
Total current liabilities	452,564	420,588
Long-term debt (Notes 5 and 12)	15,033	69,476
Non-current deferred income taxes (Note 6)	29,965	27,074
Other non-current liabilities (Note 1)	43,575	23,728
Commitments and contingencies (Note 11)	—	—
Redeemable Preferred Stock (Note 7)	300	300
Shareholders' equity (Note 8):		
Common Stock at stated value:		
Class A convertible—26,691 and 26,919 shares outstanding	159	161
Class B—49,161 and 48,591 shares outstanding	2,720	2,716
Capital in excess of stated value	108,451	93,799
Foreign currency translation adjustment	(7,790)	686
Retained earnings	1,542,486	1,234,333
	1,646,026	1,331,695
	$2,187,463	$1,872,861

The accompanying notes to consolidated financial statements are an integral part of this statement.

EXHIBIT 22-3 STATEMENT OF CASH FLOWS—NIKE, INC.

(in thousands) Year Ended May 31,	1993	1992	1991
Cash provided (used) by operations:			
Net income	$ 365,016	$ 329,218	$ 287,046
Income charges (credits) not affecting cash:			
Depreciation	60,393	47,665	34,473
Deferred income taxes and purchased tax benefits	4,310	8,222	(2,668)
Other non-current liabilities	19,847	9,992	4,769
Other, including amortization	12,951	9,355	5,626
Changes in certain working capital components:			
(Increase) decrease in inventory	(97,471)	115,392	(274,966)
Increase in accounts receivable	(62,538)	(74,430)	(119,958)
Increase in other current assets	(5,133)	(6,239)	(6,261)
(Decrease) increase in accounts payable, accrued liabilities and income taxes payable	(32,083)	(3,337)	83,061
Cash provided by operations	265,292	435,838	11,122
Cash provided (used) by investing activities:			
Additions to property, plant and equipment	(97,041)	(106,492)	(164,843)
Disposals of property, plant and equipment	5,006	4,065	1,730
Acquisition of subsidiaries:			
Goodwill	(52,003)	—	(31,482)
Net assets acquired	(25,858)	—	(6,081)
Additions to other non-current assets	(3,036)	(7,494)	(10,511)
Cash used by investing activities	(172,932)	(109,921)	(211,187)

(in thousands) Year Ended May 31,	1993	1992	1991
Cash provided (used) by financing activities:			
Additions to long-term debt	1,536	45,901	5,149
Reductions in long-term debt including current portion	(5,817)	(3,467)	(9,974)
(Decrease) increase in notes payable	(2,017)	(194,668)	269,262
Proceeds from exercise of options	7,055	4,159	3,211
Dividends—common and preferred	(53,017)	(43,760)	(36,070)
Cash (used) provided by financing activities	(52,260)	(191,835)	231,578
Effect of exchange rate changes on cash	(8,866)	6,164	(2,158)
Net increase in cash and equivalents	31,234	140,246	29,355
Cash and equivalents, beginning of year	260,050	119,804	90,449
Cash and equivalents, end of year	$291,284	$ 260,050	$ 119,804
Supplemental disclosure of cash flow information:			
Cash paid during the year for:			
Interest (net of amount capitalized)	$ 20,800	$ 29,200	$ 27,200
Income taxes	235,200	184,100	159,900

The accompanying notes to consolidated financial statements are an integral part of this statement.

EXHIBIT 22-4 STATEMENT OF STOCKHOLDERS' EQUITY—NIKE, INC.

(in thousands)	Common Stock				Capital In Excess of Stated Value	Foreign Currency Translation Adjustment	Retained Earnings	Total
	Class A		Class B					
	Shares	Amount	Shares	Amount				
Balance at May 31, 1990	14,051	$168	23,435	$2,706	$78,582	$ 1,035	$ 701,728	$ 784,219
Stock options exercised			276	2	6,099			6,101
Conversion to Class B Common Stock	(393)	(4)	393	4				—
Two-for-one Stock Split October 5, 1990	13,780	—	23,754	—				—
Translation of statements of foreign operations						(5,463)		(5,463)
Net income							287,046	287,046
Dividends on Redeemable Preferred Stock							(30)	(30)
Dividends on Common Stock							(39,084)	(39,084)
Balance at May 31, 1991	27,438	164	47,858	2,712	84,681	(4,428)	949,660	1,032,789
Stock options exercised			214	1	9,118			9,119
Conversion to Class B Common Stock	(519)	(3)	519	3				—
Translation of statements of foreign operations						5,114		5,114
Net income							329,218	329,218
Dividends on Redeemable Preferred Stock							(30)	(30)
Dividends on Common Stock							(44,515)	(44,515)
Balance at May 31, 1992	26,919	161	48,591	2,716	93,799	686	1,234,333	1,331,695
Stock options exercised			342	2	14,652			14,654
Conversion to Class B Common Stock	(228)	(2)	228	2				—
Translation of statements of foreign operations						(8,476)		(8,476)
Net income							365,016	365,016
Dividends on Redeemable Preferred Stock							(30)	(30)
Dividends on Common Stock							(56,833)	(56,833)
Balance at May 31, 1993	26,691	$159	49,161	$2,720	$108,451	$ (7,790)	$1,542,486	$1,646,026

The accompanying notes to consolidated financial statements are an integral part of this statement.

EXHIBIT 22-5 FINANCIAL HIGHLIGHTS—NIKE, INC.

(in thousands, except per share data)

	1993	1992	% Change
Year Ended May 31:			
Revenues	$3,930,984	$3,405,211	15.4%
Gross profit	1,543,991	1,316,122	17.3
Gross profit %	39.3%	38.-%	
Net income	365,016	329,218	10.9
Net income per common share	4.74	4.30	10.2
Return on equity	24.5%	27.8%	
Stock price at May 31	72½	58	25.0

Selected Quarterly Financial Data (unaudited)

(in thousands, except per share data)

	1st Quarter		2nd Quarter		3rd Quarter		4th Quarter	
	1993	1992	1993	1992	1993	1992	1993	1992
Revenues	$1,099,862	$947,161	$875,839	$743,417	972,004	$867,019	$983,279	$847,614
Gross profit	433,199	366,575	346,235	287,979	375,981	334,446	388,576	327,122
Gross profit %	39.4%	38.7%	39.5%	38.7%	38.7%	38.6%	39.5%	38.6%
Net income	122,593	114,437	76,045	61,535	89,471	82,517	76,907	70,729
Net income per common share	1.60	1.50	.98	.80	1.16	1.08	1.00	.92
Dividends declared per common share	.15	.14	.20	.15	.20	.15	.20	.15
Price range of common stock								
High	73¼	50	90¼	62½	90	77⅜	79½	74⅞
Low	55	35⅛	71⅝	47⅜	64½	57¼	67¾	56¾

Liquidity Ratios

High liquidity is evidenced by a high amount of current assets relative to the amount of current liabilities, and by a high proportion of current assets in cash and receivables, as opposed to inventory or prepaid expenses. Liquidity ratios measure the relative sizes of these components.

Working Capital

Working capital is the difference between current assets and current liabilities and provides a crude measure of liquidity. Nike, Inc. had the following amounts of working capital at the ends of 1993 and 1992.

	1993	1992
Current assets	$1,620,647	$1,387,758
Current liabilities	452,564	420,588
Working capital	$1,168,083	$ 967,170

An increase in working capital is not always a sign of increased liquidity, because working capital is a dollar amount, not a ratio. Amounts by themselves can be difficult to evaluate.

Two better measures of liquidity include the current and quick ratios. The use of different inventory cost flow methods (such as FIFO or LIFO), resulting in different inventory amounts on the balance sheet, make company comparisons of working capital and liquidity difficult.

Current Ratio

The current ratio, current assets divided by current liabilities, is probably the most basic liquidity ratio. Because it is a ratio, and not an amount, it can be used to compare companies of different sizes or the same company at different balance sheet dates.

Nike's current ratios are:

$$1993: \frac{\$1,620,647}{\$452,564} = 3.58 \qquad 1992: \frac{\$1,387,758}{\$420,588} = 3.30$$

We can say that, on the basis of the current ratio, Nike appears to be more liquid at the end of 1993. However, a major problem with the current ratio (and other ratios), is one of *composition*. That is, the use of a total, such as total current assets (or current liabilities) might mask information about individual components of the ratio. A user must look at the balance sheet to see the extent to which current assets are composed of relatively liquid items, such as cash and receivables. In addition, the current ratio does not provide any information regarding how quickly current assets will be converted into cash and liabilities paid.

What should the current ratio be? Some analysts use a rule of thumb of 2.0 to 1; however, there is no definite answer. The ratio needs to be interpreted with respect to an industry norm or as part of a trend. In addition, the ratio should be evaluated in terms of its components.

Quick Ratio (Acid–Test Ratio)

The quick ratio, or acid-test ratio, is quick assets divided by current liabilities. Quick assets are cash, temporary investments, and accounts receivable. The quick ratio is a stricter test of liquidity (the "acid test") than the current ratio because it indicates whether a company could extinguish its current liabilities if they came due within a fairly short period of time.

$$\text{Quick Ratio} = \frac{\text{Cash} + \text{Temporary Investments} + \text{Receivables}}{\text{Current Liabilities}}$$

Nike's quick ratios are as follows.

$$1993: \quad \frac{\$291,284 + \$667,547}{\$452,546} = 2.12$$

$$1992: \quad \frac{\$260,050 + \$596,018}{\$420,588} = 2.04$$

Nike's liquidity seems to have increased slightly, because its quick ratio increased. We could say that the company is in a better position to meet current liabilities at the end of 1993 because the ratio of its most liquid assets to its current liabilities increased. In examining the balance sheet of Nike, Inc. for 1993 and 1992 (Exhibit 22-2), we can see that the cause of the increase in the ratio is that accounts receivable and cash increased by a greater amount than the increase in current liabilities.

Current Asset Activity Ratios

The next two ratios tell us about how quickly receivables and inventory will be turned into cash. Neither the current ratio nor the quick ratio provide this type of information, but instead focus on the coverage of current liabilities. Activity ratios are called turnover ratios and generally take the following form:

$$\text{Activity Ratio} = \frac{\text{Best Measure of Asset Activity}}{\text{Asset}}$$

Accounts Receivable Turnover and Days' Sales in Accounts Receivable

Accounts receivable turnover measures how rapidly receivables are collected, or turned over. The ratio is sales divided by average net accounts receivable.

$$\frac{\text{Accounts Receivable}}{\text{Turnover}} = \frac{\text{Net Sales}}{\text{Average Net Accounts Receivables}}$$

The numerator should be net *credit* sales, because cash sales do not generate accounts receivable; in most cases the user does not know credit sales and must use net sales. Average net accounts receivable is normally the beginning balance of accounts receivable plus the ending balance, divided by 2. Some users employ the end-of-year figure, instead of the average. A user must be careful in the use of either averages or year-end balances because those amounts might not be representative of the year, leading to erroneous conclusions.

The ratio shows the number of times during the year that the average accounts receivable balance was converted into cash. Normally, the higher the turnover is, the better, because receivables are being collected rapidly. This reduces the amount of sales dollars tied up in accounts receivable and creates more cash that is available for other purposes. However, a high turnover ratio might also indicate that the company's credit policies are too stringent, resulting in lost sales and reduced profitability. The accounts receivable turnover ratio for Nike, Inc. for 1993 follows.

$$\frac{\$3,930,984}{(\$667,457 + \$596,018)/2} = 6.22$$

The numerator is the revenues figure from the income statement, and the denominator is the accounts receivable figures from the balance sheets in Exhibit 22-2.

Another related ratio is called *days' sales in accounts receivable*. It is used to assess the efficiency of accounts receivable management. This figure represents the average age of ending accounts receivable and is calculated as follows.

$$\text{Days' Sales in Accounts Receivable} = \frac{\text{Ending Accounts Receivable}}{\text{Average Daily Sales}}$$

Average daily sales is the annual net credit sales divided by 365. (Net sales are normally used because net credit sales are unavailable.) This ratio also has the same problem as the accounts receivable turnover ratio, in that the ending balance may not be representative of the year.

Nike has average daily sales of $10,770 ($3,930,984/365) for 1993 and $9,329 ($3,405,211/365) for 1992. Hence, days' sales in accounts receivable are:

1993: $\dfrac{\$667,547}{\$10,770} = 62$ days   1992: $\dfrac{\$596,018}{\$9,329} = 64$ days

On average, Nike's accounts receivable were 64 days old at the end of 1992 and 62 days old at the end of 1993. The collection period has decreased in one year, perhaps because of a loosening of credit policies. It is more important to consider the trend in the number of days' sales in accounts receivable than simply to look at any single number.

As a general rule, the faster customers pay, the better. But a company always must consider the fact that there are trade-offs. If the company loses sales because of tight credit policies, the advantage of faster collection might be more than offset by the loss of profits because of lower total sales.

Inventory Turnover and Days' Sales in Inventory

Inventory turnover is extremely important, because the faster the inventory is sold, the quicker the company turns its investment in inventory into cash. Inventory turnover is calculated as follows:

$$\text{Inventory Turnover} = \frac{\text{Cost of Goods Sold}}{\text{Average Inventory}}$$

Again, average inventory is usually the beginning balance plus the ending balance divided by 2; the year-end balance could instead be used. The problem of representativeness applies here, as with accounts receivable.

Because investment in inventory is expensive, inventory turnover is important. The costs of holding inventory include personal property taxes, insurance, pilferage, obsolescence, and, probably most important, interest on the funds tied up in inventory. These costs must be balanced against the costs of a stockout. Generally, the higher the turnover, the better, although high turnover can also mean that the company is experiencing stockouts by not maintaining enough inventory. Therefore, a company seeks to maintain a turnover that balances carrying costs and stockouts. This trade-off results in the most profitable turnover rate, not necessarily the highest rate.

Nike's inventory turnover for 1993 is about 4.5 times, calculated as follows.

$$\frac{\$2,386,993}{(\$592,986 + \$471,202)/2} = 4.5$$

Inventory turnover is a critical measure for businesses such as food stores. Foods stores have low profit margins and need rapid turnover to earn satisfactory returns. On the other hand, companies that have high profit margins, such as automobile dealers, can be profitable with lower turnover ratios.

Like accounts receivable turnover, inventory turnover has a counterpart, *days' sales in inventory*, calculated as follows.

$$\text{Days' Sales in Inventory} = \frac{\text{Ending Inventory}}{\text{Average Daily Cost of Goods Sold}}$$

Average daily cost of goods sold is simply cost of goods sold for the year divided by 365. For Nike this figure is $6,540 ($2,386,993/365) for 1993 and $5,724 ($2,089,089/365) for 1992. The days' sales in inventory are:

$$1993: \quad \frac{\$592,986}{\$6,540} = 90.7 \text{ days}$$

$$1992: \quad \frac{\$471,202}{\$5,724} = 82.3 \text{ days}$$

The increase in days' sales in inventory could indicate a change in inventory policy, or just a temporary increase in inventory because of purchases made near the end of the year. Inventory turnover rates vary widely and are related to a company's profit margin. Because of this, the user should compare the rate to industry norms and also observe the trend of the ratio over time.

Profitability Ratios

The income statement has at least three important ratios relating to profitability. One is the *gross profit ratio*, gross profit divided by net sales; the second is the *operating ratio*, income before interest and taxes and other income (or expense) divided by net sales*; and the third is *return on sales* (ROS), net income divided by net sales. These ratios for Nike, Inc. in 1993 are 39.3%, 15.8%, and 9.3%, respectively. The gross profit ratio increased slightly in 1993 over 1991, but ROS and the operating ratio declined.

Income statement ratios are principally concerned with profitability but can also provide hints as to operating efficiency. Operating efficiency tells the user how well the company's managers were able to turn each dollar of sales into gross profit, operating profit, and net income.

Other profitability measures use information from the income statement and the balance sheet. Most common measures of profitability relate to return on investment (ROI), a group of ratios having the general form:

$$\text{Return on Investment} = \frac{\text{Income}}{\text{Investment}}$$

Most measures relate an income statement item (such as net income) to a balance sheet item (such as stockholders' equity). Stockholders, as well as potential stockholders, are interested in their return on investment. Company managers are concerned with earning satisfactory returns on the investments they control. There are different forms of the ratio, because different users define income and investment in distinctive ways when measuring the same basic relationship.

---

*The operating ratio is sometimes defined as operating income divided by net sales. Operating income equals net income plus interest expense plus income tax expense plus other expense (or minus income). In the example, Nike, Inc. had 1993 net income of $365,016, interest expense of $25,739, income tax expense of $229,500, and other expense of $1,479. Therefore, its operating ratio for 1993 is calculated as follows.

$$\frac{\$365,016 + \$25,739 + \$229,500 + \$1,479}{\$3,930,984} = \frac{\$621,734}{\$3,930,984} = 15.8\%$$

Return on Assets

Return on assets (ROA) measures operating efficiency. It indicates how well a company has used the assets under its control to create income. The most common calculation of the ratio follows.

$$\text{Return on Assets} = \frac{\text{Income Before Interest, Taxes, and Other Income (Expense)}}{\text{Average Total Assets}}$$

For Nike, Inc. ROA was 30.6 for 1993, calculated as follows.

$$\frac{\$594,516 + \$25,739 + \$1,475}{(\$2,187,463 + \$1,872,861)/2} = \frac{\$621,730}{\$2,030,162} = 30.6\%$$

Notice that income before interest and income taxes and other income (expense) is the same as net income plus interest and income taxes and other income (expense) ($365,016 + $25,739 + $229,500 + $1,475) = $621,730. The ratio relates to operations. Interest and income taxes depend on how the company finances assets, so we exclude them. We adjust the numerator for other income (or expense) because these items do not directly relate to operations. Other variations are also used, such as adding back interest but not taxes. There are arguments to support several measures of the numerator and denominator in the ROA calculation, so the choice is one of personal preference.

The most common measure of average total assets is the sum of the beginning and ending balance sheet amounts divided by 2. Average total assets is used in the calculation, be-cause income, the numerator, is earned throughout the year. The balance of total assets at the end of the year is also sometimes used as the denominator.

Note that intercompany comparisons are hindered by the use of different inventory cost flow assumptions, depreciation methods, and asset service lives.

Return on Common Equity (ROE)

Common stockholders are concerned about the return on their investment. Return on investment depends on profitable operations, as well as on the amount of debt and preferred stock in the company's capital structure.

Return on common equity (ROE) is computed as follows.

$$\frac{\text{Return on}}{\text{Common Equity}} = \frac{\text{Net Income} - \text{Preferred Dividends}}{\text{Average Common Stockholders' Equity}}$$

For a company without preferred stock, average common stockholders' equity is the sum of the beginning and ending amounts of total stockholders' equity divided by 2. If the company has preferred stock, preferred dividends must be subtracted from net income in the numerator. The equity attributable to preferred stock must also be subtracted from total stockholders' equity in the denominator. The denominator in the following equation does not include Nike's preferred stock. Nike's preferred dividends are also excluded from the numerator. ROE for Nike, Inc. in 1993 is almost 25%.

$$\frac{\$365,016 - \$30}{(\$1,646,026 + \$1,331,695)/2} = 24.5\%$$

Creditors receive a fixed amount of interest. Companies can therefore increase ROE by using debt, provided that ROA is greater than the interest rate it pays to creditors. Using debt (or preferred stock) to increase ROE is called *leverage* or *trading on the equity*. Leverage increases risk as it provides the potential for greater return.

Earnings per Share and the Growth Rate of EPS

Earnings per share (EPS) is the most widely reported statistic in the financial press and in recommendations by investment services. In the absence of complicating factors, EPS is calculated as follows.

$$\text{Earnings per Share} =$$

$$\frac{\text{Net Income Available for Common Stockholders}}{\text{Weighted-Average Common Shares Outstanding}}$$

(Complicating factors relating to earnings per share are discussed in Chapter 15.) Notice that in computing EPS, the denominator is the weighted-average number of shares outstanding during the year, not the number of shares outstanding at year-end.) Preferred stock dividends are subtracted from net income to arrive at earnings available to the common stockholders, because preferred stockholders are paid dividends before common stockholders. The weighted-average is the best measure of the number of shares outstanding throughout the period. Adding shares of Class A and Class B common stock together, Exhibit 22-4 indicates that Nike, Inc. had 75,852 shares outstanding at the end of 1993 and 75,510 shares outstanding at the end of 1992. However, using weighted-average shares outstanding (as shown in Exhibit 22-1), Nike's EPS figures are

$$1993: \quad \frac{\$365,016 - \$30}{77,063 \text{ shares}} = \$4.74$$

$$1992: \quad \frac{\$329,218 - \$30}{76,602 \text{ shares}} = \$4.30$$

EPS in 1993 was $0.44 higher than in 1992, a 10% growth rate, calculated as follows:

$$\text{Growth Rate of EPS} = \frac{\text{EPS Current Year} - \text{EPS Prior Year}}{\text{EPS Prior Year}}$$

$$\frac{\$4.74 - \$4.30}{\$4.30} = 10.2\%$$

In general, the higher the company's EPS growth rate, the more the investing public will pay for the company's common stock. Like other ratios, growth rates should be viewed over a number of years, rather than for a single year, because to be significant, growth must be sustained.

Price-Earnings Ratio

The price-earnings (PE) ratio is the market price of a share of common stock divided by its EPS.

$$\text{Price-Earnings Ratio} = \frac{\text{Market Price per Share}}{\text{Earnings per Share}}$$

The PE ratio is a factor in an investor's decision to buy, hold, or sell shares of stock. PE ratios are reported in the financial press and represent the amount an investor pays for a dollar of earnings. That is, it is a common measure of how expensive stock prices are relative to corporate profits. High-growth companies usually have high PE ratios, whereas low-growth, stable, or declining companies have low ratios. In Exhibit 22-5, we see that Nike's common stock sold at $58.00 per share at the end of 1992 and $72.50 at the end of 1993. The PE ratios are as follows.

$$1992: \quad \frac{\$58.00}{\$4.30} = 13.5 \qquad 1993: \quad \frac{\$72.50}{\$4.74} = 15.3$$

The PE ratio increased from 1992 to 1993, indicating investors' willingness to pay more for each dollar of earnings. The increase could have occurred because the company's earnings prospects were more optimistic or because PE ratios in general increased because of investor sentiment regarding a better economic climate.

The return that common stockholders receive has two components, dividends and increases in share prices. If investor expectations are that earnings and dividends will increase, they generally are willing to pay more for that share of stock. The PE ratio incorporates both of these interrelated factors.

Dividend Yield and Payout Ratio

Investors benefit from dividends and increases in the market value of their shares of stock. The *dividend yield* measures the percentage of market value that is paid annually in dividends to stockholders.

$$\text{Dividend Yield} = \frac{\text{Dividend per Share}}{\text{Market Price per Share}}$$

Nike's annual report indicates that the company had dividends per share of $0.59 and $0.75 for 1992 and 1993, respectively (see Exhibit 22-5). With the share prices of $58.00 and $72.50 at the ends of 1992 and 1993, dividend yields are as follows.

$$1992: \quad \frac{\$.59}{\$58.00} = 1.02\% \qquad 1993: \quad \frac{\$.75}{\$72.50} = 1.03\%$$

Investors compare dividend yields to other investment options. Normally investors accept lower yields from companies that reinvest earnings, because they feel that reinvestment will lead to increased future earnings and dividends. Investors in growth companies are not seeking dividends as much as capital appreciation; that is, increases in the market price of their common stock. Dividend yields vary widely. Older, more established companies can have a dividend yield of 4% to 8%, whereas growth companies can have a dividend yield of 0% to 3%. Nike falls into this second group.

The *dividend payout ratio* is the ratio of dividends per share to earnings per share. For Nike, Inc. the payout ratio in 1993 was 16% ($0.75/$4.74) and in 1992 was 14% ($0.59/$4.30). Companies with high growth rates generally have relatively low dividend yields and payout ratios because they reinvest the cash that could be used to pay dividends.

Solvency Ratios

Solvency relates to a company's ability to pay its long-term liabilities. Stockholders and long-term creditors are both concerned with solvency. Long-term creditors are interested in receiving interest payments and repayment of the principal amount of debt. Stockholders are interested in solvency, because if the company cannot pay its long-term liabilities, it cannot pay dividends and its share price will not increase.

Debt Ratio

A very common measure of solvency is the *debt ratio*, which is computed as follows:

$$\text{Debt Ratio} = \frac{\text{Total Liabilities}}{\text{Total Assets}}$$

This ratio measures the percentage of debt in the capital structure. Like other ratios, it has several variations, including the debt-to-equity ratio.

$$\frac{\text{Total Liabilities}}{\text{Total Stockholders' Equity}}$$

Other users like the ratio of long-term liabilities to total assets or of long-term liabilities to fixed assets. All forms of the ratio attempt to measure the debt burden of a company to determine whether the company is too highly leveraged. In general, the higher the debt ratio, the riskier the company.

Nike's debt ratios for 1992 and 1993 are as follows.

$$1992: \ \frac{\$540,866}{\$1,872,861} = 29\% \qquad 1993: \ \frac{\$541,137}{\$2,187,463} = 25\%$$

The debt ratio decreased from 1992 to 1993. The result is a larger proportion of the assets being financed by the owners rather than by the creditors. This takes some of the pressure off Nike to pay principal and interest payments on its debts. Moreover, if Nike attempts to borrow, the interest rate charged by a lender might be lower, although decreasing the ratio also reduces leverage and therefore can reduce ROE.

Times Interest Earned

Additional information on a company's debt burden is obtained by calculating times interest earned. *Times interest earned*, or interest coverage, measures the extent to which operations cover interest expense. The higher the ratio, the more likely that the company will be able to continue meeting the interest payments.

$$\text{Times Interest Earned} = \frac{\text{Income Before Interest and Taxes and Other Income (Expense)}}{\text{Interest Expense}}$$

Income before interest and taxes and other income (expense) is operating income. Nike had interest coverage of 18.09 times in 1992 and 24.16 times in 1993, indicating an improvement in this ratio.

$$1992: \quad \frac{\$554,624}{\$30,665} = 18.09 \qquad 1993: \quad \frac{\$621,730}{\$25,739} = 24.16$$

Cash Flow Ratios

Cash flow ratios are discussed in Chapter 17. Cash flow ratios are used to examine solvency in terms of a company's cash flows. Three cash flow ratios are:

$$\text{Overall Cash Flow Ratio} = \frac{\text{Cash Flow from Operations}}{\text{Financing} + \text{Investing} \atop \text{Cash Outflows}}$$

$$\text{Cash Flow to Net Income} = \frac{\text{Cash Flow from Operations}}{\text{Net Income}}$$

$$\text{Cash Return on Sales} = \frac{\text{Cash Flow from Operations}}{\text{Sales}}$$

The overall cash flow ratio measures the extent to which cash flow from operations supplies the cash needed for a company's investing and financing activities. Cash flow to net income is used to determine how closely a company's cash flows are correlated with its income. All things being equal, the higher the correlation, the better. Cash return on sales is a very similar measure to the conventional return on sales figure, that is, net income divided by sales.

Nike's cash flow ratios for 1993 are:

$$\text{Overall Cash Flow Ratio} = \frac{\$265{,}292}{\$238{,}789} = \$1.11$$

$$\text{Cash Return on Sales} = \frac{\$265{,}292}{\$3{,}930{,}984} = \$0.07$$

$$\text{Cash Flow to Net Income} = \frac{\$265{,}292}{\$365{,}016} = \$0.73$$

In reviewing Nike's overall cash flow ratio, we see that the company's cash flow from operations is slightly more than needed for financing and investing activities, which is a good sign. The company generates $.73 in cash flows from net income, but only $.07 from sales. As with all other ratios, in order to assess Nike's cash flow ratios we would need to make comparisons to a norm, such as industry averages, or view the ratios over time.

Exhibit 22-6 provides a summary of the ratios discussed in this chapter.

EXHIBIT 22-6   SUMMARY OF RATIOS AND ANALYTICAL MEASUREMENTS

LIQUIDITY

1. Working Capital = Current Assets − Current Liabilities

2. Current Ratio = $\dfrac{\text{Current Assets}}{\text{Current Liabilities}}$

3. Quick Ratio = $\dfrac{\text{Cash} + \text{Temporary Investments} + \text{Receivables}}{\text{Current Liabilities}}$

ACTIVITY

4. Accounts Receivable Turnover = $\dfrac{\text{Net Sales}}{\text{Average Net Accounts Receivables}}$

5. Days' Sales in Accounts Receivable = $\dfrac{\text{Ending Accounts Receivable}}{\text{Average Daily Sales}}$

6. Inventory Turnover = $\dfrac{\text{Cost of Goods Sold}}{\text{Average Inventory}}$

7. Days' Sales in Inventory = $\dfrac{\text{Ending Inventory}}{\text{Average Daily Cost of Goods Sold}}$

PROFITABILITY

8. Gross Profit = $\dfrac{\text{Gross Profit}}{\text{Net Sales}}$

9. Operating Ratio = $\dfrac{\text{Income Before Interest and Taxes and Other Income (Expense)}}{\text{Net Sales}}$

10. Return on Sales = $\dfrac{\text{Net Income}}{\text{Net Sales}}$

11. Return on Investment = $\dfrac{\text{Income}}{\text{Investment}}$

12. Return on Assets = $\dfrac{\text{Income Before Interest and Taxes and Other Income (Expense)}}{\text{Average Total Assets}}$

13. Return on Common Equity (ROE) = $\dfrac{\text{Net Income} - \text{Preferred Dividends}}{\text{Average Common Stockholders' Equity}}$

14. Earnings per Share = $\dfrac{\text{Net Income Available for Common Stockholders}}{\text{Weighted-Average Common Shares Outstanding}}$

15. Growth Rate of EPS = $\dfrac{\text{EPS Current Year} - \text{EPS Prior Year}}{\text{EPS Prior Year}}$

16. Price-Earnings Ratio = $\dfrac{\text{Market Price per Share}}{\text{Earnings per Share}}$

17. Dividend Yield = $\dfrac{\text{Dividend per Share}}{\text{Market Price per Share}}$

18. Dividend Payout Ratio = $\dfrac{\text{Dividend per Share}}{\text{Earnings per Share}}$

SOLVENCY

19. Debt Ratio = $\dfrac{\text{Total Liabilities}}{\text{Total Assets}}$

20. Debt to Equity Ratio = $\dfrac{\text{Total Liabilities}}{\text{Total Stockholders' Equity}}$

21. Times Interest Earned = $\dfrac{\text{Income Before Interest and Taxes and Other Income (Expense)}}{\text{Interest Expense}}$

CASH FLOW

22. Overall Cash Flow Ratio = $\dfrac{\text{Cash Flow from Operations}}{\text{Financing} + \text{Investing Cash Outflows}}$

23. Cash Flow to Net Income = $\dfrac{\text{Cash Flow from Operations}}{\text{Net Income}}$

24. Cash Return on Sales = $\dfrac{\text{Cash Flow from Operations}}{\text{Sales}}$

23

THE QUALITY OF EARNINGS

Investors' perception of the quality of a company's earnings relates to the extent to which the company's reported net income is different from its "true" net income. The quality of a company's earnings affects the market value of its stock. The lower investors perceive the quality of a company's earnings to be, the lower value they place on the company's stock.

Investors believe earnings are of low quality (1) when they cannot be sustained or (2) when accounting or "paper" gains increase earnings without a corresponding increase in a "real" asset. Conversely, investors believe earnings that can be sustained and that are accompanied by cash inflows are of high quality.

Some analysts worry that the quality of reported earnings has been declining. This chapter examines some of the factors that affect earnings quality and tells how you might analyze the quality of a company's earnings.

Sustainable Earnings

Investors tend to believe earnings cannot be sustained when managers attempt to "manage" earnings rather than operations. One way managers increase reported profits is by changing the timing of revenue and expense recognition. A manufacturer may offer liberal credit terms to entice customers to buy who would customarily wait until next year. A company that advertises "No payment or interest until June" may motivate customers to buy appliances or furniture in December, increasing current year earnings but stealing sales from next year. Earnings this year may thus be increased but earnings next year may be reduced.

Managers may defer or accelerate discretionary expenses. Managers defer expenses to improve current earnings; they accelerate expenses to take the "hit" in a current year of low earnings and improve prospects for next year. Travel, maintenance, or advertising expenditures may be delayed from December to January to reduce expenses. In early fall, managers may be able to set the date for repainting the equipment and factory buildings, or for the annual sales meeting. Delaying these expenses will improve current earnings; accelerating them will improve next year's.

Changing the timing of revenues and expenses can produce an increase in current reported earnings that cannot be sustained in the future periods.

Questionable Practices

Some management efforts to manage earnings go beyond timing changes. Managers may increase sales through "loose" credit standards that later also increase bad debts, or may bias estimates of expense items—such as obsolete inventories or bad debts—to delay recognition of the full amount of these expenses. Actions such as these are ethically questionable and result (if successful) in earnings increases that cannot be sustained and do not provide an accompanying increased inflow of cash or other assets.

Accounting Methods and Perceived Quality of Earnings

Companies frequently must choose among alternative accounting methods, some of which affect taxable income, and some of which do not. When a company chooses an accounting method because it maximizes reported earnings, investors view the resulting reported earnings as lower quality. Studies have shown, for instance, that a company that chooses to use straight-line depreciation is seen by investors as having lower quality earnings than a company that uses an accelerated method.*

Exhibit 23-1 shows the difference between straight-line and accelerated sum-of-the-years'-digits (SYD) depreciation for a $10,000 machine with a four-year life and no salvage value. SYD depreciation yields higher depreciation expense and lower net income than straight-line in the first two years of the machine's life, but the situation is exactly reversed in the last two years. Over the machine's four-year life, both methods result in the same total depreciation expense and earnings.

Moreover, regardless of the depreciation method used for financial reporting, for tax reporting a company is free to use the depreciation method that results in the lowest tax liability—so

*See Frances L. Ayres, "Perceptions of Earnings Quality: What Managers Need to Know," *Management Accounting* (March 1994): 27–29.

the choice of depreciation method for earnings does not result in different cash flows, only in different reported earnings.

The theory is that investors (as a group) must "see" the company's real earnings, regardless of the accounting method used. Thus, the higher earnings brought about solely by accounting treatment are "seen" as lower quality than earnings that use accelerated depreciation and more closely match the inflow of cash from operations. (Despite this, a study, some years ago, by the National Accounting Association found that straight-line depreciation is the most appropriate method for most manufacturers because it best matches the way most machines wear out.)

EXHIBIT 23-1 STRAIGHT-LINE AND ACCELERATED DEPRECIATION EXPENSE

Year	Straight-Line Depreciation (1)	Sum-of-the-Years'-Digits Depreciation (2)	Difference (2) − (1)
1	$ 2,500	$ 4,000	$1,500
2	2,500	3,000	500
3	2,500	2,000	(500)
4	2,500	1,000	(1,500)
Total	$10,000	$10,000	$ -0-

This exhibit shows the difference between straight-line and the accelerated sum-of-the-years'-digits depreciation for a $10,000 machine with a four-year life.

Accounting Methods That Change Cash Flows

When accountants choose between accounting methods, some choices affect cash flows, because sometimes the same accounting method must be used for both financial reporting and tax reporting. Inventory methods (Chapter 12) fall into this group; a company that uses LIFO inventory must use the same method for both financial and tax reporting. Because they affect both reported earnings and cash flows for taxes, LIFO and FIFO inventory methods are used to illustrate the effect of such accounting methods on the quality of earnings.

Assume, in a period of rising prices, a company has beginning inventory of one unit costing $5 and purchases two more units for $6 each.

Beginning inventory	1 unit @ $5/unit	$ 5
Purchase	2 units @ $6/unit	12
Total available for sale	3 units	$17

If the company sells one unit for $10, LIFO and FIFO inventory methods give gross profit and ending inventory amounts as follows.

	LIFO	FIFO
In the Income Statement:		
Sales	$10	$10
Cost of Goods Sold	6	5
Gross Profit	4	5
In the Balance Sheet:		
Inventory	11	12
	(5 + 6)	(6 + 6)

When a company uses FIFO inventory during a period of rising inventory replacement costs, the company charges the cost of old, lower cost inventory to cost of goods sold: here, $5. This results in a cost-of-goods-sold expense that is less than the cash required to replace the inventory sold. In our example, $6 is the cost of units most recently purchased. To replace the unit sold, the company can be expected to spend $6 cash, or more. If the company must spend $6 (or more) to replace the unit sold, operating cash flows using FIFO are as follows.

Cash inflow from sales	$10
Cash outflow to replace the unit sold	6
Net cash inflow from operations	$ 4
Reported gross profit	5
Excess gross profit over cash inflow	$ 1

Reported earnings (reported gross profit) are greater than the increase in real net assets (cash from operations), and this reduces the quality of reported earnings.

If, instead, the company uses LIFO inventory, the $6 cost of the most recent inventory purchased is charged to cost of goods sold. If the company must spend $6 (or more) to replace the unit sold, operating cash flows using LIFO are as follows.

Cash inflow from sales	$10
Cash outflow to replace the unit sold	6
Net cash inflow from operations	$ 4
Reported gross profit	4
Excess gross profit over cash inflow	$ 0

This cost-of-goods-sold expense is much closer to the amount of cash required to replace the inventory sold, and reported earnings are closer to cash from operations.

Thus, investors perceive earnings to be of higher quality when companies use LIFO rather than FIFO. This is true when prices are rising or falling: the most current prices expensed using LIFO are always closer to replacement cost than the older costs expensed under FIFO.

The Effect on Taxes

In addition to the effect on the difference between reported earnings and cash flows, the choice of LIFO inventory method also has an effect on taxes paid, because a company must use the same method for filing taxes. When prices are rising, companies that use FIFO pay more income tax than those that use LIFO.

Assume in the preceding example that the company had $2 in other expenses and the tax rate was 50%.

	LIFO	FIFO
Sales	$10	$ 10
Cost of Goods Sold	6	5
Gross Profit	4	5
Other Expenses	2	2
Net Income Before Tax	2	3
Income Tax	1	1.5
Net Income	$ 1	$1.5

The company pays higher taxes using FIFO than when using LIFO. If prices were falling instead of rising, the reverse would be true; the most current prices (charged to cost of goods sold under LIFO) would be the lower, and LIFO would result in the higher income and the higher income tax paid.

LIFO Reserve in the Financial Statements

A LIFO reserve (see Chapter 12) is the difference between LIFO cost and the replacement cost of the inventory (usually assumed to be FIFO cost). We can use the LIFO reserve to determine the effect of the LIFO/FIFO choice on the quality of earnings. For example, Exhibit 23-2 shows that Upjohn Company reported cost of goods sold of $919,667,000 using LIFO for its domestic inventories in 1993. The inventory note to the Upjohn financial statements show a LIFO reserve of $150,578,000 in 1993 and $139,395,000 in 1992.

The increase in LIFO reserve from 1992 to 1993 is $11,183,000 ($150,578,000 − $139,395,000). Thus, if FIFO inventory had been used, cost of goods sold and, consequently, earnings before tax would have been $11,183,000 higher, inflated by the company's choice of accounting method, and consequently of lower quality than the earnings reported using LIFO.

EXHIBIT 23-2   LIFO RESERVE—UPJOHN COMPANY INCOME STATEMENT

Dollar amounts in thousands, except per-share data

For the years ended December 31	1993	1992	1991
Operating revenue:			
Net sales	**$3,611,180**	$3,548,570	3,320,249
Other revenue	**42,184**	29,941	24,514
Total	**3,653,364**	3,578,511	3,344,763
Operating costs and expenses:			
Cost of products sold	**919,667**	904,756	804,955
Research and development	**642,033**	581,534	522,875
Marketing and administrative	**1,409,149**	1,389,734	1,301,400
Restructuring	**216,000**	23,956	5,000
Total	**3,186,849**	2,899,980	2,634,230
Operating income	**466,515**	678,531	710,533
Interest income	**54,155**	55,295	51,511
Interest expense	**(31,496)**	(31,253)	(19,956)
Foreign exchange (losses) gains	**(4,926)**	(4,212)	4,165
All other, net	**6,174**	(1,654)	(30,700)
Earnings from continuing operations before income taxes and minority equity	**490,422**	696,707	715,553
Provision for income taxes	**89,001**	153,300	178,700
Minority equity in (losses) earnings	**(1,062)**	(1,034)	2,685
Earnings from continuing operations	**402,483**	544,441	534,168
Discontinued operation:			
Earnings from operations (net of tax)	**3,894**	2,776	3,251
Gain on disposal of discontinued operation (net of tax)	**4,926**		
Earnings before cumulative effect of accounting changes	**411,303**	547,217	537,419
Cumulative effect of accounting changes (net of tax)	**(18,906)**	(222,895)	
Net earnings	**392,397**	324,322	537,419
Dividends on preferred stock (net of tax)	**12,125**	12,084	12,356
Net earnings on common stock	**$ 380,272**	$ 312,238	$ 525,063

Dollar amounts in thousands, except per-share data

For the years ended December 31	1993	1992	1991
Earnings per common share:			
Primary			
Earnings from continuing operations before accounting changes	**$2.24**	$3.03	$2.94
Discontinued operation	**.05**	.01	.02
Cumulative effect of accounting changes	**(.11)**	(1.26)	
Net earnings	**$2.18**	$1.78	$2.96
Fully diluted			
Earnings from continuing operations before accounting changes	**$2.19**	$2.94	$2.85
Discontinued operation	**.04**	.01	.02
Cumulative effect of accounting changes	**(.10)**	(1.21)	
Net earnings	**$2.13**	$1.74	$2.87

The accompanying notes are an integral part of the consolidated financial statements.

NOTE: **Inventories**

Inventories are summarized as follows:

December 31	1993	1992
Estimated replacement cost (FIFO basis):		
Pharmaceutical and other finished products	**$ 174,615**	$ 187,070
Seeds	**171,716**	163,413
Raw materials, supplies and work in process	**375,170**	329,580
	721,501	680,063
Less reduction to LIFO cost	**(150,578)**	(139,395)
	$ 570,923	$ 540,668

Inventories valued on the LIFO method had an estimated replacement cost (FIFO basis) of $461,090 at December 31, 1993, and $421,924 at December 31, 1992.

Cash Flow Ratios

Analysts have developed two ratios that help to assess a company's cash flow relative to its earnings.*

$$\text{Cash Return on Sales} = \frac{\text{Cash Flow from Operations}}{\text{Sales}}$$

$$\text{Cash Flow to Net Income} = \frac{\text{Cash Flow from Operations}}{\text{Net Income}}$$

Cash return on sales and the cash flow to net income ratio help analysts determine whether the company's sales and earnings are matched by appropriate cash flows. This in turn helps investors determine the quality of the company's earnings. Exhibit 23-3 contains the statements of net income and cash flow for Dayton Hudson Corporation and Subsidiaries. Cash flow ratios for Dayton Hudson follow.

$$\text{Cash Return on Sales} = \frac{\text{Cash Flow from Operations}}{\text{Sales}}$$

1993	= $1,219/$19,233 = .063
1992	= $984/$17,927 = .055

$$\text{Return on Sales} = \frac{\text{Net Income}}{\text{Sales}}$$

1993	= $375/$19,233 = .019
1992	= $383/$17,927 = .021

$$\text{Cash Flow to Net Income} = \frac{\text{Cash Flow from Operations}}{\text{Net Income}}$$

1993	= $1,219/$375 = 3.25
1992	= $984/$383 = 2.57

Dayton Hudson generated about $.06 in cash flow from each sales dollar in both years, a greater amount than the approximately $.02 in accrual accounting earnings per dollar of sales in both years. This is in agreement with our finding that cash provided by operations is more than three times net income in 1993 and more than two and one-half times net income in 1992.

Dayton Hudson has an inflow of "real" assets equal to two or three times its reported earnings. Nothing indicates to us that its earnings are not sustainable. Investors probably see Dayton Hudson's earnings as high quality.

*For a discussion of ratios used to analyze cash flows, see Lloyd Brant, Jr., Joseph R. Danos, and J. Herman Brasseaux, "Financial Statement Analysis: Benefits and Pitfalls" (Part II), *The Practical Accountant* (June 1989): 69–78.

EXHIBIT 23-3 INCOME STATEMENT AND STATEMENT OF CASH FLOWS— DAYTON HUDSON CORPORATION AND SUBSIDIARIES

(Millions of Dollars, Except Per-Share Data)	1993	1992	1991
Revenues	**$19,233**	$17,927	$16,115
Costs and Expenses			
Cost of retail sales, buying and occupancy	**14,164**	13,129	11,751
Selling, publicity and administrative	**3,175**	2,978	2,801
Depreciation	**498**	459	410
Interest expense, net	**446**	437	398
Taxes other than income taxes	**343**	313	283
Total Costs and Expenses	**18,626**	17,316	15,643
Earnings Before Income Taxes	**607**	611	472
Provision for Income Taxes	**232**	228	171
Net Earnings	**$ 375**	$ 383	$ 301
Primary Earnings Per Share	**$ 4.99**	$ 5.02	$ 3.86
Fully Diluted Earnings Per Share	**$ 4.77**	$ 4.82	$ 3.72
Average Common Shares Outstanding (Millions):			
Primary	**71.8**	71.6	71.5
Fully Diluted	**76.1**	75.9	75.9

(Millions of Dollars)	1993	1992	1991
Operating Activities			
Net earnings	**$ 375**	$ 383	$ 301
Reconciliation to cash flow:			
Depreciation	**498**	459	410
Deferred tax provision	**29**	11	34
Other noncash items affecting earnings	**60**	48	26
Changes in operating accounts providing/(requiring) cash:			
Accounts receivable	**(22)**	(84)	(23)
Merchandise inventories	**121**	(237)	(365)
Accounts payable	**58**	272	57
Accrued liabilities	**63**	142	59
Income taxes payable	**20**	27	(62)
Other	**17**	(37)	
Cash Flow Provided by Operations	**1,219**	984	437
Investing Activities			
Expenditures for property and equipment	**(969)**	(918)	(1,009)
Disposals of property and equipment	**79**	10	19
Cash Flow Required for Investing Activities	**(890)**	(908)	(990)
Net Financing Sources/(Requirements)	**329**	76	(553)
Financing Activities			
(Decrease)/increase in notes payable	**(23)**	(242)	161
Additions to long-term debt	**528**	550	756
Reductions of long-term debt	**(581)**	(290)	(280)
Principal payments received on loan to ESOP	**61**	58	49
Dividends paid	**(138)**	(133)	(128)
Other	**28**	2	(1)
Cash Flow (Used)/Provided by Financing Activities	**(125)**	(55)	557
Net Increase in Cash and Cash Equivalents	**204**	21	4
Cash and Cash Equivalents at Beginning of Year	**117**	96	92
Cash and Cash Equivalents at End of Year	**$ 321**	$ 117	$ 96

The financial statements should be read in conjunction with the Notes and Analysis contained throughout.

24

INCOME STATEMENTS OF FOREIGN COMPANIES

Accounting in the United States is driven by the needs of companies to attract investors in a competitive, highly efficient capital market. However, not all financial reporting is driven by concern for capital markets. In fact, a large part of the world still produces financial statements that are difficult for investors to read and interpret. There are at least six accounting models. Each of these models reflects key aspects of the cultures and economic climates of the countries that use them.*

1. British-North American-Dutch

2. Continental

3. South American

4. Eastern Europe/Communist Bloc

5. Islamic

6. International Standards

This chapter briefly discusses these six accounting models and tells how the various countries adapt their statements for U.S. readers.

*The discussion of accounting models is based on the report on "accounting clusters" by Gerhard G. Mueller, Helen Gernon, and Gary K. Meek, 1994, Boston, Irwin, *Accounting: An International Perspective*, 8–13.

British–North American–Dutch Accounting

The British–North American–Dutch accounting model is focused on the needs of investors and common law. Countries using this model have large, well-developed markets for stocks and bonds, and financial reporting is directed to the needs of capital providers. The private sector establishes generally accepted accounting principles (GAAP) that tend to be innovative and adaptive. Accountants must exercise judgment and choose among equally acceptable methods of accounting for similar transactions.

In general, the education levels in countries using this model are high, and users of accounting information sophisticated. These countries have many large, multinational corporations.

Exhibit 24-1 shows the income statement of the Dutch company Koninklijke Ahold nv. Outside the Netherlands, the company uses the name Royal Ahold. Royal Ahold operates grocery stores in Europe and the United States. Its statements are published in English for the convenience of its English-speaking employees. The company's stock is not traded in the United States. Its income statement is prepared using Dutch GAAP, and amounts are given in both U.S. dollars and Dutch guilders.

EXHIBIT 24-1 AN INCOME STATEMENT USING DUTCH ACCOUNTING PRINCIPLES

Consolidated Statement of Earnings of Royal Ahold

(x000)	1992 $	1992 NLG	1991 NLG
Sales	12,302,100	22,317,239	20,789,784
Less: Value added tax	398,548	723,006	667,805
Net sales	11,903,552	21,594,233	20,121,979
Less: Cost of sales	9,345,152	16,953,039	15,929,785
Gross profit	2,558,400	4,641,194	4,192,194
Less: Selling expenses	1,926,674	3,495,180	3,177,937
General and administrative expenses	345,401	626,592	547,760
Operating results	286,325	519,422	466,497
Income from unconsolidated subsidiaries and affiliates	27,060	49,089	44,348
Interest income	11,408	20,695	15,135
Interest expense	(97,391)	(176,677)	(154,570)
Net financial expense	(58,923)	(106,893)	(95,087)
Operating earnings before income taxes	227,402	412,529	371,410
Income taxes	(58,196)	(105,574)	(95,303)
Operating earnings after income taxes	169,206	306,955	276,107
Gain on sale of real estate	289	525	(409)
Income taxes	(89)	(162)	194
Net income from sale of real estate	200	363	(215)
Third parties	(1,255)	(2,276)	(77)
Net earnings	168,151	305,042	275,815
Appropriation of earnings:			
Reserves (Retained earnings)	113,477	205,858	188,554
Dividend common stock	54,674	99,184	87,261
	168,151	305,042	275,815

Note: Dollar figures herein are translated from the underlying guilder figures for reader convenience at NLG 1.8141 = $1

Continental Accounting

Accounting in Europe is historically driven by government needs. Because of this, GAAP is frequently established by code law in each country. GAAP is national law and includes detailed, procedural rules, requiring strict compliance. There is little or no room for individual judgment.

Continental accounting and financial reporting are not oriented to the needs of capital providers, because European companies tend to have close ties with one primary source of capital, usually a bank. The Continental accounting model is used by companies in Europe and in most French-speaking African countries.

Exhibit 24-2 presents the income statement of the Italian bank CRT. The statement is in an account format foreign to U.S. readers and follows detailed accounting regulations set down by the Italian government. (A translation of the CRT income statement is shown in Exhibit 24-5 and discussed later in this chapter.)

COMPONENTI CONTO ECONOMICO	Esercizio 1990	Esercizio 1989	Scarto %
INTERESSI ATTIVI	**271.340.225.437**	**252.897.735.15**	**77,292**
Da clientela	117.373.342.707	105.039.326.429	11,742
Da istituzioni creditizie	46.901.064.061	40.736.340.167	15,133
Da Tesoro e C.R. postali	1.341.210.438	867.814.710	54,550
Da certificati di deposito	271.572.278	505.976.757	−46,327
Da titoli e partecipazioni	105.453.035.953	105.748.277.094	−0,279
INTERESSI PASSIVI	**163.648.852.086**	**160.954.159.555**	**1,674**
A clientela	128.675.667.346	138.157.514.318	−6,863
A istituzioni creditizie	9.633.862.792	5.841.605.024	64,918
Su buoni fruttiferi e certificati di deposito	25.339.321.948	16.955.040.213	49,450
Margine finanziario	**107.691.373.351**	**91.943.575.602**	**17,128**
PROVENTI DA SERVIZI	**54.874.693.364**	**46.483.623.552**	**18,052**
Utili da negoziazione titoli	22.023.985.576	11.231.956.012	96,083
Utili da negoziazione cambi	674.732.421	553.020.717	22,009
Commissioni, provvigioni ed altri ricavi al netto commiss. e provv. pass.	19.193.105.288	17.109.945.241	12,175
Proventi diversi	7.446.352.626	15.314.817.859	−51,378
Saldo utili e perdite da realizzi	3.883.755.793	288.675.375	1.245,371
Saldo sopravvenienze attive e passive	1.652.761.660	1.985.208.348	−16,746
Margine Intermediazione	**162.566.066.715**	**138.427.199.154**	**17,438**

COMPONENTI CONTO ECONOMICO	Esercizio 1990	Esercizio 1989	Scarto %
ALTRI COSTI ED ONERI DI GESTIONE	**110.576.194.644**	**96.568.511.943**	**14,505**
Spese per il personale (—utilizzo fondi)	73.272.910.948	63.974.779.471	14,534
Imposte e tasse (—utilizzo fondi)	3.219.022.054	2.081.301.269	54,664
Costi e spese div. (—utilizzo fondo beneficenza)	24.624.576.145	22.626.011.050	8,833
Perdite su crediti (—utilizzo fondi)	27.760.972	57.172.928	−51,444
Ammortamenti ordinari	7.992.785.495	6.763.983.320	18,167
Ammortamenti anticipati	1.439.139.030	1.065.263.905	35,097
Utile lordo	**51.989.872.071**	**41.858.687.211**	**24,203**
ACCANTONAMENTI	**10.782.046.905**	**15.133.835.024**	**28,755**
Ai fondi rischi e perdite su crediti	10.280.507.731	13.492.532.958	−23,806
Accantonamenti diversi	501.539.174	1.641.302.066	−69,443
Utile dell'esercizio prima delle imposte	**41.207.825.166**	**26.724.852.187**	**54,193**
ACCANTONAMENTO PER IMPOSTE DELL'ESERCIZIO	**17.449.700.000**	**15.250.000.000**	**14,424**
Utile dell'esercizio	**23.758.125.166**	**11.474.852.187**	**107,045**
Al fondo rischi e perdite FRIE	126.340.000	239.860.000	−47,328
Al fondo riserva straordinaria	11.000.000.000	0	—
Utile da ripartire	**12.631.785.166**	**11.234.992.187**	**12,433**

South American Accounting

Perhaps the most significant factor affecting business in South America is the historic, pervasive inflation. So, as you might expect, South American accounting and financial reporting are controlled by inflation accounting adjustments, by which companies periodically revise costs upward to reflect the rise in the replacement cost of assets. This can be confusing to financial statement readers in the United States, because each upward revision of assets may be accompanied by an equal "inflation gain" in income or owners' equity.

Assets	= Liabilities +	Owners' Equity
Inflation		Inflation
Adjustment		Gain
+ $100		+$100

South American GAAP is oriented to government planners' needs (especially for comparability). Countries in South America frequently require the same uniform, codified methods for both tax and financial reporting.

This model is used by most countries in South America. Their financial statements are in Spanish, with the notable exception of Brazil, for which the language is Portuguese.

Eastern European Accounting

Eastern European accounting and financial reporting is in a state of almost continual change, as these former Communist countries seek investors and evolve toward the more capital-oriented, investor-oriented models of Europe and North America. Accounting in Eastern Europe has been historically determined by:

1. The needs of government planners for tight economic control,

2. The lack of private ownership,

3. The lack of income as a measure of success, and

4. The requirement that companies produce a predetermined level (quota) of output from a specific, allocated amount of resources.

Because under Communism there was no emphasis on income, fixed asset valuation was not important. Owners' equity showed only the equity of the state. Truly, under Communism there was no real financial accounting, and this situation still exists in those countries that retain state-operated industry. Controlled economies are disappearing, however, and you can expect that accounting and financial reporting in Eastern Europe will quickly adopt more informative accounting standards.

The translation of a Polish pro forma format for an income statement is shown in Exhibit 24-3. But new Polish financial reporting standards are proposed and, just as for standards in the rest of Eastern Europe, what is now correct will soon be obsolete.

**EXHIBIT 24-3   PRO FORMA FORMAT FOR AN INCOME
STATEMENT IN POLAND**

INCOME STATEMENT

Expenses and Losses

A. Cost of obtained revenues
 I. Costs by nature*)
  1. Depreciation and amortization
  2. Materials and energy used
  3. Services
  4. Salaries and wages
  5. Charges on salaries and wages
  6.
  7.
  8.
  9. Other expenses
 II. Change in stock*)
  1. Decrease
  2. Increase
A. Cost of obtained revenues
 I. Cost of goods sold (product costs)**)
  1.
  2.
  3.
  4.
  5.
 II. Administrative and selling expenses**)
 III. Trade activity expenses**)
 IV. Purchases
 V. Financial expenses
  1. Interests
  2. Other
 VI. Turnover tax and other charges on
  sale
  1. Turnover tax
  2. Other charges on sale
B. Profit on normal activity
C. Extraordinary losses
 I. natural disasters
 II. other losses
  1.
  2.
  3.
  4.

D. Profit before taxes and charges
E. Obligatory charges on profit
 I. Corporate tax
 II. Other obligatory charges
F. Net profit

Revenues and Gains

A. Revenue from sale
 I. Product sale
  1.
  2.
  3.
  4.
  5.
 II. Resale of goods
 III. Financial revenues
  1. Dividends
  2. Interests
  3. Other
 IV. Profit or loss on other sale
  1. Profit
  2. Loss
 V. Subsidies and other increase of sale
B. Loss on normal activity
C. Extraordinary gains
 I. Windful gains
 II. Other extraordinary gains
  1.
  2.
  3.
  4.
D. Loss before taxes and charges
E. Obligatory charges on loss
 I.
 II.
F. Net loss

Source:
Rozporządzenie Ministra Finansów z
dn. 15.01.1991 w sprawie
zasad prowadzenia rachunkowości—
Dziennik Ustaw Nr 10 1991 poz.35

Islamic Accounting

Not much is known by scholars in the United States about the Islamic accounting model. The model is based on Islamic theology and uses current market values rather than historical cost. How Islamic theology affects Islamic GAAP is uncertain, only that it prohibits the use of interest. (This model is not well developed but does have its impact. A recent meeting of the international accounting issues group of the United Nations altered the wording of a position paper to avoid the use of the term *interest*.)

Accounting Using International Standards

The development of uniform international accounting standards is driven by the needs of companies to access international capital markets. Without this need, there is little incentive to create statements that can be read outside a company's home country. The International Accounting Standards Committee (IASC) is the leading worldwide accounting standard setter. The IASC was formed in 1973 and represents more than 75 countries. The Committee is currently promulgating accounting standards to establish the tone and format for accounting and financial reporting in the international capital markets.

Many of the IASC standards parallel the accounting standards in the United States. In most cases, a U.S. company that is in compliance with U.S. GAAP is also in compliance with IASC international GAAP.

Exhibit 24-4 presents a list of accounting standards developed by IASC. Where appropriate, each standard is shown beside the section of the financial report to which it applies. Compliance with the standards promulgated by IASC is completely voluntary. The standards will gain acceptance only as companies around the globe find them useful.

EXHIBIT 24-4   STANDARDS PROMULGATED BY THE INTERNATIONAL ACCOUNTING STANDARDS COMMITTEE

	IASC Current Status		IASC Current Status
GENERAL		**BALANCE SHEET** (continued)	
Disclosure of accounting policies	IAS 1/Presentation of Financial Statements	Foreign currency	IAS 21 (revised 11/93)
Changes in accounting policies	IAS 8 (revised 11/93)	Investments	IAS 25/E48, Financial Instruments
Information to be disclosed in financial statements	IAS 5/Presentation of Financial Statements	Financial instruments/off balance sheet transactions	E48, Financial Instruments
		Joint ventures	IAS 31
INCOME STATEMENT		Contingencies	IAS 10
Revenue recognition	IAS 18 (revised 11/93)	Events occurring after the balance sheet date	IAS 10
Construction contracts	IAS 11 (revised 11/93)	Current assets and current liabilities	IAS 13/Presentation of Financial Statements
Production and purchase costs	IAS 2 (revised 11/93)		
Depreciation	IAS 4/IAS 16 (revised 11/93)	Business combinations (including goodwill)	IAS 22 (revised 11/93)
Impairment	IAS 4/IAS 16 (revised) — PP&E — plus all specific IASs	Other intangibles	DSOP (1/94)
Taxes	IAS 12 — under review	**CASH FLOW STATEMENTS**	
Extraordinary items	IAS 8 (revised 11/93)	Cash flow	IAS 7 (revised 12/92)
Government grants	IAS 20		
Retirement benefits	IAS 19 (revised 11/93) — Board identified need for further review	**OTHER STANDARDS**	
		Consolidated financial statements	IAS 27
Employee benefits	IAS 19 (revised 11/93) — Board identified need for separate project	Subsidiaries operating in hyperinflationary economies	IAS 21 (revised 11/93) /IAS 29
Research and development	IAS 9 (revised 11/93)	Associates/equity accounting	IAS 28
Interest	IAS 23 (revised 11/93)	Segments	IAS 14 — under review
Hedging	E48, Financial Instruments	Interim reporting	
		Earnings per share	DSOP 9/93
BALANCE SHEET		Related party disclosures	IAS 24
Balance sheet impact of income statement items listed above	Various IASs and current projects	Discontinued operations	IAS 8 (revised 11/93) — disclosure only — Board identified need to deal with recognition and measurement issues
Property, plant and equipment	IAS 16 (revised 11/93)	Fundamental errors	IAS 8 (revised 11/93)
Leases	IAS 17	Changes in estimates	IAS 8 (revised 11/93)
Inventories	IAS 2 (revised 11/93)		
Deferred taxes	IAS 12 — under review		

This exhibit is adapted from "Core International Accounting Standards," IASC Insight, December 1993, p. 5.

Approaches to Accommodate Foreign Readers

Companies that want to accommodate foreign readers take one of several measures.* The simplest and least expensive for the accommodating company is to prepare convenience translations. At the lowest level, the company may translate the language but retain the home country's GAAP and monetary unit.

Exhibit 24-5 shows the translated income statement of the Italian bank CRT, also shown in Italian in Exhibit 24-2. The income statement is called the Reclassified Profit and Loss Account and is still based on Italian GAAP, in an Italian accounting format, and is in lira, not dollars. The CRT annual report also contains translations to German and French. Clearly, these statements are for the convenience of foreign customers, rather than investors.

*Ibid., 56–60.

Reclassified Profit and Loss Account as at December 31, 1990

(lire in millions)	1990		1989	(lire in millions)	1990		1989
INTEREST RECEIVED		271,340	252,898	NET PROFIT ON SERVICES		54,875	46,484
Interest from customers	117,373		105,039	INTERMEDIATION MARGIN		162,566	138,428
Interest from banks	48,514		42,111	Personnel costs (net of allocations used)	73,273		63,975
Interest and dividends on securities	105,453		105,748	Taxes (net of allocations used)	3,219		2,081
INTEREST PAID		163,649	160,954	Sundry costs and charges (net of charity fund)	24,625		22,626
Interest to customers	128,676		138,157	Credit losses (net of allocations used)	28		57
Interest to banks	34,973		22,797	Depreciation funds	9,431		7,830
INTEREST MARGIN		107,691	91,944	OTHER EXPENSES AND CHARGES		110,576	96,569
Profits on securities' negotiation (net of depreciations)	22,024		11,232	GROSS MARGIN		51,990	41,859
Shareholdings' appreciations	—		—	Provisions to reserves and other funds		21,908	15,374
Profits from foreign exchange transactions	675		557	PROFIT BEFORE TAXATION		30,082	26,485
Commissions, fees and other earnings (net of costs)	19,193		17,110	Provision for taxation		17,450	15,250
Sundry income and non-recurring receipts (net of charges)	12,983		17,589	**NET PROFIT FOR THE YEAR**		**12,632**	**11,235**

At the next level of accommodation, convenience statements translate both the language and currency, using a year-end exchange rate. Such statements still retain the home country's GAAP, which may mislead readers because the statements no longer look foreign.

The next level of accommodation to foreign readers is to restate the financial statements on a limited basis, often with U.S. or international GAAP earnings reconciled to the foreign GAAP earnings. Although these statements can still be mis-leading because individual components of the reports cannot be examined within the reader's GAAP, they are far better than convenience translations.

A company seriously interested in a foreign capital market will completely restate its financial statements using the GAAP of the foreign country. Companies that want to trade their stock on the New York Stock Exchange must provide statements completely converted to U.S. GAAP, regardless of the company's home country GAAP.

An Example of International Accounting Differences

Accounting standards in the various countries often treat items in very different ways. We illustrate the difference in accounting methods by examining how countries treat goodwill.

Goodwill is the premium paid for a subsidiary company above its fair market (current) value because of the subsidiary's promising future earnings. There are three main ways to account for goodwill.

1. Capitalize but don't amortize.

2. Capitalize and amortize.

3. Don't capitalize, write off immediately.

Capitalize but Don't Amortize

Countries that allow companies to capitalize goodwill as an asset, but not to amortize it, rationalize this position by maintaining that goodwill is a premium paid for benefits to be received, and that the value of goodwill does not decline because it (the excellent earnings) is continuously maintained. Therefore, they submit, if goodwill is amortized, double counting results, because companies must expense both the goodwill and the cost of maintaining the goodwill. Switzerland is the only major industrial country to permit this approach.

Capitalize and Amortize

Countries that capitalize goodwill as an asset and then amortize (expense) it maintain that goodwill is a purchased resource that is consumed over time. Because goodwill is consumed, it must be amortized or earnings will be overstated. This is the most popular method of accounting for goodwill, permitted by most industrialized countries.

Still, the period benefited is arbitrary and differs among countries. The example that follows shows the maximum allowable lives used and the annual amortization expense for $100,000 in goodwill under each life.

Country	Allowable Life	Amortization Expense
United States	Maximum 40 years	$ 2,500
Austria and Sweden	Maximum 20 years	$ 5,000
The Netherlands	Maximum 10 years	$10,000
Japan	Maximum 5 years	$20,000

Don't Capitalize, Write Off Immediately

Countries that write off goodwill immediately against owners' equity or against earnings as an extraordinary item, maintain that goodwill is not a premium paid for benefits to be received and that goodwill results only because the company is valued as a whole (rather than asset by asset). In this view, goodwill is not a resource that can be consumed. Internally generated goodwill is not capitalized, say these countries, and purchased goodwill should not be either.

Immediate write-off of goodwill against earnings or owners' equity improves the comparability of companies' earnings but may deplete equity in service companies (that have few tangible assets) and highly acquisitive companies (where much goodwill is acquired). Immediate write-off is permitted by several countries, including France, Germany, Hong Kong, Italy, Mexico, Nigeria, Switzerland, Japan, and the United Kingdom. These countries are home to many of the companies that compete most successfully with U.S. companies in the world markets and that seek to acquire the same subsidiaries desired by U.S. companies.

Given there are three ways to account for goodwill, how do U.S. companies fare versus foreign companies in acquisitions?

Foreign companies tend to prefer immediate write-off when it is available, and not having to reduce future earnings with goodwill amortization gives foreign companies an advantage over U.S. companies. U.S. companies amortizing goodwill report lower incremental earnings from acquisitions than do foreign companies that don't amortize goodwill.

For example, the U.K. company Blue Arrow recently reported earnings of 65 million pounds using U.K. rules, but losses of $686 million under U.S. rules, primarily because of goodwill amortization. This is an important difference. Companies are often valued based on a multiple of reported earnings.

Furthermore, in Japan, Canada, and Germany an immediate or accelerated write-off of goodwill has been especially desirable because it was deductible for taxes in those countries, but until 1994 was not deductible in the United States. This gave companies in those countries a cash flow advantage over U.S. companies and made it difficult for U.S. companies to compete in bidding, even for acquisitions of companies inside the United States. As of 1994, however, Congress made goodwill deductible for tax purposes in the United States and somewhat leveled the acquisition playing field.

A Word of Caution

From time to time investments in Europe or on the Pacific Rim are widely promoted in the United States. However, financial statement readers should be extremely cautious when considering investments in foreign companies not traded on a U.S. stock exchange. Unless you read the foreign company's language fluently and are knowledgeable in the foreign country's GAAP, you will not be able to evaluate the company from its financial statements. Financial statements translated into English are perhaps even more dangerous, for they do not look foreign and may beguile readers who incorrectly interpret the statements based on U.S. accounting principles.

If you want to invest in foreign companies not listed on a U.S. stock exchange, do it through a U.S. mutual fund that is either global or international. Global funds invest in the stocks of foreign companies but may also invest in U.S. companies. International funds invest only in countries outside the United States, frequently in a specific geographical area.

INDEX

Note: Numbers in **boldface** indicate those pages where terms are defined.

About the Authors

Franklin J. Plewa, Jr., is Professor of Accounting at Idaho State University and the recipient of honors and awards for both teaching and research. He is the author of many books and articles, and is coauthor with George T. Friedlob of *Keys to Improving Your Return on Investment (ROI)* and *Financial and Business Statements*.

George T. Friedlob is Professor and Institute of Internal Auditors Research Foundation Faculty Fellow in the School of Accountancy at Clemson University. He has received numerous academic and professional awards and is the author of a wide variety of professional publications.